MULTICULTURAL ISSUES
AND LITERACY ACHIEVEMENT

MULTICULTURAL ISSUES AND LITERACY ACHIEVEMENT

Kathryn H. Au
University of Hawaii

 LAWRENCE ERLBAUM ASSOCIATES, PUBLISHERS
2006   Mahwah, New Jersey   London

Lawrence Erlbaum Associates, Inc., Publishers
10 Industrial Avenue
Mahwah, New Jersey 07430
www.erlbaum.com

Cover design by Kathryn Houghtaling Lacey

Library of Congress Cataloging-in-Publication Data

Au, Kathryn Hu-Pei.
 Multicultural issues and literacy achievement / Kathryn H. Au.
  p. cm.
 Includes bibliographical references and index.
 ISBN 0-8058-4400-7 (cloth : alk. paper)
 ISBN 0-8058-4401-5 (paper : alk. paper)
  1. Literacy—Social aspects—United States.   2. Language arts—Social aspects—
United States.   3. Multicultural education—United States.   I. Title.

LC151.A94   2005
302.2'244—dc22   2004060687
                                                                       CIP

To the teachers
of the public schools of Hawaii,
especially those who have taken the journey
that is the Standards-Based Change Process—
I am proud to stand beside you.

Contents

Preface

The growing numbers of students of diverse cultural and linguistic backgrounds in schools present educators with unprecedented challenges. This volume is intended to help educators meet these challenges. I wrote this volume with preservice teachers in mind. At the same time, I believe that complexities of theory and research have been treated in sufficient depth to make the book suitable for graduate courses and for teacher study groups.

The phrase in the title likely to capture the attention of many educators is *literacy achievement*. As I write this preface, the effects of the No Child Left Behind Act (2001), the reauthorization of the Elementary and Secondary Education Act, are reverberating throughout the United States. The literacy achievement of students of diverse backgrounds, already a concern of long standing, has been brought to the nation's attention as never before. Yet answers to the questions of how to improve the literacy achievement of these students seem as elusive as ever to many educators.

How do we as educators turn the situation around? What does the research tell us about improving the literacy achievement of students of diverse backgrounds? What can be done in classrooms and schools to help students of diverse backgrounds achieve high levels of literacy in school? These are the questions driving this volume.

Each chapter is organized around key issues that need to be addressed in schools and classrooms with many students of diverse backgrounds. I identified these key issues not only on the basis of research but also on the basis of my experience with preservice and inservice teachers working in schools in diverse, low-income communities. Each chapter explores the issues from

angles that I know many teachers have not previously encountered. By taking the approach of looking at familiar issues through new lenses, I hope to
stimulate readers' thinking and spark discussion and reflection.

I wrote this volume from the perspective of social constructivism. My underlying thesis is that teachers must be able to recognize negative, socially
sustained patterns that hamper the literacy achievement of students of diverse backgrounds, and put new, positive patterns in their place. Critical
theory, discourse theory, and an historical perspective are introduced to
help teachers see how patterns of success and failure in school literacy attainment have been socially constructed over time. However, my overall
emphasis is not on the macrolevel. Rather, it is on the actions that educators
can take on a daily basis to improve the literacy achievement of students of
diverse backgrounds.

In chapter 1, I lay out the big picture, providing teachers with an orientation to the literacy achievement gap. I introduce key variables and discuss
the larger societal context, including rising standards, globalization, and
the need for higher level thinking. In chapter 2, I address the question of
why the literacy achievement gap exists. I present the major explanations
for the gap operating at both the macrolevel and at the classroom level. In
chapter 3, I turn to the common problem of attributing the poor literacy
achievement of students of diverse backgrounds to the vagaries of parents
and communities. I give an overview of discourse theory, discuss research
on literacy practices in diverse communities, and explore how mainstream
discourse is used to devalue the language and literacy of students of diverse
backgrounds and their families.

In chapter 4, I move from the community to the classroom and deal with
questions of effective literacy instruction. I explain the benefits of workshop approaches from the perspective of discourse theory and illustrate
key points using the example of a program called Book Club *Plus*. In chapter 5, I continue to focus on the classroom, delving into anthropological research on student resistance and peer group dynamics. I look at how classrooms may be organized and managed as communities of learners in which
teachers establish positive relationships with students and motivate them
to become literate, or develop ownership of literacy, in school. In chapter 6,
I deal in detail with the teaching of reading comprehension strategies, an often neglected part of the literacy instruction of students of diverse backgrounds. This chapter reviews the importance of higher level thinking with
text and provides guidelines about when comprehension strategies should
be taught, which strategies should be highlighted, and the specific steps to
be taken in teaching these strategies.

In chapter 7, I take a fresh look at culturally responsive instruction, exploring in particular how this approach may be applied to classrooms with students of many different ethnicities, a common situation in urban settings. I explain how culturally responsive instruction does not involve a precise matching of cultural elements, but rather an incorporation of instructional options that reflect a diverse worldview rooted in the values of cooperation and the well-being of the group. In chapter 8, I examine issues of language that affect English Language Learners, such as speakers of Spanish, as well as students whose primary language is a nonmainstream variety of English, such as speakers of African American Vernacular English. I look at actions teachers can take to build on the language strengths students bring to the classroom and suggest ways that multiliteracy can be supported, even when teachers themselves are monolingual.

In chapter 9, I focus on phonics and skill instruction, often a topic of concern in schools enrolling large numbers of students of diverse backgrounds. I examine skill instruction from the perspective of discourse theory and suggest how teachers can and should teach skills effectively, including such approaches as providing lessons consistent with students' stages of word identification and integrating the teaching of phonics and spelling. In chapter 10, I move from the classroom to the whole school, addressing school change and the need to implement systems for improving students' literacy achievement through standards. I describe the Standards-Based Change Process as an example of an approach that meets the criteria for an effective school change effort.

Instructors familiar with my earlier volume, *Literacy Instruction in Multicultural Settings* (Au, 1993), may be wondering about similarities and differences between that volume and this one. I treated this volume as a sequel, not a revision. I feel that much of the content of the earlier book has stood the test of time. However, in addition to providing an update on research in the field, I have attempted to correct some omissions in that book, specifically, the need to address issues of power, attitudes, and systemic change through the application of discourse theory and critical theory. Instructors indicated that they liked the brevity, terseness, and clarity of the earlier text, and I kept these characteristics in mind while writing this new book.

I have one suggestion for instructors, and that is to have students maintain a running list of negative patterns affecting the literacy achievement of students of diverse backgrounds, along with the alternative, positive patterns. Each chapter presents new patterns or delves more deeply into patterns mentioned earlier. Students can be asked to look for patterns in their practicum placements and their own school experiences, as well as in this volume. Keeping a list of patterns helps students to put together the pieces of the puzzle, to understand better why the literacy achievement gap exists and how it can be closed.

The intellectual influences on this volume have been many, but I want to acknowledge the contributions of my friend and colleague, Taffy Raphael, who was the first reader of several of the more challenging chapters. Her comments were insightful, constructive, and greatly appreciated. Chapters 4 and 6 would surely have been coauthored with Taffy, had she not been writing a volume of her own for this series. Many of the ideas discussed in chapter 10 grew from conversations over the years with Sheila Valencia, who is the first person I contact if I have a question about assessment. Jennifer Stone did a thorough review of the manuscript and made many suggestions that enabled me to fill in gaps and present concepts more clearly and completely.

I have often seen in schools and classrooms with students of diverse backgrounds that failure is robust, whereas success is fragile. I hope that this book may help more teachers to find success in bringing all of their students to high levels of literacy.

—Kathy Au
Honolulu, Hawaii
August 2004

1

Students of Diverse Backgrounds and the Literacy Achievement Gap

My purpose in this volume is to discuss what educators can do to bring all students to high levels of literacy. In this opening chapter, I start with underlying beliefs, comparing the pluralist and assimilationist stances. I then turn to facts and figures about students of diverse cultural and linguistic backgrounds, the students that teachers typically struggle to reach. To gain a deeper understanding of these issues, I explore the concept of culture and show how this concept applies to teachers and schools, as well as to students. I then address the topic of literacy—how it has spread and how standards for literacy have changed over time. I close the chapter by considering the literacy achievement gap and differences between the reading performance of students of diverse backgrounds and their mainstream peers.

A recurring theme in this volume is that there are patterns in the ways that schools and classrooms usually operate, and that these patterns often have negative effects on the literacy achievement of students of diverse backgrounds. First, educators must learn to recognize these patterns in their own schools and classrooms. Second, they must know how to put new patterns in place to be successful in bringing students of diverse backgrounds to high levels of literacy. You read about these patterns in detail in chapter 2. The general idea is that success and failure in the teaching and learning of literacy are social constructions, resulting from the beliefs, expectations, and actions of human beings—not the innate states of individuals.

The theoretical perspective underlying this view is known as *social constructivism* (Au, 1998; Spivey, 1997). Throughout this book you will learn more about the social constructivist perspective and the insights it offers for improving students' literacy achievement. The essence of the social constructivist perspective is that it focuses on the social conditions under which learning takes place. Failure in learning to read and write is seen to occur because of societal patterns collaboratively produced and maintained by the participants, including teachers, students, families, politicians, and others. Similarly, success in learning to read and write can occur if new patterns are put in place and carried out by these same participants.

By introducing the idea that people's actions create and sustain negative patterns in schools, I am not calling into question the good intentions of educators. Most educators in schools with poor records of literacy achievement show a strong dedication to their students. Nevertheless, we must recognize that good intentions have not been enough. Many schools are still failing to bring most students of diverse backgrounds to high levels of literacy. This book will guide you through research that provides insights about why schools fail to help many students reach high levels of literacy, as well as research that provides ideas about how schools can improve students' literacy achievement.

PLURALIST AND ASSIMILATIONIST STANCES

Let us begin by looking at the larger societal context in which educational issues involving students of diverse backgrounds are routinely debated. There are two contrasting points of view it is helpful to understand, which you will easily be able to identify, whether the topic is high-stakes testing or bilingual education. These points of view are assimilationism and pluralism (see also Gollnick & Chinn, 2002). In chapter 2, I discuss the notion that societies have dominant and subordinate groups. In general, the assimilationist perspective tends to favor the interests of the dominant groups, whereas the pluralist perspective lends support to the interests of the subordinate groups, including students of diverse backgrounds and their families.

Those who take an assimilationist stance argue that it is essential for all members of the society to have a common base of knowledge. The metaphor for the assimilationist stance is the melting pot. The key element in this point of view is that all ethnic groups within the society should accept and adopt the same values as the dominant group. In the United States, for example, everyone should have a common understanding of the nation's history and read the classic works of Western civilization. Mastery of a common language, English, facilitates national discussions and communication. The implication of the assimilationist point of view is that students of diverse backgrounds should accept mainstream values, adjust to main-stream schooling, learn only standard American English, and receive in-struction just like that given to mainstream students. These arguments gain considerable weight through constant reinforcement by the dominant dis-course, the various means that members of the dominant group use to keep their worldview at the forefront, as explained further in chapter 3.

Those who advocate a pluralist stance argue that different ethnic groups can live side by side without the less powerful groups having to be assimi-lated into the more powerful ones. Furthermore, all ethnic groups should have equal opportunities to advance in society. Pluralists see the metaphor of the melting pot as quite frightening, if the inference is that people's cul-tural identities must be melted away before they can contribute to and par-ticipate effectively in the larger society. Pluralists prefer the metaphor of the salad or the stew, in which the individual ingredients still retain their own distinct identities. Pluralists note that national conversations on key issues can be enriched by the differing perspectives of those from a variety of cul-tural backgrounds.

As you have no doubt inferred, I have written this textbook from a plural-ist perspective. My interest is in improving literacy achievement through means that build on, rather than work against, students' cultural back-grounds. To this end, we must be aware of weaknesses in the logic of the assimilationist position. Consider the notion of a core curriculum. On the surface, it certainly seems to make sense for schools to have a core curricu-lum for the purpose of giving students a common base of knowledge (e.g., Hirsch & Trefil, 1987). As we probe a little further, however, we encounter the question of what that common base of knowledge should be. A core cur-riculum must be carefully devised, because of the influence it can have in shaping students' thoughts and attitudes. Pluralists caution that decisions about what to include in the curriculum are usually controlled by the domi-nant groups. Mandating such a curriculum generally leads to the continued imposition of dominant-group views on students of diverse backgrounds. For example, earlier generations of native Hawaiian students were taught that the Hawaiian Islands were discovered by the British explorer James Cook in 1783. This view of history had the effect of denying the accomplish-ments of the Polynesian navigators who sailed between Hawaii and the Marquesas centuries before. As this example shows, the slant taken in the curriculum can celebrate the accomplishments of one group, while render-ing invisible the accomplishments of another (cf. Loewen, 1995).

Although assimilationists tend to favor literary classics, pluralists see value in multicultural literature, including modern works that celebrate the contributions of African Americans, Latinos, Asian Americans, and Native Americans. Pluralists point out that the imposition of an English-only language policy in the United States runs counter to that of all other developed countries, in which educated people are expected to be fluent in two, if not three or four, different languages. The pluralist perspective is that individuals need not leave behind or deny the cultural heritage of their families to be good citizens who contribute to the larger society.

The differences between the assimilationist and pluralist perspectives are matters of philosophy and values that cannot be resolved through debate. My advocacy of the pluralist perspective, evident throughout this book, stems from repeated observations, as well as considerable research, showing that maintaining the status quo and an assimilationist perspective in schools has led to patterns of continuing inequality in educational outcomes for students of diverse backgrounds. The literacy achievement gap is an example of these patterns. Assimilationist thinking does not lead to the new patterns that allow teachers to bring students of diverse backgrounds to high levels of literacy in school.

Within a pluralist perspective, however, educators need to think carefully about the futures of students of diverse backgrounds in the larger society, to ensure that these students will have the same life opportunities afforded to mainstream students. Students of diverse backgrounds must receive schooling that prepares them to participate effectively in the larger society, for example, to advance as teachers or scientists, if that is their choice. For this reason, the interpretation of pluralism promoted here emphasizes the importance of making certain that students of diverse backgrounds learn strategies of higher level thinking with text and become proficient in reading, writing, listening, and speaking in the standard language. This view is consistent with Delpit's (1988, 1991) arguments that students of diverse backgrounds need to become thinkers, not just workers, and that they need to acquire the linguistic codes of the culture of power.

STUDENTS OF DIVERSE BACKGROUNDS:
FACTS AND FIGURES

The term *students of diverse backgrounds* has already been used a number of times, and I now describe these students in more specific terms. Students of diverse backgrounds show cultural differences along three lines: ethnicity, socioeconomic status, and primary language (Au, 1993). First, these students come from diverse ethnic backgrounds. In the United States, these students are often African American, Latino or Latina, Asian American, or

Native American in ethnicity. Second, these students are from low-income families and families living in poverty. These families are part of the working or underclass. Third, these students are speakers of a home language other than the language of power. In the United States, the language of power is standard American English. In contrast, students' home languages may be Spanish or African American Vernacular English. Throughout this volume, I give preference to the terms *students of diverse backgrounds, African American, Latino and Latina,* and *European American.* However, for the sake of accuracy, *minority students, Black, Hispanic,* and *White* are substituted if these were the terms used in the sources cited.

Along with many researchers who study these issues, I have seen that it is the intersection of all three of these dimensions of cultural diversity that presents the greatest challenge to schools. I have worked primarily in schools and classrooms with many native Hawaiian students, and many of the examples in this book come from these settings. As used here, the term *native Hawaiian* or *Hawaiian* refers to descendants of the original Polynesian inhabitants of the Hawaiian Islands. Although these students are ethnically diverse, they are also diverse in terms of their socioeconomic background. At most schools in predominantly Hawaiian communities, over 80% of the students are eligible for free or reduced-cost lunch. In this volume and elsewhere, you see low-income students in U.S. public schools described as students eligible for subsidized lunch. Finally, these students are speakers of a home language other than standard American English. Most grow up speaking Hawaii Creole English, a nonmainstream variety of English, as their first language.

At this point a few words need to be said about generalizations versus stereotyping. Social scientists make generalizations based on the results of research. For example, anthropologists studying native Hawaiian families have observed a pattern of sibling caretaking (Gallimore, Boggs, & Jordan, 1974). Sibling caretaking occurs when an older sister or brother receives the responsibility for looking after a younger child in the family. For example, the older child may see that the younger one wakes at the proper time in the morning, eats breakfast, and gets walked to the door of the classroom. Parents supervise the household and monitor the children's activities overall, but leave many specific responsibilities to the older siblings. It is a generalization to state that sibling caretaking occurs in many Hawaiian families. This generalization acknowledges that sibling caretaking does not occur in all Hawaiian families, because there will be differences among these families, just as there are differences among families within any cultural group. Stereotyping differs from generalizing by putting forth blanket or all-encompassing statements. For example, it would be stereotyping to state that sibling caretaking occurs in all Hawaiian families. Generalizations presented in this volume should be understood to apply often but certainly not always.

To continue our discussion of students of diverse backgrounds: What do the statistics show us about the ethnicity, socioeconomic status, and primary language of students in the United States? One obvious conclusion is that the number of students of diverse ethnic backgrounds is steadily increasing. In 2000, approximately 47,051,000 students in kindergarten through 12th grade were enrolled in public schools in the United States (U.S. Department of Education, 2002). Students who were members of minority groups accounted for 38.7% of the total, compared to only 22.2% in 1972. This increase is attributable largely to the growth in the number of Hispanic students. In 2000, Hispanic students accounted for 16.6% of the enrollment in public schools, up from only 6.0% in 1972. Black students accounted for 16.6%, up slightly from 14.8% in 1972. Students from other minority groups made up 5.4% of public school enrollment, up from 1.4% in 1972. Asian Americans accounted for about 4% of these students, Native Americans about 1%. White students made up 61.3% of enrollment, compared to 77.8% in 1972.

In terms of socioeconomic status, we know that growing up in poverty seriously affects students' opportunities for school success. Although the percentage of school-age children living in poverty decreased slightly between 1994 and 2001, 15% of all children ages 5 to 17 lived in households where the annual income fell below the poverty level (U.S. Department of Education, 2002). To determine who is poor, the U.S. Bureau of the Census uses a set of income thresholds that vary by family size and composition. In 2001, a family of four with two children was judged to be poor if their income fell below $17,960. By this standard, 30.0% of Black families with children age 18 or younger had income levels below the poverty line (U.S. Census Bureau, 2002). For Hispanic families, the figure was 27.4%, compared to 9.0% for White, non-Hispanic families.

The proportion of children growing up in poverty can vary widely depending on location, ranging from an average of 28.5% in large cities to an average of 12.1% in the suburbs (U.S. Department of Education, 2002). The rate for rural areas falls in between, with an estimated 20.6% of children being raised in poverty.

Poverty is certainly a factor, and some educators may believe that it is the only factor that needs to be addressed. However, studies as far back as the 1960s indicate that Black, Hispanic, and Native American students across different socioeconomic levels do not perform as well on standardized tests as White and Asian American students (The College Board, 1999). An achievement gap exists even for Black and Hispanic students from middle or professional class backgrounds. For example, a "within-socioeconomic-class" analysis of the 1994 NAEP reading results for twelfth graders revealed that the Black-White gap was actually larger for students with a parent who had a college degree (30 points) than it was for students whose parents both lacked a high school diploma (16 points) (The College Board, 1999). The achievement gap is noticeable in affluent suburban districts enrolling African American students from middle class and upper middle class families, and not just in urban districts (Viadero, 2000).

What do the statistics show about students who speak a primary language other than standard American English? In the United States, an estimated 4.5 million students in preschool through grade 12, about 9.3% of all students, are considered to be English Language Learners (ELLs; Kindler, 2002). These students speak home languages such as Spanish or Cantonese and are in the process of becoming proficient in English. Hispanic students make up by far the largest group of ELLs in the United States. However, Hispanic students vary in their patterns of language use. In 1999, the majority of Hispanic students, 57%, spoke English, or mostly English, at home (U.S. Department of Education, 2002). Nearly 90% of these students had mothers born in the United States. About 17% of Hispanic students spoke English and Spanish to an equal extent, whereas 25% spoke Spanish at home. Students' use of Spanish at home varied depending on their grade level. Twenty-eight percent of students in kindergarten through fifth grade spoke Spanish at home, compared to 21% of students in Grades 6 to 8, and 22% in Grades 9 to 12.

The states of California and Texas encompassed the major school districts reporting the highest percentages of students served in ELL programs in the 1999 to 2000 school year (Hoffman, 2001). These included the following:

- Los Angeles Unified School District, 44.1%
- Long Beach Unified School District, 36.0%
- Dallas Independent School District, 32.8%
- Fresno Unified School District, 32.3%
- San Diego City Unified School District, 27.5%
- Houston Independent School District, 26.5%.

These statistics cover students who speak Spanish or another home language other than English, such as Cantonese. However, neither the U.S. Bureau of the Census nor the U.S. Department of Education provides information on the number of students who speak nonmainstream varieties of English, such as African American Vernacular English (AAVE) or Hawaii Creole English. For example, we do not know the percentage of African American students who speak standard American English at home, who speak both standard American English and AAVE, and who primarily speak AAVE. Further discussion of these issues is presented in chapter 8.

The mindset educators should have about these factors follows. Students of diverse backgrounds often do present a challenge to schools. However, each of the three factors discussed—ethnicity, socioeconomic status, and primary language—is not necessarily a barrier to school success. Although these three factors are beyond their control, some students of diverse backgrounds still achieve at high levels. What is troubling is that these students tend to be the exception rather than the rule. The challenge for educators is to create new patterns in schools that capitalize on the strengths of students, families, and communities. A major issue is that systems in place in schools tend to rely on strengths more typical of many mainstream students, rather than on strengths held by many students of diverse backgrounds. An obvious example is that schools generally rely on students to speak standard American English and do not know how to build on students' strengths in other languages.

The Concept of Culture

I have mentioned culture and students' cultural identity, and it is now time to look more closely at the concept of culture. This concept can be complex and slippery, to say the least. I open this discussion by considering the concept of culture as it applies to students of diverse backgrounds. After that I consider how the concept of culture applies as well to teachers and schools.

Two Dimensions of Culture. One reason culture is such a difficult concept to grasp is that it has two different, and seemingly contradictory, dimensions. However, if you can understand these two different dimensions of culture, you will see why the cultural identity of students of diverse backgrounds—ethnicity, socioeconomic status, and primary language—does not prevent students and teachers from collaborating to create new patterns in classrooms.

First, we can think of culture as long-lasting values, beliefs, and practices that are passed down from generation to generation. This is what Lowe (1996) referred to as the *vertical dimension of culture*. For example, Hmong refugees from Laos and Thailand have been entering the United

States since the late 1970s. Hmong culture has been described as patriarchal, with an emphasis on the traditional roles of women as daughters, wives, and mothers (Ngo, 2002). Researchers have observed that young women in Hmong families tend to marry at a young age, rather than pursuing an education, apparently in keeping with the traditional values and practices of Hmong culture. These descriptions are a way of looking at the vertical dimension of Hmong culture, the dimension that relates to the continuity or sameness of culture.

Second, we can think of culture as involving dynamic processes of change. This is what Lowe (1996) termed the *horizontal dimension of culture*. Even as members of a cultural group are guided by its long-lasting values, they may simultaneously be adjusting to new circumstances and surroundings. Group members may change their cultural values and practices because of the new environment. In some cases, there will be a clear break with traditional practice. For example, in Laos and Thailand, most Hmong families had not encouraged young women to become highly educated. In contrast, Ngo (2002) found that the Hmong families she studied were encouraging young women to go on to higher education, because education was seen to offer opportunities for advancement in American society.

In other cases, change is shown when a traditional practice is kept in place but for new reasons. Ngo (2002) observed that young Hmong women were following the traditional pattern of marrying at a relatively young age, but not for traditional reasons. These young women wanted to show respect for their elders. At the same time, they wanted to participate in activities popular with other young Americans, such as being able to go out on a date to the movies unaccompanied by a parent. They saw getting married as a means of gaining freedom from parental control and of escaping from college environments perceived as unfriendly. On the surface, these young women appeared to be adhering to tradition, but beneath the surface, they were acting for reasons of their own that might be seen as rebellion or resistance rather than as compliance. This is a more subtle example of the horizontal—dynamic or changing—dimension of Hmong culture in the United States.

Educators must be aware that the vertical and horizontal dimensions of culture are simultaneously at work in the classroom. In chapter 7, I discuss the concept of culturally responsive instruction, or teaching that builds on the values and experiences students bring from the home. A common misconception about culturally responsive instruction is that it involves matching or replicating the home culture in the classroom. This view is incorrect because it overemphasizes the vertical or stable dimension of culture at the expense of the horizontal or changing dimension. The idea of culturally responsive instruction is not to recreate the home culture in the classroom. Rather, we want to allow teachers and students to construct new, hybrid classroom cultures that build on long-lasting cultural values while fostering academic achievement (Au, 2001). The idea is to allow students to succeed at academic learning by viewing their cultural heritage as an asset and a strength to be built upon in school. In this way, students can achieve at high levels in school without having to reject their own heritages (Au, 1993).

How Culture Applies to Teachers as Well as Students. Most teachers can readily see how the concept of culture applies to students of diverse backgrounds. It seems obvious that the more we know about our students and their cultural identities, the better we can tailor instruction to meet their needs as literacy learners. Earlier, I discussed three aspects of the cultural identity of students of diverse backgrounds: ethnicity, social class, and primary language.

It is more difficult to understand how the concept of culture applies to ourselves as teachers. Yet teachers have cultural identities, just like students. Recognizing and reflecting on our own cultural identity is central to the task of improving the literacy achievement of students of diverse backgrounds. One reason is that many teachers who work in schools with large numbers of students of diverse backgrounds do not share the cultural identity of their students. For example, in many schools in low-income Hawaiian communities, the majority of teachers are Asian Americans who commute from other residential areas. These teachers differ from their students in terms of ethnicity as well as social class, although they may share the same primary language, Hawaii Creole English.

The majority of teachers in the United States are from mainstream backgrounds: European American in ethnicity, from middle-income families, and monolingual speakers of standard American English. Teachers of mainstream backgrounds who have been raised in mainstream communities may not have had the opportunity to reflect on their cultural identities and may even believe that they "have no culture" (Florio-Ruane, 2001). As educators, we must recognize that each one of us has a cultural identity, and we must understand our own cultural identity to recognize the lenses through which we see other people, including our students (Schmidt, 1999).

The situation in which students of diverse backgrounds are taught by teachers of mainstream backgrounds is common throughout the United States. Teachers who do not share their students' cultural identity, and who are unfamiliar with the community in which the school is located, often bring views and values to the classroom that differ from those of their students. These differences in perspective may cause teachers to misinterpret students' behavior, resulting in misunderstandings and problems with classroom management. For example, consider the following situation. A Hawaiian child in a first-grade classroom is having trouble with a seatwork assignment. Because she wants to complete the task correctly, she asks other children for help and begins to copy their answers. Noticing these interactions, the teacher reminds the children to "do your own work." When the child persists in seeking help from other children, the teacher interprets this behavior as cheating and disobedience. This teacher does not know that many Hawaiian children have been brought up in households with sibling caretaking, as discussed earlier, and so are accustomed to turning to other children when in need of assistance. From the child's point of view, it makes little sense to struggle on one's own to complete a task, when assistance is close at hand.

How might this situation be adjusted to yield a positive result? The teacher could benefit from recognizing this child's ability to learn from other children, developed by being raised in a household with sibling caretaking. The teacher could turn this child's ability into an asset by having the children work in small, cooperative groups (Jordan, 1985). Later, she could explain to the children that there are times in school when we can ask others for help, and times when we must do our best on our own.

The Culture of the School. The concept of culture applies to schools as social institutions, as well as to students and teachers. Many studies have been conducted on the typical patterns of Western schooling or the way that we routinely "do school" (e.g., Henry, 1972; Mehan, 1979), including the patterns typically in place in schools with a high percentage of students of diverse backgrounds (Allington, 1991). A typical pattern is to focus the instruction of students of diverse backgrounds mainly on lower level skills as opposed to higher level thinking (Fitzgerald, 1995). Another typical pattern is to center the reading curriculum primarily on books written by authors with a mainstream perspective (Diamond & Moore, 1995). Still another typical pattern is to rely on standardized tests, or tests based on state standards, as the primary means of evaluating students' literacy learning (Hoffman, Assaf, & Paris, 2001). These typical patterns are what we have been calling the vertical or stable dimension of school culture. As made clear in chapter 2, a problem with these typical patterns is that they often contribute to the poor literacy achievement of students of diverse backgrounds. To help students achieve at higher levels, we must break away from these typical patterns and put new patterns in their place. This is where the horizontal or changing dimension of school culture comes into play. In chapter 2, I address specific steps educators can take to put new patterns in place in schools, including making changes in instruction, texts, and assessment. In chapter 4, I present literature-based instruction and the readers' workshop as a framework for organizing literacy learning according to new patterns.

Literacy in the Age of Globalization

In common with the concept of culture, the concept of literacy is also quite complex and slippery. The historical record shows that literacy has been a moving target in two different ways. First, over the centuries, literacy has been spreading out to a wider and wider audience. Second, standards for literacy have changed over time, so that literacy expectations today are higher than in the past.

Venezky (1991) traced the development of literacy in the industrialized West. He pointed out that literacy began as a monopoly of the church. By the 9th century, literacy had begun to spread to the nobility. In the 11th and 12th centuries, with the development of towns and cities, literacy moved into the ranks of the professions, to fill the need for greater administration, record keeping, and communication. The Protestant Reformation, in the early 16th century, spurred the spread of literacy as a means of gaining direct access to the word of God. In the 19th century, governments decided to provide many with a basic education for the purposes of building a citizenry that could participate productively in civic, economic, and military affairs. As public education expanded in both urban and rural areas, literacy spread to the masses. At the same time, new approaches to making paper, to printing, and to transportation, made books, such as the American dime novel, more affordable. Reading materials became available to more people than ever before.

Venezky (1991) observed that literacy moved through Western society in a patterned manner. The spread of literacy proceeded slowly from the clergy to the layman, from the wealthy to the laboring class, from men to women, from the cities to the countryside. In the United States, literacy reached large numbers of Whites before Blacks (Stedman & Kaestle, 1991).

Research conducted by Stedman and Kaestle (1991) showed that the big story of American education from 1880 to 1990 was the steady increase in school attainment. A rise in school attainment was evident for both Black and White Americans. However, although the gap between the educational accomplishments of the two groups narrowed, it remained substantial. Stedman and Kaestle explained the gap in the following way:

> A large, durable portion of the literacy differences between black and white Americans clearly cannot be explained by measurable economic and family characteristics. In the unexplained portion of the variation lie such elusive but real factors as the effects of prejudice, cultural alienation, discouragement, and differential aspirations, all related to race. (p. 126)

Standards for literacy in the United States have risen rapidly over the past century. In the early 1900s, the average American had a third-grade education, and a literate American was someone who could read and write at the third-grade level. In the 1940s, the average American had an eighth-grade education, and reading and writing at the eighth-grade level were considered acceptable. By the year 2000, expectations for literacy rose to the point where the average American was expected to graduate from high school and to read and write at the 12th-grade level.

Two important points can be taken from the historical record. First, standards for literacy have risen rapidly in the past, and it is logical to assume that they will continue to rise. As literacy educators today, we face a different challenge from educators in the past. We must aim to bring students to higher levels of literacy than ever before demanded. Literacy today involves the ability to read and write about complex documents, including literature and informational texts, as well as to interpret visual and audio information, such as photographs, movies, television programs, and other media. Second, although in the past only a privileged few were expected to attain high levels of literacy, at present, all students are expected to achieve at these levels. Literacy educators face the challenge of bringing all students to high levels of literacy, regardless of ethnicity, primary language, and family income.

A common misconception held by the general public is that there was a golden age of American education, a time not too long ago when most Americans could read and write well, and certainly much better than the average student can read and write today. To the contrary, studies show that today's students are achieving at higher levels than in the past. Berliner and Biddle (1997) conducted studies of the results of the Scholastic Aptitude Test (SAT). The SAT is taken by about half of the students in the United States; those who are planning to attend college. Scores on the SAT range from 200 to 800. Critics have cited declines in SAT scores as evidence of the failure of the nation's schools. The analysis by Berliner and Biddle demonstrates that the purported drop in test scores during the period from 1976 to 1993 occurred because a larger pool of students than ever before took the SAT, including many more students of diverse backgrounds. When the results are disaggregated by subgroup, it can be seen that the scores of White students remained almost constant. The 6-point decline seen in the scores of White students occurred because a higher number of students from low-income backgrounds took the test, and scores are highly related to family income. At the same time, the scores of students in every minority group (Black, Asian American, Native American, Mexican American, and Puerto Rican) actually increased. The most dramatic increase was seen in the results for Black students, who achieved an average score 55 points higher in 1993 than in 1976.

Fueling the push for higher test scores and higher standards for students' achievement is the present era of globalization. The essence of globalization is the spread of free-market capitalism to all corners of the world (Friedman, 2000). According to Burbules and Torres (2000), the following are among the elements that characterize globalization: (a) an integration of what were once separate national economies, as seen in the rise of the European Union; (b) the emergence of new exchange relationships and arrangements, such as those that enable financial traders in one country to buy and sell stocks and bonds from another country; and (c) the rise of multinational corporations with the ability to connect markets around the globe, enabling 600 such corporations to control 25% of the world's economy.

The economies of countries around the world are more closely linked than ever before, due to unprecedented advances in technology. The Internet and high-speed communication systems allow news to race around the globe. The knowledge and service economy is the dominant force, not manufacturing and agriculture. This is the shift from Fordist models of production, such as that of the assembly line used in the typical auto plant, to post-Fordist models that emphasize the flexible use of workers, inventories, and labor processes (Burbules & Torres, 2000). This shift is leading to a polarized labor market, with well compensated, highly skilled workers on one hand, and poorly compensated, unskilled or low-skilled workers on the other. Workers in the knowledge and service economy include teachers, software developers, insurance salespeople, and scientists, as well as workers in the fast-food restaurants, hotels, and landscaping companies. According to Friedman (2000), 93% of the workers of the future will be part of the knowledge and service economy, whereas only 5% will be employed in manufacturing and 2% in agriculture.

Decision makers in the United States and other developed nations realize that continued economic prosperity depends on workers who can outthink workers in other parts of the world. For this reason, the emphasis on rote learning in school, considered logical in an age when many students were expected to become factory workers, has gradually been replaced by an emphasis on higher level thinking (Smith, 2000). In literacy, students are expected not just to read with expression but to comprehend, summarize, and interpret texts. In mathematics, students are expected not just to perform calculations but to describe the process of thinking that they followed to solve a problem. Because of the economic shifts brought about by globalization, today's young people should be able to engage in higher level thinking, to communicate across sociocultural groups, and to use a variety of technologies.

Certainly, the purpose of literacy learning in school cannot be merely to build a highly trained workforce. Purposes for literacy such as citizenship and personal fulfillment are perhaps more important and must continue to have a place. Furthermore, literacy practices within diverse communities may differ from the mainstream literacy practices demanded by the workplace and valued by the larger society (a point discussed in chapter 3, when I contrast the idea of autonomous literacy with multiple literacies). It is clear, however, that forces impelling the United States and other nations toward higher standards for literacy achievement are at a macrolevel and long-lasting in their significance.

For educators working in schools with many students of diverse backgrounds, the question is how these students can be helped to achieve at the high levels of literacy presently demanded. School reform policies based on globalization and economic restructuring can have the dangerous effect of increasing rather than decreasing educational inequality and economic stratification (Lipman, 2002). Yet, if students of diverse backgrounds continue to perform at low levels, they will be denied the opportunities for social, political, and economic advancement available to other students. This is the very problem facing educators today, made evident by the literacy achievement gap.

The Literacy Achievement Gap

Considerable evidence documents the existence of a gap between the literacy achievement of students of diverse backgrounds and their more privileged peers. In the United States, this gap is readily apparent in the results of tests administered by the National Assessment of Educational Progress (NAEP), popularly known as the "Nation's Report Card." The NAEP is the only large-scale, federally funded testing program in the United States, and its results on students' reading achievement date back to 1971. Long-term results are available for three major subgroups: White, Black, and Hispanic students. Students are tested at Grades 4, 8, and 12.

In discussing recent results, I refer to average scale scores, the scores obtained when the performance of all the students in a group are considered. Average scores do not tell us about the performance of individual students. It is important to remember that some Black and Hispanic students at all grade levels received high scores, whereas some White and Asian or Pacific Islander students received low scores.

Figure 1.1 shows the average scale scores, by group, for the NAEP reading tests administered in 2002 (Grigg, Daane, Yin, & Campbell, 2003). At all three grade levels, White and Asian or Pacific Islander students had higher average scores than Hispanic and Black students. For example, at Grade 12, the average score for White students was 292; for Asian or Pacific Islander students, 286; for Hispanic students, 273; and for Black students, 267. Looking at these differences another way, the average score for Hispanic students at Grade 12 (273) is just 1 point above the average score for White students at Grade 8 (272). The average score for Black students at Grade 12 (267) is identical to that for Asian or Pacific Islander students at Grade 8 (267). These results suggest that, by Grade 12, the average level of reading achievement of Hispanic and Black students, as groups, is about four grades below the average level for White and Asian or Pacific Islander students, as groups—a significant gap, indeed.

The 2002 NAEP reading results did show some positive signs. At Grade 4, the average scale scores for Black and Hispanic students, as well as White

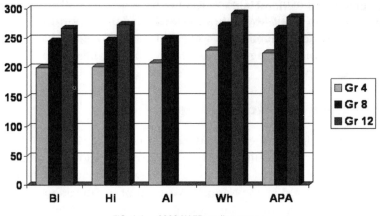

FIG. 1.1.   2002 NAEP reading scores.

students, reached their highest levels in a decade. The same promising pattern is seen at Grade 8, although not at Grade 12. Although the literacy achievement gap remained sizeable, it did not appear to be increasing. In 2002, the gap between the average scores of White and Black fourth graders was not significantly different from 1992, and the same was true for the gap between White and Hispanic fourth graders. At Grades 8 and 12, gaps between White and Black students, and between White and Hispanic students, were not significantly different when the 2002 results were compared to those of previous assessment years. On one hand, these findings showed that the literacy achievement gap had not worsened. On the other hand, the size of the gap remained substantial.

SUMMARY

Students of diverse backgrounds—those who differ from mainstream students in terms of ethnicity, socioeconomic status, and primary language— are entering schools in growing numbers. Of great concern to educators is the gap that exists between the literacy achievement of these students and their mainstream peers. Taking a pluralist perspective will help educators in their efforts to close the gap. Socially sustained patterns in place in schools and classrooms prevent students of diverse backgrounds from achieving high levels of literacy. To put new patterns in place, educators must consider their own cultural backgrounds and identities, as well as that of their students. Culture is both stable and changing. Educators must recognize the strengths that students bring from the home, identify negative patterns detrimental to students' literacy learning in school, and create positive patterns that promote higher levels of literacy achievement. Closing the literacy achievement gap is critical in the current era of globalization and rising standards, if students of diverse backgrounds are to enjoy the economic, as well as political and social, benefits, offered by the larger society.

2

Understanding the Gap: Explanations and Solutions

In chapter 1, I described the literacy achievement gap between students of diverse backgrounds and their mainstream peers. In this chapter, I consider explanations for the gap, plausible from a social constructivist perspective. A common response is to attribute the gap to deficiencies, perhaps of intellect or motivation, in students from the lower achieving groups. Social constructivism helps us to see weaknesses in such a deficit perspective. In a social constructivist view, a first category of explanations is related to societal patterns at a macrolevel and beyond the immediate control of educators. A second category of explanations is related to patterns at a more microlevel, within schools and classrooms and subject to the influence of educators. The first category is discussed to provide a broader context for understanding the issues. However, my focus is on the second category of explanations, because these relate to steps that teachers can take to make a difference in closing the literacy achievement gap. I describe patterns likely to be effective in improving the school literacy learning of students of diverse backgrounds and make the contrast to ineffective patterns. The key issues reflected in these patterns are all explored in greater detail in later chapters.

EXPLANATIONS FOR THE LITERACY ACHIEVEMENT GAP

Given the clear evidence for the existence of a literacy achievement gap, the obvious question is why such a gap exists. I have pointed out that historical patterns in society contributed to the creation of a gap between the literacy achievement of mainstream students and students of diverse backgrounds. In addition, present patterns in society operate to keep the gap in place. These patterns are reflected at a macrolevel in the social, political, and economic conditions that affect the lives of students and their families, as well as at the microlevel in students' daily interactions and experiences in schools and classrooms. These patterns are part of the culture of Western schooling and the way educators typically "do school" with students of diverse backgrounds. As discussed in chapter 1, it is important to keep in mind that culture is both stable and dynamic. By looking at the stable dimension of school culture, we can hone in on the problem. By considering the dynamic dimension of school culture, we can see how to turn situations around to improve the literacy learning of students of diverse backgrounds.

There is no one simple explanation for the literacy achievement gap. Rather, research consistent with a social constructivist perspective supports multiple explanations (Au, 1998; see also Jacob & Jordan, 1993; Strickland & Ascher, 1992). As various explanations are discussed, you will see that they are interconnected and overlap one another.

Explanations at a Macrolevel

Discrimination. The first explanation has to do with discrimination (also called societal racism; Strickland & Ascher, 1992). From a social constructivist perspective, poverty and school failure may both be seen as manifestations of historical and systemic conditions rooted in discrimination. Sociologists known as critical theorists argue that society in the United States and other nations is structured to favor the continued advancement of those already in power. According to this view, the major institutions in a society, including the schools, are run for the benefit of mainstream students, those with ethnic and linguistic backgrounds like those of the wealthy and powerful members of that society, not for the benefit of students of diverse backgrounds and their families. Critical theory (e.g., Kincheloe & McLaren, 2000) is discussed further in chapter 5.

An implication of the discrimination explanation is that teaching and learning in school tends to revolve around the culture, language, values, and behaviors familiar to most mainstream students. In contrast, the culture, language, values, and behaviors familiar to students of diverse backgrounds is usually discounted or rendered invisible. For example, students may find that they are not allowed to teach or learn from peers, that their home languages are ignored, and that school texts reflect only mainstream content (Au, 1993). Discrimination, intentional or unintentional, can be a contributing factor in all of the other explanations that are discussed.

To take another example, the belief that a focus on lower level skills is appropriate for students of diverse backgrounds may stem from lowered expectations for the academic performance of these students, which in turn may arise from beliefs that students of diverse backgrounds lack the intellectual ability and drive to benefit from challenging curricula. This belief has deep roots in the history of Western education in which schooling has often been used by one cultural group as a tool group to establish superiority over another. In the process of colonization, members of the subordinate culture become marked as inferior to members of the dominant culture. In the United States, there has been a centuries-long struggle to impose mainstream values, rooted in the English and Protestant heritage of the American colonies, on all people. This process of deculturalization has been described by Spring (2001):

> *Deculturalization is the educational process of destroying a people's culture and replacing it with a new culture.* In the case of the United States, schools have used varying forms of this method in attempts to eradicate the cultures of Native Americans; African Americans; Mexican Americans; Puerto Ricans; and immigrants from Ireland, Southern and Eastern Europe, and Asia. Believing that Anglo-American culture—the culture of the descendants of the British colonists and immigrants—was a superior culture and the only culture that would support republican and democratic institutions, educators forbade the speaking of non-English languages, particularly Spanish and Native American tongues, and forced students to learn an Anglo-American centered curriculum. (p. 4; italics in the original)

The treatment of Native Americans vividly illustrates the dynamics outlined by Spring. Lomowaima (1995) outlined the four methods used by Western nations and churches to subjugate Native Americans and take away their land. First, Native Americans were relocated to controlled communities separate from European settlements. Second, they were instructed in the language of the conquering nation, such as French, English, or Spanish. Third, their communities came under the religious influence of the colonizers, with the conversion of Native Americans to Catholicism or Protestantism. Fourth, native communities were restructured economically, with men receiving training in trades or agriculture and women in domestic skills. Such a powerfully damaging legacy is bound to be difficult to overcome. According to Lomowaima, "[t]hese four components of colonization—relocation under political control, replacement of language, religious conversion, and gendered economic reconstruction—permeate American Indian education to the present day" (pp. 334–335).

In his classic work, Carnoy (1974) described education as a process of cultural imperialism. As educators, we must be aware of the controversial history of schooling as a process of imposing mainstream culture on students of diverse backgrounds. We must acknowledge the lingering effects of this long history on education today. Teachers, whether of mainstream or nonmainstream backgrounds, are usually individuals who were themselves successful in school. As a result, they may find it difficult to recognize the subtle influences of colonization and deculturalization in their own lives and in the lives of their students, and the underlying attitudes that these harmful processes have propagated.

Inferior Education. One of the effects of discrimination is the unequal allocation of educational resources. The second explanation attributes the literacy achievement gap to the inferior education received by students of diverse backgrounds, due to inferior physical facilities and resources as well as to less expert teaching (Strickland & Ascher, 1992). For example, consider the patterns seen in the typical suburban school versus the typical urban school. Suburban schools in affluent communities, where there are few students of diverse cultural and linguistic backgrounds, are located in safe neighborhoods, have well maintained buildings, up-to-date textbooks, and ready access to technology. In contrast, urban schools in low-income communities, where most of the students are of diverse cultural and linguistic backgrounds, usually are located in neighborhoods that expose students to violence, have poorly maintained buildings and out-of-date textbooks, and offer limited access to technology (see Kozol, 1992, for illustrations of these "savage inequalities"). Further exacerbating these differences is the quality of teaching students receive. Suburban schools in affluent areas are usually able to attract highly qualified, experienced teachers, and these teachers tend to remain in the schools. Urban and rural schools, in which teaching conditions may be much more challenging, find it difficult to attract and retain teachers. At many of these schools, the majority of teachers are inexperienced and less qualified than those in suburban districts, and rates of teacher turnover tend to be high (Darling-Hammond, 1995).

As shown in later chapters, the forms of instruction likely to be effective with students of diverse backgrounds tend to require high levels of teacher expertise. Students of diverse backgrounds often receive an inferior education because teachers who are inexperienced and less qualified often find it difficult to implement these effective forms of instruction. This difficulty is often compounded by the response of policymakers. Rather than investing in the professional development that will build teachers' expertise in effective instruction, policymakers tend to see packaged programs as the "quick fix" that will improve students' achievement (Allington & Walmsley, 1995). The danger is that many of these packaged programs are built around scripted lessons and lower level skills and do not encourage culturally responsive forms of instruction or higher level thinking with text. For these reasons, packaged programs chosen to simplify teaching may further contribute to the inferior education received by students of diverse backgrounds.

Although factors at the macrolevel are beyond the control of an individual teacher, groups of teachers can and should work together to counter the effects of discrimination and inferior education on their students. Countering these effects might begin with professional development, for example through forming a study group to read and learn more about the issues. The next step might be for members of the study group to begin sharing the ideas they have learned with the whole faculty at their school. Teachers can join professional organizations to upgrade their knowledge of literacy issues and to promote high-quality literacy instruction for their students. Teachers can join with parents and community groups to address the effects of discrimination and inferior education, perhaps by lobbying decision makers for changes, such as increased funding for professional development, books, or technology.

Explanations at the Classroom Level

Teaching That Fails to Build on Students' Culture.　As suggested in chapter 1, the lack of school success experienced by many students of diverse backgrounds may be due to a mismatch between the culture of the home and the culture of the school (Au & Mason, 1981; Heath, 1983; Philips, 1983). Because the school is a mainstream institution, instruction is usually carried out in ways following mainstream standards for behavior and reflecting mainstream cultural values. Students of diverse backgrounds may have difficulty learning in school because instruction does not draw on the knowledge, values, and standards for behavior of their own culture and community.

An example of research supporting this explanation is seen in an ethnographic study conducted by McMillon and McMillon (2004) of the empowering literacy practices of an African American church. (My intention in focusing on this research is to give examples of values developed in a community setting, not to privilege Christianity or going to church.) The researchers pointed out the importance of considering community settings in which children's literacy learning takes place, often before they enter school. The church is one such setting for many African American children. Historically, the African American church has been of great significance to the community. Through its spiritual and social influence, it has provided leadership, a firm foundation for families in unstable times, a place where African Americans could exert control without having to answer to outsiders, and a strong voice for equality. The church continues to be a source of encouragement and validation to African Americans, as this institution supports schools, businesses, and low-income housing, and nurtures the artistic talents of young people. McMillon and McMillon discussed how Black theology, the central beliefs carried forward by the African American church, emphasizes (a) the fighting of racial discrimination; (b) the building of Black resources, including people, institutions, and movements; and (c) a relentless, absolute faith in freedom.

African American children who are immersed in the church as a community context learn to interpret their world according to a particular set of values. McMillon and McMillon (2004) described how children find themselves enmeshed in a complex social network that teaches them the importance of personal, family-like relationships, or what Fordham and Ogbu (1986) called *fictive kinship*. The term fictive kinship refers to the closeness of ties to other people in the community. Kinship indicates that these ties or relationships are as strong as those among kin or family members. Fictive indicates that the people involved may not actually be related by blood or by marriage. Children are taught to address adults using kinship terms such as *Brother, Sister,* or *Mother,* and they learn to respect adults for the wisdom acquired through life experience without regard for educational background or social status. The close-knit network of social relationships in the church creates an atmosphere of trust, mutual commitment, and personal connections among teachers, students, and students' families. Teachers in the church establish close, caring relationships with students and constantly offer advice and encouragement, especially when students encounter personal difficulties. Teachers maintain high expectations for students' performance and delight in their progress. As children participate in Sunday school classes and other church activities, they learn to emulate the ethic of caring modeled by their teachers and other adults, as they help their peers and sometimes serve as teachers themselves.

According to McMillon and McMillon (2004), literacy is made meaningful to children because authentic literacy practices are taught in a natural environment with an emphasis on the application to real life of lessons learned through reading:

The most valued artifact and important learning tool in the African American Church is the *Holy Bible*, which is considered "God's Word"—the roadmap for life. Students are taught that it is the most important book they will ever read and are admonished to read it frequently and obey (apply) what they read. . . . We found that, based on these beliefs, the students understood the importance of learning the "lessons" that they are taught each week. They understand that biblical knowledge acquired will be applicable throughout their lives. In this way, we believe that teachers' use of authentic print helps students understand the value of learning in the church environment, by explicitly teaching the purpose and relevance of learning. (pp. 291–292)

Besides learning the practical applications of "lessons" from their reading, children develop language and literacy skills such as speaking clearly, using proper inflection and expressing emotions, speaking extemporaneously, retelling traditional tales and nursery rhymes, and memorizing and sharing stories from the Bible.

One of the responsibilities of fictive kinship is to help others succeed. McMillon and McMillon (2004) pointed out how an orientation toward fictive kinship may create a conflict in school if competition and outshining others is rewarded, rather than cooperation and assisting others. A second source of cultural conflict may develop if teachers treat students in a distant, alienating manner, because students have come to expect the close and nurturing experiences formed in the atmosphere of the African American church. A third source of conflict may arise if students are taught literacy skills outside of a context they find meaningful to their own lives.

Action Recommendation: Show Respect for Students' Cultures and Build on Their Cultural Knowledge. What can teachers do to build on the orientation toward fictive kinship that many African American children may bring from the church or other family and community settings? Ladson-Billings (1994) cited the case of Patricia Hilliard, an African American teacher who created relationships in the classroom similar to those in an extended family. She and her class began the school year by developing an "undefined contract." Hilliard helped the students arrive at expectations they believed they could meet and consequences they judged to be fair. She had the students form "extended family groups." Students chose the names for their families, adhering only to guidelines that these names not be offensive or have gang connotations. Students in the extended family groups took responsibility for monitoring each other's academic work and classroom behavior and for resolving any problems that arose within the group.

Here is an example of a discussion in Hilliard's classroom:

Hilliard: What happens in your house when you do something good?

Student: My momma is real happy.

Hilliard: How do you know she's happy?

Student: Sometimes she hugs and kisses me. Sometimes she just smiles and tells me.

Hilliard: Right! And that's what we're going to do here. When your "family member" does a good job you're going to show him or her just how proud you are. And when someone doesn't do a good job, you're not going to laugh at him or tease him. You're going to do your best to help him do better. When one of us does well, we'll all do well. When one of us fails, we all fail. (Ladson-Billings, 1994, p. 62)

Note in this example how the idea of the extended family builds on the values of fictive kinship, cooperation, and supporting others. Ladson-Billings found that cooperative learning was a strategy used by all of the exemplary teachers in her study, which included both African American and European American teachers.

Ladson-Billings (1994) pointed out that the ideology underlying these exemplary teachers' use of cooperative learning strategies was "to prepare their students for collective growth and liberation" (p. 60). As students worked in groups, teachers recognized and rewarded joint effort, rather than elevating the importance of individual achievement. This emphasis on collective action was shown even in class discussions of heroes or role models. Here is what Pauline Dupree told her fourth graders:

Now I know your book talks about Rosa Parks being a seamstress with tired feet who decided to sit down on a bus one day. But, that's not the *whole* story. . . . You see, Rosa was an activist. (She writes the word "activist" on the chalkboard.) That means she was someone who didn't wait for things to happen. She made things happen! For years Rosa had been going to a place called Highlander Folk School (she writes "Highlander Folk School" on the board) learning how to educate black people in their struggle against racism. She was a member of the local NAACP and was just waiting for a chance to confront racism. She was a woman with a plan.

This story teaches us that we can't just do something without thinking first. You can't do things you're not prepared to do. And you probably can't do very much by yourself. You need help. I need help. We all need help. That's how we make things happen—by working together. (Ladson-Billings, 1994, pp. 60–61)

Dupree's emphasis on collective action and on taking responsibility for helping others provides another example of how a teacher can build on students' orientation toward fictive kinship. In addition, Dupree spelled out the lesson students should take from their books and the application of that lesson to their own lives. Dupree made it easy for students to see the connections between their reading and their lives outside the classroom.

Example of an Ineffective Pattern.   Now let's look at what happens when the teacher creates a classroom atmosphere that does not reflect the students' cultural values, such as fictive kinship. Sometimes teachers who do not understand the students' culture unintentionally create barriers that prevent the growth of relationships supportive of literacy learning. Larson and Irvine (1999) used the term *reciprocal distancing* for "a discourse process in which teachers and students invoke existing sociohistorical and political distances between their communities in classroom interaction" (p. 395). Reciprocal distancing comes about when the teacher fails to recognize or dismisses students' cultural and linguistic knowledge. In essence, the classroom becomes contested ground, with teachers and students vying to determine whether the usual mainstream school content and practices will dominate, or whether culturally relevant content and practices will have a place. If students find that their preferences and interests are continually rebuffed, they will react by widening the gulf between themselves and the teacher. The term reciprocal distancing reflects the notion that separation between teacher and students is collaboratively enacted and reinforced in their daily interactions in the classroom.

Larson and Irvine (1999) made the following observation in a first-grade classroom on January 15th, the birthday of acclaimed civil rights leader Martin Luther King, Jr. The interaction occurred during a transition between a whole-class reading lesson on constructing a "hard words" list and an exercise on word families:

[An African American boy takes a picture of Martin Luther King out of his desk to color.]

Teacher: Let's not look at that now! That's for after lunch.

Student: I like him. I just want to look at him.

Teacher: Well that's nice. Put him away. We'll do Martin Luther King after lunch.

[An African American boy across the room calls out, "We call him Dr. King."]

Teacher: He's not a *real* doctor like you go to for a cold or sore throat. [1 second pause] He's a *different* kind of doctor.

[The boy who called out "We call him Dr. King" slumps down in his chair and looks down at his desk. An African American girl in front calls, "It's his birthday."]

Teacher: Then I guess we'll have to talk about it later. We'll talk about it this afternoon. (p. 395)

This brief interaction illustrates how quickly a rift can develop between the teacher and students. Larson and Irvine pointed out how the teacher and students used pronouns to take sides against one another in a struggle over the value of Dr. King as a significant historical figure. In her haste to move on to the next activity, the teacher used the pronoun "that" to refer to the picture of Dr. King she planned to have the children color later in the day. By using the more personal pronoun "him," the African American boy who had taken out the picture resisted the teacher's order and expressed his regard for Dr. King. The teacher tried to appease the boy by talking about what "we"—the teacher and students together—would be doing after lunch. But the term *we* was appropriated and given a different spin by the African American boy who called out, "*We* call him Dr. King." By emphasizing the word "we," this boy put the teacher outside of the students' community and reinforced Dr. King's position of significance in their lives. In her declaration, "He's not a *real* doctor," the teacher showed a refusal to accept the students' point of view. When an African American girl reminded the teacher that it was Dr. King's birthday, the teacher at last recognized the depth of the students' interest. However, her grudging acceptance could not undo the damage done.

Larson and Irvine (1999) concluded the following: "In this classroom, students may be learning some forms of literacy knowledge, but they are also learning that their sociocultural knowledge and literacy practices are not valuable resources" (p. 396). The reciprocal distancing occurring through interactions in this classroom worked strongly against the values of fictive kinship, making teaching more difficult for the teacher and learning more difficult for the children.

Teaching That Fails to Build on Students' Language.   Another explanation for the literacy achievement gap centers on linguistic differences. This explanation grows from the fact that many students of diverse backgrounds speak a home language other than standard American English (e.g., the home language of many Latino and Latina students is Spanish, whereas the home language of many African American students is AAVE). Current theory and research in bilingual education, consistent with a social constructivist perspective (e.g., Brock, Boyd, & Moore, 2003), suggest that students' poor academic achievement generally is not due to their limited proficiency in English, or standard English in particular. Rather, it is due to the exclusion or limited use of instruction in the home language in many school programs (Snow, 1990) or to the low status accorded the home language. Students of diverse backgrounds enter school with strengths in their home language, if not the standard language. The challenge for schools is to tailor instruction to build on these language strengths (e.g., Schwarzer, Haywood, & Lorenzen, 2003). When schools provide instruction that ignores these strengths, they limit students' academic progress and may cause students to lose confidence in themselves as language and literacy learners.

The denigration of the home languages of students of diverse backgrounds has taken its toll over generations. Barrera (in Jimenez, Moll, Rodriguez-Brown, & Barrera, 1999), a well known Latina literacy researcher, described these negative effects:

> So many of us are in need of healing from the *culturalectomies* that we endured as children in U.S. schools. There are many scars left from the process. For example, many currently practicing Latino educators in the U.S. southwest, in particular those of Mexican American heritage, never saw their culture, language, and literacy reflected in the school curriculum as they moved through the elementary and secondary grades. In fact, some faced school biases related to both English and Spanish language learning.
>
> In the elementary grades, the school's message to them was that English mattered and Spanish did not. In the secondary grades, the message to those who studied Spanish was that their dialect was not good enough compared to standard Spanish. (pp. 217–218)

A negative attitude toward ELLs can lead to the denigration of students' home languages, as well as to mistaken assumptions about the kinds of instruction they should receive. A review of research conducted by Fitzgerald (1995) summarized the findings confirmed in study after study of the literacy instruction most frequently experienced by ELLs in the United States. At least in the primary grades, most students received instruction in small groups with an emphasis on word identification and oral reading, rather than on higher level thinking such as comprehension and vocabulary meaning. Teachers generally spent much more time correcting students' pronunciation than engaging them in discussions of text ideas. Fitzgerald found that the typical discourse patterns in reading lessons (see discussion of the teacher initiation, student response, teacher evaluation pattern in chapter 5) were incompatible with those of students' home cultures, although some teachers were observed to use culturally responsive discourse patterns. Teachers working with ELLs in groups labeled as *low ability* placed an even greater focus on lower level skills than when working with ELLs in groups judged to be of higher ability.

Action Recommendation: Show Respect for Students' Home Languages and Build on Their Linguistic Knowledge. In terms of promoting students' literacy learning, teachers who know their students' home languages have a considerable advantage over teachers who do not. I first discuss positive practices observed in the classroom of a bilingual teacher, then positive practices that may be followed by monolingual teachers or teachers whose students speak many different home languages.

Manyak (2001) studied a first- and second-grade English immersion classroom in a Title I school where 65% of the children were Latino or Latina. (In the United States, schools in low-income communities are called Title I schools because they qualify for federal monies under Title I of the Elementary and Secondary Education Act.) The teacher, Ms. Page, featured a literacy activity called the Daily News as part of her morning routine. Ms. Page instructed the children to share "cosas de verdad" (true stories) and "cosas que nos interesa" (interesting things) for the Daily News, and she taught them to present their ideas in a big voice that everyone could hear. Because many of the children knew very little English at the start of the school year, the majority of their contributions were made in Spanish. When this happened, Ms. Page asked the children to translate their classmates' words. Children collaborated with one another during the sharing and translating, so that their voices often overlapped. Ms. Page wrote the children's ideas down on a large sheet of paper. When she had finished writing, she led the class in a choral reading of the Daily News. Ms. Page frequently used the oral cloze technique to guide the children as they watched her write and then read the Daily News together in a chorus. In oral cloze, the teacher begins the phrase and pauses to allow the children to complete it. Ms. Page's skillful use of this technique engaged the children, and they chimed in eagerly.

Here is an example of translation that occurred after Ana had shared in Spanish that she was going to the movies.

Ms. Page: Let's try to do that in English. Ana, can you help me out and think how to say that in English?
(Ana shakes head, "no." Karen raises her hand.)
Ms. Page: Are you sure? Sandra.

Sandra: Ana went to a movie.

Karen: Is going to a movie.

Student 1: A movie.

Student 2: The movies.

Ms. Page: The movies. Which day is she going to the movies?

Students: El sábado.

Ms. Page: On Saturday. OK, all eyes up here on the board. Ana, help me out
           with the words. (Ms. Page begins to write.). (Manyak, 2001, p.
           444)

This transcript illustrates collaboration, as four children volunteered information. By working together, the class could tackle problems of translation that might have been beyond the reach of any one child. Ms. Page guided the translation activity by inviting participation, posing questions, and summarizing the key points made. All the while, she modeled the use of English for the children. Manyak observed that children could participate in the Daily News in a variety of ways, depending on their confidence and proficiency in English and Spanish. Those who spoke Spanish could start to experiment with English by saying words quietly to themselves, imitating other children or the teacher, or contributing just a word or phrase.

Ms. Page could build on the children's home language because she spoke Spanish. However, with a little creativity, monolingual teachers or teachers in classrooms where students speak a variety of home languages can incorporate these languages into the classroom. For example, Gay (2000) described a kindergarten classroom with children who were immigrants or whose parents were immigrants, from a mixture of ethnic groups. School had been in session just over 4 months when Gay made the following observations:

> Attached to the entrance door is a huge welcome sign brightly decorated with the children's own art. The sign reads "Welcome to Our Academic Home." This message is accompanied by a group photograph of the members of the class and "welcome" in different languages (Spanish, Japanese, German, French, various U.S. dialects, etc.). (p. 39)

Books in the classroom library reflected the children's cultures and languages as well. Because the teacher had enlisted the help of the parents, she gained access to their linguistic resources and could easily bring different languages into the classroom.

I present evidence in chapter 8 suggesting that two-way immersion appears to be the strongest approach for improving the literacy achievement of ELLs. In two-way immersion programs, ELLs develop oral proficiency and literacy in their home language (such as Spanish, Portuguese, or Korean) as well as in English. At the same time, their classmates who are native speakers of English develop oral proficiency and literacy in a second language, such as Spanish. Two-way immersion programs continue until students graduate from high school, so students do not experience the problem of leaving bilingual education, a departure associated with a loss of support for growth in the home language.

Teaching That Fails to Promote Higher Level Thinking. In chapter 1, we pointed out the importance of providing students of diverse backgrounds with ample instruction in higher level thinking with text, given rising standards for literacy achievement spurred by globalization. Research reviewed by Fitzgerald (1995) documented that the very opposite usually happens. Students of diverse backgrounds, and ELLs in particular, tend to receive instruction heavily oriented toward lower level skills. Educators need to understand why this focus on lower level skills persists and what can be done to shift the focus toward higher level thinking.

Without realizing it, teachers may subconsciously absorb long-standing stereotypes that lead them to expect a lower level of academic performance from students of diverse backgrounds. For example, Oakes and Guiton (1995) conducted a study of tracking in high school. Students who were assigned to lower tracks received courses in vocational education and did not have the opportunity to gain the advanced academic skills necessary for college. These researchers found that a disproportionate number of Latino students were placed in the lower tracks, and that these placements were related to teachers' low expectations for their academic performance:

Latino students suffered the most negative judgments about their culture's impact on school effort and motivation and, as a consequence, on their class placements. Educators at all three schools characterized Latinos as having poor basic skills, little interest in school, and being "culturally disinclined" to aspire to postsecondary education. One Coolidge teacher said that Latinos, "as a result of the way they were raised, do not want to learn and view school only as something to get away from." Another attributed their low representation in higher level courses to their home environment and lack of parental support. Other teachers and administrators mentioned the likely transience of Latino students as a factor. (Oakes & Guiton, 1995, pp. 18–19)

This study documented how low expectations for academic achievement contributed to students' placement in low-track classes that failed to provide challenging curricula. In elementary schools, similar effects are seen in the disproportionate placement of students of diverse backgrounds in remedial reading classes and in the bottom reading groups in their classrooms (e.g., Bartoli, 1995). Research conducted by Allington (1983), Shannon (1989), and others, demonstrated that students in classes and groups deemed to be of lower ability received instruction heavily weighted toward lower level skills of word identification, with little instruction in comprehension and reasoning with text.

Some educators may hold the mistaken belief that programs focusing on lower level skills are somehow a better match to the abilities of students of diverse backgrounds. Lomowaima (1995) described how research, such as certain studies conducted in the United States in the 1960s and 1970s, gave a false aura of scientific respectability to notions of the inherent inferiority of students of diverse backgrounds. For example, studies conducted during this time found that Native American children had poor visual perception and weak language skills; other studies from this period documented similar deficits in children from other diverse ethnic groups. These children were deemed to come from a "culture of poverty," and they were labeled as "disadvantaged." As a result, programs were designed to provide these students with the lower level cognitive and linguistic skills they were assumed to lack. These skills were taught to students in a rote manner, again in keeping with assumptions about students' limited intellectual capacities. These programs, and others based on similar notions, resurfaced in the 1990s and were promoted as solutions for addressing the increasing diversity in the U.S. student population and rising standards for achievement. From a historical perspective, such programs, based on assumptions about the inferior intellectual abilities of students of diverse backgrounds, can be seen as part of the long and unfortunate legacy of colonization and deculturalization.

Teachers attempting to improve the literacy achievement of students of diverse backgrounds must be willing to strike off in new directions, rather than continuing with familiar practices that have served students poorly in the past. For example, what would happen if students of diverse backgrounds were given access to advanced classes, asked to engage in higher level thinking, and guided toward taking responsibility for their own learning? To answer this question, Mehan and his colleagues (Mehan, Hubbard, Lintz, & Villanueva, 1994; Mehan, Hubbard, & Villanueva, 1994) conducted research on Achievement Via Individual Determination (AVID), a high school program in San Diego, California, designed to increase access to advanced classes and promote the college enrollment of students of diverse backgrounds. In a process of untracking, students of diverse backgrounds (primarily African American and Latino or Latina) with previous records of low achievement were placed in college-prep courses alongside high-achieving mainstream students. These students had performed at below-average levels in school but showed academic potential, as indicated by standardized test scores.

For 3 of their 4 years in high school, students took a special AVID course daily. Teachers in this course used a distinctive approach to instruction termed WIC, for writing, inquiry, and collaboration. The writing component required students to take notes in their classes and to generate questions based on these notes. Students kept learning logs in which they wrote their reflections on classes and what they had learned. In the inquiry component of the program, AVID students were tutored by students recruited from area colleges. Study sessions focused on the questions students had drafted about their classes. Tutors were specifically instructed not to provide answers but to guide AVID students in working out answers on their own. In the collaboration component, students formed study teams. Team members provided one another with information and feedback. As with the inquiry component, the purpose was to develop students' ability to take responsibility for their own learning.

Besides learning study and test-taking strategies, AVID students received what Mehan, Hubbard, and Villanueva (1994) called *social scaffolding*. Students were taught conflict-resolution strategies so that they could negotiate successfully or make amends with teachers when problems arose. AVID teachers acted as students' advocates, for example, in cases when family problems prevented students from meeting the demands of school. AVID students received college counseling and considerable support in completing application forms for admission and financial aid.

Mehan, Hubbard, and Villanueva (1994) examined the effects of access to college-prep courses and increased academic support on students' likelihood of enrolling in college. The results showed that 48% of the AVID students reported enrolling in 4-year colleges. In comparison, 34% of the students who had participated in AVID for 1 year or less reported enrolling in 4-year colleges. The rate for AVID students was higher than the 37% enrollment rate for San Diego high schools and the 39% rate for U.S. high school graduates.

Normally, higher levels of family income and parental education are associated with higher levels of college enrollment. However, Mehan, Hubbard, and Villanueva (1994) found that family income and parents' education did not predict the 4-year college enrollment rates of students who had participated in AVID for 3 years. Among 3-year AVID students, college enrollment rates were highest for those in families with income of $19,000 a year or less (57%), second in families with income of $40,000 to $59,000 (49%), and third in families with income of $20,000 to $39,000 (46%). The relation to parental education was nonlinear as well, with college enrollment rates of 44% for students whose parents had less than a high school education, 51% for those whose parents were high school graduates, 51% for those whose parents had some college, and 48% for those whose parents were college graduates. Students who had participated in AVID for 1 year or less showed the expected linear relations to family income (except for families earning $60,000 or more) and to parental education.

The success of AVID indicates that high expectations for academic achievement can and should be held for students of diverse backgrounds. Students' ethnicity, family income, and previous achievement do not necessarily determine their academic futures. The research on AVID shows that schools can offer all students, not just a select few, the opportunity to benefit from demanding coursework. Clearly, the achievement of students of diverse backgrounds is improved when they have access to challenging curriculum plus the social and academic support that will enable them to succeed.

Action Recommendation: Engage Students in Literacy Activities With an Emphasis on Higher Level Thinking About Text. One way to engage students of diverse backgrounds in higher level thinking about text is to have them read, write, and discuss literature, especially multicultural works, that present complex ideas. A growing body of research confirms the benefits of literature-based instruction for students of diverse backgrounds (e.g., Morrow, 1992), as well as for mainstream students, a point elaborated on in chapters 4 and 6. Students' thinking is stimulated through small-group discussions that allow them to exchange ideas with their classmates.

Torry Montes, a fourth-grade teacher in a Title I school, found success with an approach called Book Club (Montes & Au, 2003; Raphael, 1994). The majority of Montes's students were of native Hawaiian ancestry. Many of the students entered fourth grade reading a year or two below grade level. At the start of the school year, Montes found that her students lacked an interest in reading, and that their written responses and discussions showed superficial thinking. Montes taught her students different forms they could follow in their written responses, such as predictions, retelling and summarization, and putting themselves in the character's situation.

Students learned to draw webs to depict relationships among characters. When students found that their webs were becoming too complex and confusing, a boy in the class converted his web to a matrix. This new form of written response, introduced by a student, was soon adopted by others in the class.

Montes organized her class into small groups of four students each. Each small group became a book club in which students led their own discussions of literature. Montes's students needed guidance to develop the skills for sustaining a worthwhile exchange of ideas. She and the students developed guidelines to be followed during book clubs. She had students participate in fishbowls (Scherer, 1997), in which the rest of the class observed the discussion processes of a single book club. After each fishbowl, she helped the students to critique and make suggestions for improving discussions.

Here is an exchange that took place between two boys in a book club in April, near the end of the school year. This group was reading *Call It Courage* (Sperry, 1940), and the boys made predictions about what might happen to the main character, a boy named Mafatu.

Kaleo: I wonder if he, when he is going to be back home from the canoe, or if he lives or dies?

Brian: If he lives or dies?

Kaleo: I hope he lives.

Brian: He could die on the canoe, 'cause then he could run out of water. He could run out of food.

Kaleo: He could die—of the shark.

Brian: Or he could live of the shark, but we don't know that yet. So—

Kaleo: And he could, I think he, when his father dies, after he's proven he has a stout heart, when his father dies, he'll take his father's place as the chief.

Brian: Yeah, but when he comes back, the father's going to tell them, this is my son and his name is brave heart or something. And he's going to, the father's going to die in a war and he is going to survive and he's going to like take his father's place as chief. (Montes & Au, 2003, p. 86)

The dashes indicate overlapping speech, times when the conversation became especially animated. Kaleo started this exchange by wondering what will happen to Mafatu. Brian made an observation about the dangers facing Mafatu on the canoe. When Kaleo speculated that Mafatu might be killed by the shark, Brian cautioned that "we don't know that yet." Both boys then formulated detailed predictions, consistent with text information, based on the assumption that Mafatu would survive, prove himself, and win recognition.

Montes's teaching approach illustrates many of the principles seen as well in the AVID program. She held high expectations for her students' literacy learning, although many of them began the year reading far below grade level. She emphasized higher level thinking with text, requiring students to engage in reading, writing, and discussion of works of literature. She helped students to develop the necessary social skills, in this case, those needed to participate in small-group discussions of literature. Finally, she encouraged students to take responsibility for their own learning.

SUMMARY

This chapter addressed five explanations for the literacy achievement gap consistent with a social constructivist perspective: (a) discrimination, (b) inferior education, (c) teaching that fails to build on students' culture, (d) teaching that fails to build on students' language, and (e) teaching that fails to promote higher level thinking. Research supports all five of these explanations, a testimony to the complexity of the challenge posed by the literacy achievement gap. Obviously, a series of changes—not just a single change—is required to solve the problem. Action steps were presented for the last three explanations because these explanations relate to patterns that educators can change in their schools and classrooms. These action steps, as illustrated in classroom examples, allow educators to put in place new patterns likely to be beneficial to the literacy learning of students of diverse backgrounds.

3

Discourses and Literacy
in the Home and Community

In chapter 2, I discussed the importance of teachers maintaining high expectations for students of diverse backgrounds to reverse three common
patterns that hamper students' literacy learning in school. In this chapter, I
present research showing how students of diverse backgrounds and members of their families show competence and resilience within their own cultural settings. This finding, well supported by research, makes it clear that
students of diverse backgrounds have the ability to reach high levels of literacy in school. Educators should assume that students are competent and
move forward on that basis (cf. McDermott, 1993). The concepts of multiple literacies (Street, 1995) and discourse (Gee, 1990) are explored, and
these concepts form the background for interpreting research about the literacy shown by students of diverse backgrounds and their families in the
home and community. I consider as well the reasons why the competence
and literacy of students and their families often goes unrecognized by
schools.

MULTIPLE LITERACIES

Questioning Assumptions

In chapter 1, I discussed the gap in literacy achievement between students
of diverse backgrounds and students of mainstream backgrounds, as indicated by the results of the NAEP. Now I examine the literacy achievement

gap from a different point of view. I start by questioning the key assumptions made in large-scale tests such as those designed for the NAEP, as well as in standardized and state tests. These key assumptions are that (a) literacy consists of a particular set of skills, and (b) there is only one type of literacy. A corollary notion is that, even if there were more than one type of literacy, there is only one type that really matters.

Autonomous Model

The view of literacy reflected in large-scale tests is what Street (1995) called the autonomous model of literacy. In the autonomous model, literacy is treated as a collection of skills. According to this model, students' results on large-scale tests are an accurate reflection of their cognitive skills of reading and writing and thus show students' literacy levels. The type of literacy measured on these tests is termed *essayist literacy*, and this is the type of literacy valued in Western academic circles. Essayist literacy is centered on forms of reading and writing favored by the mainstream or dominant groups, and it incorporates what Delpit (1986) termed the *codes of the culture of power*, such as standard American English.

Street (1995) pointed out problems with the autonomous model of literacy. He argued that literacy is never carried out in a vacuum, that literacy always occurs in a social context. Literacy is much more than a collection of skills. It always involves particular practices, carried out in particular cultural settings, for particular purposes. In other words, literacy is a cultural practice, and it may take different forms in different times and places and among different groups of people.

In the autonomous model of literacy, students' performance on a large-scale test is seen as an accurate way of demonstrating literacy. This view ignores other ways of demonstrating literacy that may be more useful and important to students and their families. For example, another way of demonstrating literacy is translating documents from English into Spanish, a task some students of diverse backgrounds encounter on a daily basis in the home and community. Students often can perform well on complex, real-world literacy tasks such as those involving translation, as is discussed later in this chapter. However, large-scale tests usually require students of diverse backgrounds to engage in literacy practices very different from those in which they have shown competence in the home and community. Students may do poorly on large-scale tests because the type of literacy being assessed is largely unfamiliar to them.

The literacy of large-scale tests, however, is likely to be highly familiar to students of mainstream backgrounds. The autonomous model gives a natural advantage to mainstream students who have ready access to essayist literacy, including the codes of the culture of power. Many mainstream students grow up in homes and communities in which essayist literacy is a common cultural practice. Students begin to learn essayist literacy, the discourse of the dominant group, from a young age. For example, in the United States, young children learn how to respond to known-answer questions, such as "What color is your shirt?" (Heath, 1983). They become familiar with the language of books through family storybook reading. Of course, they grow up speaking standard American English, the code of the culture of power. In contrast, many students of diverse backgrounds do not have easy access to essayist literacy outside of school. Different types of literacy may well be practiced in their homes and communities, and they often grow up speaking languages other than the language of power.

Because the school is an institution that reflects dominant-group values, essayist literacy tends to be favored in the classroom. Most mainstream students will have the background to benefit from the essayist literacy activities presented by teachers, whereas many students of diverse backgrounds will not. For example, mainstream students are usually familiar with responding to known-answer questions. In contrast, students of diverse backgrounds may have more experience with questions that require them to draw analogies, discussing how one thing is like another (Heath, 1983). In the classroom, teachers often conduct discussions of literature by asking a series of known-answer questions, an approach likely to be more easily understood by mainstream students than by students of diverse backgrounds. Thus, the test performance of mainstream students is generally boosted by a double advantage: their home backgrounds with essayist literacy plus their ability to benefit from essayist literacy activities in school.

Ideological Model and Multiple Literacies

What Street (1995) called the *ideological model of literacy* offers educators much brighter possibilities for working with students of diverse backgrounds than the autonomous model. In the ideological model, literacy is viewed as a social construction, as sets of practices shaped and carried out by different groups of people. Once we recognize that literacy is not a fixed entity but a set of cultural practices, we can understand that essayist literacy is only one of many types of literacy. The ideological model indicates that what it means to be literate differs among cultural groups and communities. Because families' circumstances vary considerably, the types of literacy children observe and learn may also vary considerably. When students of diverse backgrounds enter school, they may have ideas about literacy quite different from those expected from a mainstream perspective. Furthermore, the types of literacy practiced in the home and community may be more immediately valuable to students than essayist literacy (cf. Knobel, 2001).

I believe the appropriate course of action for teachers planning classroom lessons is not to choose between essayist literacy and the types of literacy valued in the community. Rather, teachers should guide students to develop multiple literacies. This means that teachers will help students learn essayist literacy along with other types of literacy that may be more meaningful and practical in family and community contexts. Furthermore, teachers may be able to use literacy strengths students have gained in the home to promote literacy learning in school.

Promoting multiple literacies does not mean that teachers ignore essayist literacy. Students of diverse backgrounds must gain a command of essayist literacy if they are to have access to the opportunities for social, political, and economic advancement that depend on literacy performances judged by dominant-group standards. However, teachers should be aware that they may do students an injustice by restricting instruction to essayist literacy alone. Students may not be able to relate to, or see the point of, instruction on essayist literacy (see chapter 9 for examples), and as a result, they may not be motivated to learn more about reading and writing. By beginning with literacy practices or texts with connections to the home and community, teachers may be able to start students on the road to reading and writing in ways that make sense to them. For example, recall the research by McMillon and McMillon (2004) about how students who attend African American churches often read texts that teach them lessons to be applied to their lives. Teachers might build on this background by having students read stories and discuss the life lessons that can be drawn from these stories.

By beginning with culturally familiar literacy practices, teachers can actively engage students with reading and writing and gradually expand their repertoires to include essayist literacy. Students will strengthen reading and writing practices they can apply in familiar home and community contexts, and then steadily gain reading and writing practices they can apply to previously unfamiliar mainstream contexts. By promoting students' learning of multiple literacies, teachers can build on literacy practices students may bring from the home, instead of ignoring these practices or placing them in a position inferior to essayist literacy. Effective classroom approaches growing from this line of thinking are presented in chapter 7. The concept of multiple literacies, stemming from Street's (1995) ideological model of literacy, reminds us that the type of literacy measured by large-scale tests is just one type of literacy. Competence in literacy is best judged by performance within particular contexts, and large-scale tests are just one context among many. However, essayist literacy and the large-scale tests that measure it have been privileged over other types of literacy and other contexts for showing one's competence as a reader and writer. The dominant group values that reinforce this privileging exert an extremely powerful influence on schooling. It has seemed natural to educators, then, to view students of diverse backgrounds, as well as their families, as incompetent when it comes to literacy.

We must work hard to overcome the biases inherent in the autonomous view. A negative pattern, commonly reflected in the views of the general public and even some educators, is to see the literacy achievement gap as the result of deficiencies on the part of students of diverse backgrounds and their families. Instead, we must establish a new pattern of understanding the gap as an indication that schools have generally been unsuccessful in helping students of diverse backgrounds acquire essayist literacy. We must consider as well a new pattern in which students of diverse backgrounds and their families are seen as highly literate and accomplished when types of literacy other than essayist literacy are considered.

TRANSLATING AS A FAMILY LITERACY PRACTICE

To illustrate the literacy accomplishments of students of diverse backgrounds, I turn to research by Orellana, Reynolds, Dorner, and Meza (2003). They studied the translating or "paraphrasing" from English to Spanish done by children in immigrant households. "*Para-phrasing* deliberately invokes a play on the Spanish word *para* and its English translation ('for'), to name what children do when they phrase things *for* others and *in order to* accomplish social goals" (Orellana et al., 2003, p. 15). Eighteen students, including 12 girls, participated in the study. These students were selected because they were the primary translators of documents for their families. Most of the students were in the fifth or sixth grade when the study began, and their families had been in the United States between 4 and 20 years.

The students kept journals in which they wrote about times when they served as translators, and they tape-recorded some translation events. In addition, other translation events were observed by the researchers. The students translated documents in all of the domains in the following list. An example of a document in each domain appears in parentheses:

- Commercial (rental application for a musical instrument).
- Community (drug prevention program manual).
- Educational (letter discussing a school's dress code).
- Family or recreational (letter written to a relative).
- Financial (informational letter from a bank).
- Legal or state (jury summons).
- Medical (label on a pharmacy bottle).
- Religious (church informational letter; adapted from Orellana et al., 2003, p. 21).

Orellana et al. found that most translating events involved students and their parents. However, on occasion, students assisted other relatives, such as aunts and uncles who had recently arrived, as well as peers or younger children in the family. Translation events most often focused on mail and documents from school.

A key feature of translation events was that they involved the coconstruction of meaning. That is, the student translator and family members collaborated to figure out the message of the text, with each supplying different kinds of knowledge. Coconstruction is clearly illustrated in the following translation event. One of the mothers received a jury summons through the mail. She set the document aside until her daughter—Adriana, age 14—came home from high school and had the time to help her with it. The summons was written in a formal tone, and some knowledge of legal terms was required to understand it. Adriana's knowledge of English enabled her to translate the general sense of the document to her mother. However, the specialized legal terms presented Adriana with a challenge. She did not know what *summons* meant, and she was unsure of the Spanish word for *juror*. However, Adriana's mother had knowledge about the courts and juries. She explained to Adriana what a jury was and described how she had gone to court because of a traffic accident. With the information her mother provided, Adriana was able to translate the rest of the summons. It seemed that Adriana's mother did not need to report for jury duty because she was not a citizen. However, her mother asked Adriana to make a phone call the next day to verify this conclusion.

Orellana et al. (2003) found that translation was a daily activity in many immigrant households. Some documents, such as the summons or the label on a vial of pills, might have significant consequences for the family.

Others, such as a letter to parents about the student dress code, might be somewhat less important. In all cases, however, the student translators had to use knowledge of both English and Spanish. They had to read a wide range of documents, some of them quite technical, as in the case of the jury summons. The students had to serve as interpreters of mainstream culture, often dealing with complex systems of law, finance, medicine, transportation, and education that are difficult to negotiate without specialized knowledge.

Clearly, many immigrant families have a pressing need for translation. In these settings, children who can read English are important resources whose literacy abilities can contribute in significant ways to the well-being of the family. In the families studied by Orellana et al. (2003), children were expected to act as interpreters in keeping with the cultural value that household members should be willing to use their skills and knowledge for the good of the whole family. Children who serve as translators may have family responsibilities much weightier than those of children from mainstream backgrounds who are seldom if ever called on to serve as interpreters.

LITERACY DEMANDS IN THE INNER CITY

Research by Cushman (1998) provides additional examples of the complex literacy practices that may be used by students of diverse backgrounds and their families in community settings. Cushman observed the oral and literate strategies used by African Americans in the inner city to improve their living conditions and the futures of their children. The women who headed the families studied by Cushman spent considerable time and energy interacting with gatekeepers, such as social workers or landlords, who controlled their access to housing, employment, afterschool programs, and other social goods. The women prepared themselves for encounters with these gatekeepers by reading and studying documents, filling out application forms, consulting with friends and neighbors, and rehearsing what they would say. For example, here are the resources consulted by Mirena and Lucy, two mothers who had to find new housing:

> Both women collected many resources that listed available housing: the typical ones, such as newspapers and rental guides, but also listings from the Housing Authority, the university's Office of Resident Life, word of mouth, the Urban League, as well as from driving, walking, and biking around the city to look for "For Rent" signs in windows. (Cushman, 1998, p. 78)

Cushman (1998) explained that these women had to do so much research because, as African Americans who relied on public assistance, they had few options for housing. In common with other large cities, Quayville was divided into distinct neighborhoods. Those who came from the inner city could not easily cross the lines established by class and ethnicity. They were marked as coming from the "ghetto" as soon as they wrote down their addresses. Landlords with properties in safer neighborhoods set rents too high to be paid by those on public assistance or would not accept payments from public assistance agencies.

Mirena and Lucy may have lacked money, but they did not lack the language and literacy abilities, or the organizational skills, required to navigate complex institutional situations. Cushman (1998) wrote the following:

> The entire five-month period that Lucy spent looking for housing, she carried with her all of the important documents she would need to complete applications, all tucked into an accordion file folder that she clutched when we went into rental offices. In this folder, she kept: birth certificates, previous rental agreements, verifications of funding, references, blank forms to be filled out by new landlords for HUD benefits, her current applications for places, a few "move-in special" coupons from the newspaper, previous utility bills, and budget statements from the utility companies. (pp. 90–91)

Cushman (1998) used the phrase *institutional language* to characterize the rhetorical strategies needed to interact with the many government agencies that control resources vital to residents of the inner city. Children began to learn about institutional language from observing interactions among adults in the community. At a young age, children had already started collaborating with one another to understand the significance of institutional documents. One day, Cushman showed a parking ticket she had just received to three youngsters: Marquis (age 11), Delilah (age 10), and Samson (age 9). When Delilah and Samson struggled with the word *prohibition,* Cushman gave examples, such as "Swimming prohibited." Marquis said, "That means you can't do it. You mess up!" (p. 108) At first, Marquis suggested that Cushman simply put the parking ticket on the windshield of another car. Then he scanned the ticket and found Cushman's license number written there. He explained to Delilah and Samson that a copy of the ticket was in the office and that Cushman would have to pay. Cushman highlighted Marquis' inventiveness in exploring different ways to think about the ticket and to exercise agency when faced with an unwanted institutional intrusion.

Cushman (1998) found that young adults could describe the social and political structure of the community and knew a great deal about power relations within it. Lucy's youngest daughter, Afriganzia, age 21, produced a diagram for Cushman based on Spades, a variation of the card game trumps, popular in the community. The diagram showed the two most influential Black women in the neighborhood on top, followed by the supervisor of two social workers, then the social workers themselves. According to Afriganzia, people who held power in the community knew how to use their language and literacy abilities to cross institutional boundaries. They were "really good talkers, good with language," she said (p. 114). They understood how institutional systems worked, and they could speak and write effectively to help their families and others achieve their goals within these systems.

GEE'S CONCEPT OF DISCOURSE

Clearly, the students and parents in the study by Orellana et al. (2003) showed a high degree of competence and resourcefulness in dealing with a wide range of documents necessary to their everyday lives. The inner-city children and parents observed by Cushman (1998) showed an equally high level of language and literacy ability in coping with institutional demands. The question raised by these studies, as well as many others (Hull & Schultz, 2001), is why the competence of students of diverse backgrounds and their families is so seldom recognized by schools. For example, Compton-Lilly (2003, p. 2) presented an excerpt from an editorial by a teacher in her school district who chastised parents for "not accepting their responsibilities" for the education of their children. Parents of students of diverse backgrounds often are blamed for the low levels of literacy their children seem to show in school.

Educators must challenge stereotypes about the intellectual competence and literacy of students of diverse backgrounds and their families, because these stereotypes often lead to a lowering of expectations for students' literacy achievement in school. To begin challenging stereotypes, let us address the question of why students and family members, who show so much competence in home and community settings, are often judged to be so incompetent from the perspective of the school. Gee's (1990) work on discourse provides a theoretical framework for helping us understand why students and their parents are typically characterized as deficient when it comes to literacy, as well as why some types of literacy are valued above others.

Gee (1990) used the term *Discourse* (with a capital *D*) to discuss the process by which people of one cultural group position themselves and others. Here is the widely cited passage in which Gee (1990) presented his definition of discourse: "A *Discourse* is a socially accepted association among ways of using language, of thinking, feeling, believing, valuing, and of acting that can be used to identify oneself as a member of a socially meaningful group or 'social network', or to signal (that one is playing) a socially meaningful 'role' " (p. 143, italics in the original). Each cultural group or subgroup has its own discourse. A discourse may be compared to an identity kit (Gee, 1989; Lopez, 1999) that allows an individual to position himself or herself as a member of a particular cultural group and to be recognized as such by members of that group. A cultural group uses a discourse to reinforce its identity and maintain its position with respect to other groups. Discourses are highly political, because the discourse of a powerful or dominant group can be used to reinforce its position over less powerful or subordinate groups.

Gee (1990) made the political nature of discourses clear. He argued that discourses are inherently ideological, in the sense that each involves a particular point of view about the relationships among people, such as who is an insider or an outsider, and who is deserving of social goods and who is not. For example, the families studied by Cushman (1998) had been positioned by institutional gatekeepers as outsiders undeserving of social goods.

Gee (1990) noted that discourses tend to resist criticism, because taking a stance against the assumptions of a discourse mark one as being an outsider. Criticisms of a discourse always come from some point of view, whether or not that point of view is acknowledged. People in the inner-city community studied by Cushman (1998) frequently did take stances in opposition to the discourse of institutional gatekeepers. However, they usually voiced their critiques when speaking with other members of the community. Because they were outsiders to the culture of power, they knew their critiques very likely would not be heard or accepted in institutional settings.

According to Gee (1990), the positions held by those exercising a particular discourse are taken with respect to opposing discourses. For example, Cushman (1998) found that many African Americans in the inner-city community she studied valued "talking Black" to show solidarity with other African Americans. In public settings, such as a shopping mall, they might even try to connect with African Americans they had not met before, to express "their shared sense of Otherness" in the larger society (p. 57). But although a discourse can be used to establish ties, it can also be used to create or maintain boundaries. This situation was illustrated in the example of reciprocal distancing cited in chapter 2, in which African American students and a European American teacher used Discourses to assume contrasting positions.

Gee (1990) argued that every discourse advances certain points of view at the expense of others. In doing so, it marginalizes viewpoints central to other discourses. An individual who has access to several discourses may accept the viewpoints from one discourse, although these viewpoints contradict those of another known discourse. The community members in Cushman's (1998) study knew the viewpoints of the institutional gatekeepers, but they often maintained their own viewpoints in the face of this knowledge, sometimes at great cost. When he had to appear before a judge, Disco, Lucy's youngest son, deliberately kept his arms folded in front of him and addressed the judge without using the phrase, "your honor." Disco's actions did not result from a lack of knowledge of the discourse expected by the court. Disco deliberately chose to be defiant, and he was sentenced to 2 weeks in jail.

Gee (1990) emphasized that discourses are closely tied to the distribution of power in a society. Control of discourses valued by the dominant group can confer power, money, and status on an individual. Afriganzia's analysis of power relations within the community, as reported by Cushman (1998), shows how this concept was understood by young people, as well as by their elders. At one point, Cushman observed Afriganzia using her knowledge of mainstream discourse during a phone call to schedule a tour of the public library:

"Hello, I'm co-directing a summer literacy program for children on 34th Ave.? I work at United Home's Neighborhood Center. I was wondering if I could schedule a tour for sometime next week? [person on the other (end of the) line responds]
"Will this cost anything?" [some reply]
"Also, what do the kids need to do to check out a book? . . . A proof of residency? You mean like a bill?" [some reply]. (Cushman, 1998, p. 126)

When the call was over, Cushman commented on the change in Afriganzia's speech, which made her sound unlike her usual self. Afriganzia replied that she liked to "mess with people" and catch them off guard when they discovered later that she was African American. She enjoyed using her language skills to counter the stereotypes held by outsiders.

The concepts presented in Gee's (1990) work on discourse provide the background needed to tackle the question posed at the beginning of this section, of why students of diverse backgrounds and their families can show such competence with literacy in community settings, yet often be judged as so incompetent by the school. A discourse is not neutral. We use discourses not only to position ourselves but to judge others. Gee's work helps us to see that the discourse of the dominant groups that exert such a strong influence on schools is often used to maintain stereotypes about the low levels of literacy of students of diverse backgrounds and their families.

Essayist literacy is part and parcel of dominant group discourse. Other literacies, such as translation or institutional language strategies, important to daily life in nonmainstream communities, are associated with the discourses of subordinate groups. Because these other literacies are outside the discourse of the dominant group, they are usually either rendered invisible or assigned a low status. A command of these other literacies signals membership in a subordinate group, and this causes individuals to be looked down on in mainstream settings. Dominant group discourse may even cause competence in nonmainstream literacies to be interpreted as incompetence.

As educators, we must grow beyond the limitations of discourses that reinforce negative views of students of diverse backgrounds and their families. Research such as that of Orellana et al. (2003) and Cushman (1998) highlights the competence and resiliency shown by students of diverse backgrounds and their families when using literacy in community settings. These findings remind us that it is essential for educators to challenge stereotypes about the literacy of students of diverse backgrounds and their families. We need to assume competence and adopt a broad view of literacy, consistent with Street's (1995) ideological model. Stereotypes about the low literacy and incompetence of students of diverse backgrounds pose a danger because they can lead to a lowering of expectations for students' literacy achievement in school.

PRIMARY AND SECONDARY DISCOURSES

Breaking away from stereotypes and having high expectations for students' literacy learning in school is a good start. However, we must also gain a deeper understanding of why it is often challenging for teachers to bring students of diverse backgrounds to high levels of achievement in essayist literacy. To tackle this issue, we need to return to Gee's (1990) theory of discourse.

Gee (1989a, 1989b) distinguishes between primary and secondary discourses. A primary discourse is acquired naturally, in the course of growing up in one's home and community. (The difference between acquisition, which is subconscious and informal, and learning, which is conscious and formally taught, as discussed by Gee, 1994, is explored in chapter 4.) Most people feel very comfortable using their primary discourse, especially in the company of others who share that discourse. In contrast, a secondary discourse is learned through conscious effort, generally in formal settings outside the home, such as the school. Secondary discourses are learned after primary discourses and are often challenging to use, especially at first. This is because, in addition to new forms of language, a secondary discourse requires an understanding of the values, beliefs, assumptions, and behaviors associated with that discourse (in other words, the culture in which the secondary discourse is embedded).

People in complex societies, such as the United States, usually move through many different settings in the course of their lifetimes. For this reason, children must grow beyond the primary discourse acquired in the home and develop the ability to employ the secondary discourses of other settings, such as the school and workplace. Afriganzia, the young woman studied by Cushman (1998), certainly had gained control over a secondary discourse. At home and at school, not all students of diverse backgrounds either have this opportunity or choose to pursue it.

Schools and other major institutions in a society tend to adhere closely to dominant-group norms. For most students from mainstream or dominant-group backgrounds, the secondary discourse of an institution, such as the school, is relatively easy to learn because it is quite similar to their primary discourse. Students of diverse backgrounds, however, face a much greater challenge in learning the secondary discourses needed to prosper in mainstream settings. In most cases, there are significant differences between these discourses and students' primary or home discourse. Lopez (1999) wrote the following of ELLs:

> These children are executing a more complex task than negotiating discourse acquisition within the official school world by using their home language, as do the rest of the English-speaking school population. Rather they are claiming a new language as a result of their multiple interactions within their social worlds, both at home and in school, through their understanding of two (or more) completely different discourses. Hispanic children speak Spanish at home to their parents, speak English and Spanish to their siblings, watch both English and Spanish television shows, and arrive in an all-English school world that has altogether different values and expectations. (p. 4)

Lopez (1999) conducted research exploring the challenges faced by students of diverse backgrounds who had to learn the secondary discourse of the school to achieve academic success. Lopez studied the home and school experiences of three fifth-grade boys who came from families of migrant workers living in Pennsylvania. The boys' families had moved to the area in search of a better life because of the work offered by apple farms. The boys all spoke Spanish as their first language. Antonio's family came from Mexico, Jose's family from Puerto Rico, and Rodolfo's family from Phoenix, Arizona.

Lopez (1999) began by identifying four major discourses in which the boys participated, associated with their roles as family member, friend, student, and classmate. In the first two roles—family member and friend—the boys could use their primary discourse. In the other two roles—student and classmate—they were required to use secondary discourses. However, as soon as she began her observations, Lopez found these neat categories becoming messy. In the community, the boys did not just interact with their parents and siblings but with extended family, family friends, neighbors, and church members. Spanish and English might both be spoken at home and in the community. Families felt the pervasive influence of popular culture, even while carrying on their own cultural traditions. In school, the boys' lives were affected by the discourses of many different groups. These included the school district administration, which influenced how much funding was available for services to migrant students; the principal; the teachers; staff in the Migrant Education Program; and the larger community.

The discourses of these groups were shaped by the families of privilege in the community, identified by Lopez (1999) as those who owned the apple farms and ran the fresh fruit packing company that served as the economic backbone of the community. Migrant farmworkers, such as the boys' parents, played a much needed role in the economic structure. However, the families of privilege looked down on the migrant farmworkers and their contributions and felt that these relative newcomers could never "belong to the land" as the longtime residents did (Lopez, 1999, p. 22). The families who owned the apple farms tended to ignore the fact that their position of privilege depended on the contributions of the farmworkers.

Lopez (1999) identified three major problems faced by the Hispanic farmworkers who entered the area. They encountered difficulties because of language, a lack of background about mainstream American culture, and prejudice. Of these three difficulties, prejudice proved the most daunting. Parents of the three boys had experienced incidents of racism. Lopez observed that interactions between the townspeople and migrant farmworkers in public settings, such as the post office and shopping centers, often seemed forced and awkward. According to newspaper articles, the families of privilege and the townspeople believed that migrant farmworkers brought crime, violence, drugs, and alcoholism into the community. Although police reports provided evidence of very low rates of crime among Hispanics, the attitudes of the townspeople were slow to change.

Obviously, the families of privilege and the townspeople, who controlled the schools, occupied a very different world and held very different worldviews from those of the migrant families. For the most part, schools in the area reflected the world of the families of privilege and the townspeople, not the migrant families. This situation had major ramifications for the three boys in Lopez's study.

Lopez (1999) reminds us that gaining the knowledge required to negotiate school successfully was extremely difficult for the boys, because they seldom had access to settings in which the secondary discourses they needed could be acquired naturally. They had to learn what they could in formal school settings, in which they were competing with classmates from privileged backgrounds.

Lopez (1999) identified specific situations that illustrated the collision between the boys' primary discourse and the secondary discourses of the school. Lopez defined a collision as a breakdown that occurs when the power of one discourse allows it to overwhelm another. Those who have command of the more powerful discourse may use it, knowingly or unknowingly, to assert their superiority and to deny opportunities to those who are marked as outsiders because they do not control this same discourse. Here are some examples of the collisions documented by Lopez.

Lopez (1999) found that parents who did not speak English could not help their children to succeed in school. A typical example occurred in Mrs. Bennett's fifth-grade classroom. The class was beginning a unit on mystery books, and Mrs. Bennett gave out a list with the assignments each student should complete in connection with the reading of each book. For their regular Tuesday assignment, the students were to write in their journals to one of their parents, and the parent was to write back. On Wednesday, the teacher collected the journals and read them. Although the boys' parents were all literate in Spanish, they could not compose such written responses in English. Although Lopez endorsed the role of parents in supporting students' learning in school, she found that schools needed to think of ways of involving parents that fit with the kind of help parents could actually provide. Lopez noted that the boys were put in the position of believing that their parents were somehow inadequate because they could not offer the kinds of help that other parents could. In school, mainstream parents were placed in a position of superiority to nonmainstream parents. The Hispanic parents felt cut off from the school, because their knowledge and the kind of help they could offer their children were not valued or recognized. Lopez stated the following: "Teachers could and did conclude that the boys would never reach their full potential because their homes did not provide the support that was necessary. Blame for the boys' poor schoolwork, therefore, went back to the home" (p. 161).

Lopez (1999) found that the mainstream discourse of the school often ignored the knowledge and experiences of those regarded as outsiders. One day Mrs. Bennett led a class discussion about a *Weekly Reader* article on the approaching presidential election. At one point, the class discussed the idea that minorities might one day run for president. Later, Mrs. Bennett raised the question of whether it was important for the president to understand the cultures of other countries. Two boys from mainstream backgrounds, Mike and Joe, stated that the president should have this understanding to avoid offending others. On the surface, Lopez commented, this class discussion seemed to go well. However, just beneath the surface it became apparent that issues of diversity were treated superficially and in the abstract. The discussion ignored the perspectives of the two Hispanic boys in the class, Rodolfo and Fernando, although these boys and their families had actual experiences with misunderstandings caused by cultural differences.

Lopez's observations showed that the very real inequalities in the classroom and the community were consistently overlooked in the mainstream, secondary discourse of the school. This situation points to complexities in the relation between students of diverse backgrounds and the secondary discourse. Because students have access to the secondary discourse in school, it seems they should be able to learn it. In practice, however, the issue may center on students' lack of willingness to learn the secondary discourse. If students see that the secondary discourse is being used to disparage them or to marginalize their experiences and concerns, they may well reject opportunities to learn this discourse in school.

Lopez (1999) observed many occasions that revealed the vast differences between the world of the boys and the world of their mainstream peers. One day Mrs. Thompson conducted a social studies lesson during which the students were to play a game following the format of the television show, "Jeopardy." When Mrs. Thompson asked if any of the students had not seen "Jeopardy" before, Jose alone raised his hand. In this case, not knowing about "Jeopardy" did not seriously affect Jose's ability to participate in the lesson. However, this incident caused Lopez to think about how different Jose's world was from that of his classmates, even with regard to something as seemingly ordinary as knowledge of television shows. The boys in her study knew many things that their classmates did not, but this knowledge was not the basis for the lessons they received in school. The knowledge held by their classmates, and not by the boys, counted for much more.

Lopez (1999) found that, in ways large and small, the boys' language and experiences were systematically excluded from school activities. It was natural, then, for the boys to retreat to their primary discourse. For example, they might converse in Spanish with a friend in the class, knowing that their mainstream classmates would be unable to understand what they were saying. In this way, Lopez noted, the boys could use their primary discourse as a form of resistance to schooling. However, she warned that a primary discourse may be limiting when compared to a secondary discourse. Access to opportunities in the larger society, such as a college education, depend on control of secondary discourses, not primary discourses. Teachers should be aware of the dangers lurking when students feel they must take refuge in their primary discourse, because they feel excluded in settings where they could learn a secondary discourse. Lopez frequently observed the exclusion experienced by students who did not speak English fluently. The boys she studied were marked as outsiders by members of the dominant group, teachers and administrators as well as students. She wrote, "The boys happily reverted back to their primary discourse as a form of resistance, but it would never provide them with the power and freedom to choose life goals that could elevate them from their current status" (p. 152). This research by Lopez highlights the importance of educators' awareness of the subtle and not-so-subtle ways that bias and discrimination may enter the classroom. Under these pressures, students may resist learning essayist literacy and lessen their chances for success in school.

SUMMARY

This chapter presented a different perspective on the literacy achievement gap. I discussed Street's (1995) distinction between the autonomous and ideological models of literacy and explained the advantages of the ideological model for educators working with students of diverse backgrounds. Street's concept of multiple literacies supports the notion of literacy as cultural practice. Given this backdrop, I looked at research on literacy in the home and community, exploring the examples of translating or paraphrasing (Orellana et al., 2003) and literacy strategies needed to deal with institutions affecting the lives of inner-city families (Cushman, 1998). I discussed

Gee's (1990) theory of discourse as a framework for better understanding why the literacy competencies of students of diverse backgrounds and their families is seldom recognized or appreciated in schools. Finally, I looked at Gee's (1990) distinction between primary and secondary discourses in an effort to explain the struggles students face in school, drawing on research by Lopez (1999) on the collision between the discourses of dominant and subordinate groups.

4

Workshop Approaches
to Literacy Learning

In the last chapter, you learned that students of diverse backgrounds have the ability to engage in complex forms of language, literacy, and higher level thinking in the home and community. The challenge faced by teachers is to motivate students to learn and use similarly complex forms of language, literacy, and higher level thinking in the classroom. This is not an easy task, because school demands for literacy are usually quite different from home demands. Teachers need to create classrooms as communities in which students of diverse backgrounds can make sense of and find meaning in the types of literacy activities favored by schools. In this chapter, we discuss the key features of programs for literacy learning that create classroom communities of readers. Specifically, building on Gee's (1990) distinction between acquisition and learning, we address the two kinds of opportunities for literacy learning that must be available in the classroom for students of diverse backgrounds. We focus on Book Club *Plus* as an approach that meets the requirements for effective literacy learning programs.

ACQUISITION VERSUS LEARNING

What two kinds of literacy learning experiences must be available in the classroom for students of diverse backgrounds? Why are both kinds of experiences important? Gee's (1990) analysis of how people gain fluency in primary and secondary discourses provides the basis for answering these questions. According to Gee, we follow a process of acquisition in mastering our primary discourse. Acquisition takes place subconsciously, as we are exposed to others who model the discourse for us. As we grow up, we witness interactions and hear talk all around us. We gain experience with the primary discourse as we engage in daily activities with family members. Through a process of trial and error, and with feedback, we acquire our primary discourse. No formal teaching or instruction takes place, Gee noted, yet acquisition must be an extremely powerful process because children everywhere acquire a primary discourse.

The situation with a secondary discourse is different, because our mastery of these discourses comes about through a process that Gee (1990) termed *learning,* not acquisition. As Gee defined it, learning involves conscious knowledge that is either imparted through teaching or gained during moments of reflection. At these times, perhaps during a classroom lesson or while we are pondering a text, we gain what Gee called metaknowledge—conscious, explicit knowledge—about the secondary discourse. This meta-knowledge enables us to consider, probe, and discuss the secondary discourse. Knowledge of the primary discourse, in contrast, is generally held in an unconscious and implicit manner and is not accessible to the same kind of probing. Gee pointed out that learning a secondary discourse is clearly a less reliable process than acquiring a primary discourse, because people do not always succeed in mastering a secondary discourse.

Gee (1990) suggested that these two processes, acquisition and learning, have different benefits. On the one hand, acquisition leads to good performance. People readily use their primary discourse to communicate with others and accomplish their purposes in the home and community. On the other hand, learning leads to metaknowledge. Although many people cannot use a secondary discourse as effectively as their primary discourse, perhaps because they began using the secondary discourse later in life or have had little experience with it, they have a conscious awareness and understanding of aspects of the secondary discourse that they do not have of the primary discourse.

Application to Classroom Literacy Learning

I now apply the distinction between acquisition and learning to the situation of students of diverse backgrounds and literacy in the classroom. This distinction and its application is easier to understand if I introduce two new phrases. Instead of acquisition, I use the phrase "learning by engaging in the full processes of reading and writing," and instead of learning, I use the phrase "learning by studying parts of reading and writing."

Learning by engaging in the full processes of reading and writing gives students the opportunity to gain proficiency in literacy in the classroom in ways similar to those they followed to gain proficiency in the primary discourse at home. In the classroom, teachers give students the chance to read and write for real purposes, just as family members involve students in using oral language to communicate for real purposes in the home. Real purposes for reading and writing are those students will find meaningful and motivating, such as reading a book on a topic of interest or composing an e-mail message to a friend. Drawing on Gee's (1990) ideas, we can deduce that the actual doing of the activity, such as reading and writing for real reasons, is the logical first step toward proficiency.

As they carry out reading and writing, students enter a process of apprenticeship in which their literacy learning is supported by those who know more about reading and writing than they do. In the classroom, these more knowledgeable or more capable others (Wood, Bruner, & Ross, 1976) include the teacher, other adults, and peers. All of those in the classroom form a community to support one another's literacy learning. As the teacher guides students' engagement in the full processes of reading and writing, students see how literacy is actually used. They witness and gain firsthand experience with literacy as a social and cultural practice in the classroom. Gee (1990) stated, "If you have no access to the social practice, you don't get in the Discourse, you don't have it" (p. 147). The process of literacy learning in the classroom is actually the learning of the secondary discourse of the school. As such, literacy learning becomes much more than a matter of letters, sounds, and words. It also entails learning about the values, beliefs, and behaviors associated with the secondary discourse of the school, which may contrast quite sharply with the values, beliefs, and behaviors associated with students' primary discourse. Becoming competent in school culture and language is a process of enculturation, of acquiring a culture, of learning the social practice. Lopez's (1999) study, discussed in chapter 3, documented the challenges faced by some students of diverse backgrounds in gaining competency in the secondary discourse of the school because of vast differences with the primary discourse.

Experience with the full processes of reading and writing helps students to become enculturated into the secondary discourse of the school and to understand the purposes for literacy in the classroom. However, engagement in the full processes of reading and writing often is not sufficient to bring students of diverse backgrounds to high levels of literacy in school. As

Gee (1990) noted, although learning by engaging in full processes is fine for performance, it does not necessarily promote the ability to be analytic and reflective about a discourse. If we want students not only to be able to be literate in a basic sense but to employ literacy in conscious, thoughtful ways, we must give them opportunities to learn by studying parts of reading and writing.

Once some proficiency in classroom literacy (the secondary discourse of the school) has been gained, learning by studying parts of reading and writing can be used to reinforce students' understandings and promote reflection and analysis. According to Gee's (1990) theory, studying parts of reading and writing will not be effective until after students have gained some sense of literacy in school. If students lack experience with how literacy works in school, they will not be able to make sense of lessons focused on particular skills, such as letter sounds, or strategies, such as determining important information. Apprenticeship within the classroom as a literacy community must precede skill and strategy instruction.

When this sequence is not observed, students of diverse backgrounds are placed at a disadvantage in literacy learning in school. As Gee (1990) warned, "Classrooms that do not properly balance acquisition and learning, and realize which is which, and which student has acquired what, simply privilege those students who have begun the acquisition process at home, engaging these students in a teaching/learning process, while the others simply 'fail' " (p. 147). The primary discourse of many students of mainstream backgrounds is usually quite similar to that of the school. For example, these students have usually experienced family storybook reading, which is similar to the reading aloud of storybooks in the classroom (Heath, 1982). Their home language, standard American English, is the language of instruction used by the teacher. These students can readily adjust to the secondary discourse of the school and often need little time with the full processes of reading and writing before being able to benefit from learning by studying parts of reading and writing.

In contrast, students of diverse backgrounds may have experienced forms of literacy, such as translation (Orellana, Reynolds, Dorner, & Meza, 2003), that do not have close parallels in the classroom. They may have been asked questions requiring them to compare one thing to another, rather than known-answer questions (Heath, 1983). Their home language, AAVE or Spanish, is not the language of instruction used by their teacher. In short, many students of diverse backgrounds face a much greater challenge in learning the secondary discourse of the school, including the types of literacy associated with school, than do students of mainstream backgrounds.

Students of diverse backgrounds may require considerable experience with the secondary discourse of the school, through engagement in the full processes of reading and writing in the classroom, before they can be expected to learn by studying parts of reading and writing. An overemphasis on the parts, or too early an emphasis on the parts, may prevent students of diverse backgrounds from ever making satisfactory progress in learning classroom forms of reading and writing and the secondary discourse of the school.

Workshop Approaches

We now discuss the readers' workshop and the writers' workshop as classroom approaches that can provide students of diverse backgrounds with both types of learning experiences: learning by engaging in the full processes of reading and writing as well as learning by studying parts of reading and writing. Workshop approaches to literacy are very much in the tradition of Dewey (1944) and progressive education, although Dewey and his colleagues held views of literacy quite different from those advocated here (Shannon, 1990).

Consider a workshop maintained by a group of artists who create pottery. If you were to visit the workshop, you might see one artist sketching a design for a new piece of pottery. Another might be shaping a piece using a potter's wheel. Another might be glazing a piece, whereas another might be placing pieces in the kiln for firing. Although all of the artists in the workshop are making pottery, each might be in a different phase of work. Similarly, in the classroom, the teacher organizes a readers' workshop and a writers' workshop. Students will all be reading and writing, but they may be in different phases of work.

The traditional classroom is completely different from a workshop, because all of the students are usually expected to be doing the same thing at the same time. The traditional classroom may provide a suitable environment for teaching about parts of reading and writing. However, it is not a suitable environment for learning by engaging in the full processes of reading and writing. The reason is that students can only participate successfully in this type of learning if they have some leeway to move through reading and writing at their own pace.

To see why this is so, consider the following situation involving the process approach to writing, which is based on teaching students to complete a piece of writing by engaging in planning, drafting, revising, editing, and publishing, the same phases used by professional authors (Graves, 1983). Teachers who are just learning about the process approach to writing

(Graves, 1983) sometimes make the mistake of trying to implement a weekly schedule in which students are to plan on Monday, draft on Tuesday, revise on Wednesday, edit on Thursday, and publish on Friday. The obvious problem with this plan is that writing is a recursive process. In a recursive process, the individual may go back and forth between different phases. For example, the writer may find that his draft is boring and wisely decide to discard the piece. This means he must return to planning to decide on another topic that will lead to a more effective finished piece. Teachers need to provide nudges (Graves, 1994) that move students forward and prevent them from stalling in a certain phase of the writing process. At the same time, teachers must realize that engagement in the full processes of reading and writing entails a certain degree of recursive or nonlinear movement among phases of activity.

This, then, is the contribution made by workshop approaches. Unlike the traditional classroom, a workshop classroom offers students the opportunity to learn by engaging in the full processes of reading and writing. In a workshop classroom, while all the students will be reading and writing, they will often be at different phases in the process, just as with the artists in the pottery workshop. For example, in the writers' workshop, some students may be planning their writing whereas others are editing or publishing. In the readers' workshop, some students may be reading the novel silently, whereas others are reading it with a partner, and still others are drafting their responses to the literature.

A workshop approach is challenging for the teacher, because it requires a sound background in teaching, learning, and literacy, as well as strong skills of classroom organization and management (Au & Carroll, 1997). Teachers need a high level of expertise to carry out a workshop approach and to bring students of diverse backgrounds to high levels of literacy in school. Providing students with ample opportunities to learn by engaging in the full processes of reading and writing is a job that cannot be accomplished by underprepared teachers or through a scripted program. Fortunately, we have a strong research base for understanding how a workshop approach works. We know that a workshop approach can be used successfully by beginning teachers, as well as experienced teachers, in classrooms with students of diverse backgrounds (Au & Carroll, 1997).

Readers' Workshop Example: Book Club *Plus*

I discuss Book Club *Plus* as an example of a program that takes a workshop approach to the teaching of reading and that provides students of diverse background with both of the necessary types of learning opportunities. In a decade of studies, Raphael and her colleagues have demonstrated the benefits to students of an approach originally known as "Book Club" but then extended to be called "Book Club *Plus*" (Raphael & McMahon, 1994; Raphael et al., 2001). (I follow the convention of referring to the program or context as Book Club, with capital letters, and to the student discussion groups as book clubs.) Book Club *Plus* centers on literature-based instruction. Literature serves as the basis for students' discussions in book clubs, as well as for teacher-led lessons aimed at strategy and skill development. Although these discussions are best based on authentic literature, they can be based as well on selections in basal readers and other texts excerpted or written for the purposes of reading instruction. Teachers select literature for use in Book Club *Plus* that promotes the goal of opening students' minds to issues of diversity, so that students will be able to contribute to a just, democratic society. Teachers in Book Club *Plus* see literature as both a mirror, reflecting our lives back to us, and a window, allowing us to glimpse the lives of people in other cultures, times, and places (Galda, 1998). Active engagement with literature promotes higher level thinking, as students make connections from text to self, from text to text, and from text to theme.

Book Club *Plus* is organized around units in a curriculum with the overall theme of "Our Storied Lives." This theme is carried out in three units, each lasting from 6 to 8 weeks: Stories of Self, Family Stories, and Stories of Culture. The units gradually branch out from familiar content to new and challenging content. Each unit is based on a set of books chosen to carry out the theme. For example, third-grade teacher Marianne George used books by Patricia Polacco—including *Babushka's Doll* (Polacco, 1994a), *The Keeping Quilt* (Polacco, 1994b), and *Thundercake* (Polacco, 1990)—in her Family Stories unit (Raphael et al., 2001). At the end of each unit, students complete a culminating project that requires them to apply language arts strategies and skills in exploring the theme. For example, George's students did research on artifacts important to their families and presented oral reports to the class.

Dual Obligations.   Raphael and her colleagues developed Book Club *Plus* to address the dual obligations that must be met in guiding students to become excellent readers (Raphael et al., 2001). The first obligation is to involve students with literacy experiences that are appropriate for their grade level. Reading literature at their grade level allows students to be involved with challenging texts that can stretch their thinking. In chapter 2, I discussed the value of literature discussions of grade-appropriate texts for promoting students' higher level thinking. If students of diverse backgrounds do not have this opportunity, their comprehension and thinking will continue to lag behind that of their peers. This first obligation identified by Raphael et al. corresponds to learning by engaging in the full processes of reading and writing. Drawing on Gee's (1990) analysis, we can state that students need to engage with the secondary discourse of the classroom that is typical for their grade level.

The second obligation is to provide students with instruction appropriate to their level of achievement or development as readers and writers. For example, consider the situation in which assessment results indicate that some students in a fifth-grade classroom are reading far below grade level. These students have weaknesses in word identification and vocabulary skills. They require lessons at their instructional level if they are to gain independence as readers and match the accomplishments of peers at their grade. Another way of describing this situation is to say that these students need lessons on parts of the secondary discourse (reading and writing) over which they are beginning to have some control. These lessons must be within what Vygotsky (1978) called the *zone of proximal development*, the region of sensitivity to instruction.

The challenge for teachers is to meet both of the obligations identified by Raphael et al. (2001)—to provide students with experiences with text appropriate to their grade level as well as with text appropriate to their achievement or developmental level. Meeting the dual obligations is not particularly difficult for teachers in classrooms where the majority of students are reading and writing at or above grade level. It can, however, be a daunting problem for teachers in classrooms with many students of diverse backgrounds who are reading below the expected level, according to measures of achievement typically used in schools. Book Club *Plus* provides a practical framework, demonstrated to be successful across a range of settings, that addresses this very problem (Raphael et al., 2001).

As shown in Fig. 4.1, the Book Club *Plus* program revolves around two contexts: Book Club and Literacy Block, along with teacher read-alouds and sustained silent reading. Book Club meets the first of the dual obligations by providing students with the opportunity to read and discuss literature appropriate for their grade level. Literacy Block meets the second of the dual obligations by providing students with the opportunity to receive systematic skill and strategy lessons tailored to their instructional level. The time set aside for Book Club *Plus* varies from classroom to classroom and may range from 35 to 120 min per day. In a schedule typical of classrooms with 60 to 75 min, the teacher will implement the Book Club context on

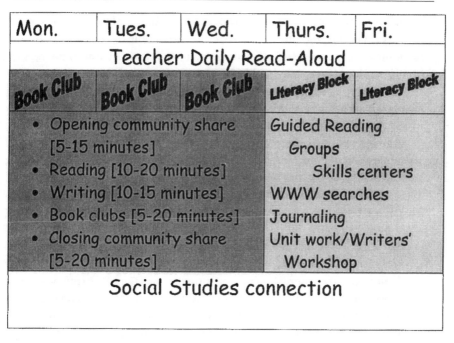

Mon.	Tues.	Wed.	Thurs.	Fri.
Teacher Daily Read-Aloud				
Book Club	Book Club	Book Club	Literacy Block	Literacy Block
• Opening community share [5-15 minutes] • Reading [10-20 minutes] • Writing [10-15 minutes] • Book clubs [5-20 minutes] • Closing community share [5-20 minutes]			Guided Reading Groups Skills centers WWW searches Journaling Unit work/Writers' Workshop	
Social Studies connection				

FIG. 4.1.   Weekly schedule for Book Club *Plus*.

Mondays, Tuesdays, and Wednesdays, devoting Thursdays and Fridays to the Literacy Block context (Raphael, Florio-Ruane, & George, 2001). In another schedule, typical of classrooms with 90 to 120 min of time, teachers have used a pattern of spending part of their time in Book Club and part in Literacy Block activities. On 2 to 3 days a week, teachers have sufficient time in Literacy Block to meet with all three of their reading groups, as well as to conduct Book Club for about 45 min. On the other days, they spend long enough in Book Club to have a sustained time for opening and closing community share, while meeting with two of their reading groups. On these days, teachers meet with the lowest group and alternate meeting with the middle and top group.

Book Club Components.   As indicated in Fig. 4.1, the Book Club context has four components: community share, reading, writing, and book club discussions. Let's look at the parts of Book Club as they might occur in order on a typical day in a fourth-grade class. The teacher opens with *community share*, the term used for lessons and discussions conducted with the whole class. The opening community share is often used for mini-lessons related to the literature. Teachers provide instruction in skills and strategies, such as making inferences, that are valuable to students regardless of reading level. The teacher may introduce a new form of written response, such as drawing a web to illustrate the relationships among characters. At another time, the teacher may introduce background, such as historical information, helpful in understanding the literature.

After the opening community share, students have time for reading and writing, two other components of Book Club. They read their group's book and prepare a written response to share during their book club meeting. Typically, students read a chapter of the novel silently to themselves. However, Raphael et al. (2001) emphasized the importance of giving struggling readers access to the literature by any convenient means. Struggling readers may read with a partner, listen to the teacher read the book aloud, or listen to an audiotape of the text.

As mentioned earlier, the teacher introduces different forms of written response through minilessons (Raphael & McMahon, 1994). Over time, students develop a repertoire and can choose the type of response they want to draft. Students become adept at combining different types of written responses (Raphael & McMahon, 1994) and may even invent new forms (Montes & Au, 2003). In chapter 2, you were introduced to the fourth-grade classroom of Torry Montes, who taught in a school in which the majority of students were of native Hawaiian ancestry. Following are the options for written responses available to her students:

When I respond I can . . .

1. Predict (before), validate (after), document (evidence from the story).
2. Retell and summarize.
3. Wonder (questions: why, how, what if).
4. Draw something from the reading that I feel is important (write a description of my picture).
5. Character web or matrix.
   Character relationships.
   Character analysis: description, feelings, attributes, actions.
6. Favorite or least favorite part, because . . .
7. If I were the character . . . , because . . .
8. Me and the book: personal connections (link it back to the story).
9. If I were the author . . . , because . . .

10. Connections with other stories I have read.
11. Create my own response type (Montes & Au, 2003, p. 76).

Book Club Discussions. The fourth component, book clubs, is at the very heart of the program. Students meet with their book club, a heterogeneous group of four to six, to discuss the novel. Teachers need to be aware that book clubs may not be an instant success. [Florio-Ruane (personal communication, October 4, 2004) indicates that an exception is seen in classrooms with many African American students, who may be quite comfortable with these discussions right from the start.] In the beginning, book club discussions may be brief and stilted, because students have not yet developed the skills to engage in a literary conversation with their peers. Observers usually note that students often read their written responses aloud in round-robin fashion, then raise their hand to tell the teacher they're finished. For book clubs to evolve in the intended manner, teachers must give students an idea of what it means to have good discussions of literature. Students benefit from seeing videotaped examples of good book club conversations. The teacher may also wish to videotape faltering discussions and allow members of that book club to analyze their own behaviors and arrive at suggestions for improvement. At the same time, teachers can offer suggestions for dealing with common problems, such as offending a classmate. In that event, teachers might suggest that students use the following wording when they disagree with the interpretation offered by someone in their book club: "Excuse me, but I have another idea."

Many teachers find that the most effective means of promoting good conversations is through a technique known as "fishbowl." In this technique, one book club meets as usual to discuss its novel, while the other students and the teacher form a large circle to observe the discussion. After the book club has finished meeting, students may direct questions or suggestions to book club members. Then the teacher guides the whole class in reflecting on the qualities of a good book club discussion. New rules or guidelines may be added to those already posted in the classroom. For example, the following items were included on a chart of "What makes a good book club?" developed by Torry Montes's students:

- All members should participate. Listening is okay.
- Ask questions to invite the shy person to jump in.
- Ask questions if you don't understand something from the story or something someone is talking about.

- Come to book club prepared to share ideas and ask questions. No yes/no answers, one-word answers, or obvious questions. Ask *why, how, what if* questions.
- Use ideas that help the book club come up with/think of new ideas (Montes & Au, 2003, p. 77).

As this example from Montes's classroom illustrates, students develop sophisticated understandings about literature discussions over time.

The following example of a book club discussion in an urban fourth-grade classroom shows how students were able to put themselves in the place of the characters. They had come to the point in *Number the Stars* (Lowry, 1990) where a German soldier ruffles a little girl's hair because the child reminds him of his daughter:

Crystal: Um, Helena, how would you feel if um, the soldier came up and hit you? What would you feel as Kirsti?

Helena: Um, I would be scared because she's Kirsti is 5 years old and the story says she was 5 years old, so if I was 5 years old I would be really scared. What would I do, I don't know cause I was so small and don't understand anything, so I don't know what I would do.

Crystal: Um, Randy, if you were one of the people in the story, how would you feel? Not the soldier but one of the people, like, how about the mother? If you were the father of the kid, what would you feel?

Randy: I would feel kind of angry and tell the soldier to not be doing, go in my daughter's hair like that because she didn't like it. She didn't. (Raphael & McMahon, 1994, p. 114)

The excerpt shows the students exploring this incident from the perspectives of different characters in the novel, imagining how they would feel and react. Crystal played a central role in the discussion, posing questions and then inviting Helena and Randy into the conversation.

Ellen Fitch, a teacher in an urban school, introduced book clubs to her fourth- and fifth-grade students (Kong & Fitch, 2003). The majority of students in her classroom were second language learners, and they came from many different cultural backgrounds: Vietnamese, Hmong, White, Latino, Haitian, Somali, and Bosnian. In expressing their thoughts and opinions about books, students learned to debate ideas and explore various perspectives. For example, here is an excerpt from a book club meeting on *Walk Two Moons* (Creech, 1996):

Tu: How are they crazy?

Andy: Of course they are crazy, because only crazy persons are going to go to rob tires from a [senator].

Tu: They didn't rob it.

Andy: Yes they did. They stole it.

Tu: They borrowed it from them.

Andy: So, they stole them.

Vong: That's kind of borrowing.

Andy: So I go and steal someone's video games and I'm just borrowing them?

Tu: To them they are borrowing and to other people they are stealing.

(Kong & Fitch, 2003, p. 352)

This example shows how students build on one another's ideas during book club to gain new insights. Tu and Andy debated about whether an action should be interpreted as stealing or borrowing. Vong entered the conversation to indicate that stealing may be a kind of borrowing. This spurred Tu to conclude that the same action may be seen as borrowing by one person and as stealing by another.

Book club discussions allow students to gain different perspectives about the literature, especially when members of the group come from different cultural backgrounds. Goatley, Brock, and Raphael (1995) conducted a year-long study of a book club with five fifth-grade students. One of the students, Mei, had left Vietnam in the second grade. On arriving in Michigan, she received 2 years of instruction in a bilingual program. In the fourth grade, she remained in the regular education classroom all day and had the opportunity to participate in Book Club. At the time of the study, she was experiencing Book Club for a second year. When her book club was reading *Park's Quest* (Paterson, 1989), Mei had the chance to share her knowledge about the war in Vietnam, including the experiences of her family. Mei gained by being able to make connections between the text and her prior knowledge and experiences, as well as by being recognized by the group for her contributions. The students in Mei's book club gained new insights about the novel and a better understanding of what life had been like for Mei and her family in Vietnam.

During the closing community share, the teacher usually has the different book clubs speak briefly about what they discussed, how they managed their interactions, or any problems they encountered. The closing community share strengthens the classroom community of readers by giving everyone access to the key ideas discussed by the different book clubs. In classrooms where book clubs are reading different novels, students often are motivated to read for themselves the novels read by other groups.

Literacy Block. Literacy Block is the other major context in Book Club *Plus.* In this context, the teacher provides systematic instruction on literacy strategies and skills. The focus in Literacy Block is on studying the parts of reading and writing (learning), in contrast to the focus in book club engagement with the full processes (acquisition). As mentioned earlier, the emphasis in Literacy Block is on instruction appropriate to students' achievement levels, which may be considerably below grade level. Much instruction takes place in small, homogeneous groups of students, where the teacher can tailor instruction to address specific needs. Teachers often divide the class into three groups for this purpose. Small group lessons typically take the form of guided reading, as described by Fountas and Pinnell (1996). Students generally read texts at their instructional level, and teachers use this time to foster skills of word identification, vocabulary, and comprehension. Because the texts are linked to the overarching theme, teachers can guide students to make connections to the texts being read in their book clubs. When not meeting with the teacher, students engage in practice activities in which they apply strategies and skills independently, for example, to theme-related writing. Skills may include grammar, spelling, and handwriting. Time in Literacy Block may also be devoted to other reading and writing activities, such as independent reading. In some classrooms, students move among different learning centers, whereas in others, they work at their desks. Ideas that teachers can follow to provide effective instruction in comprehension strategies are discussed in chapter 6; ideas for teaching phonics and vocabulary and for designing productive independent seatwork activities appear in chapter 9.

Benefits to Students. How do students, especially those of diverse backgrounds, benefit from participation in Book Club (and more recently, Book Club *Plus*)? I stated earlier that students of diverse backgrounds need to learn by engaging in the full processes of reading and writing to gain access to the secondary discourse of the school. We need to look carefully at the kinds of gains students make in the secondary discourse, as evidenced by improvements in their performance as readers, writers, speakers, and listeners. We also need to determine whether students have grown in terms of their ability to be reflective and analytic about the parts of reading and writing—skills and strategies.

Results of studies conducted in a variety of settings indicate that students in Book Club and Book Club *Plus* classrooms consistently make gains in both of these areas. Research verifies that students, including those of diverse backgrounds, improve greatly in their ability to participate in book club discussions of literature. A study set in two culturally diverse, urban classrooms showed that students learned to clarify confusing elements in the text, evaluate the behaviors and motivations of different characters, and visualize themselves in the situations portrayed (Raphael & McMahon, 1994). Students frequently draw on background knowledge, make connections among texts (Raphael et al., 2001), and monitor their own comprehension and that of the group, for example, by noting when an interpretation does not make sense (Montes & Au, 2003). Students' participation in Book Club allows them to collaborate to arrive at new interpretations of the text, showing that comprehension can be reinforced in peer-group discussions as well as in teacher-led lessons. Researchers have repeatedly found dramatic increases in the depth of students' responses to literature, in both book club discussions and written responses, over the course of the school year. The example of Mei, a second language learner, was cited earlier. Like Mei, other second language learners appear to gain in their ability to express complex ideas about literature during book clubs (Kong & Fitch, 2003).

Those who are proficient in a secondary discourse can interact comfortably with others, following accepted norms for speaking, listening, and turn-taking. Fine-grained studies of book club discussions show dramatic improvements in students' performance in this regard. Students learn to listen carefully, build on the ideas of others, invite others into the conversation, contradict one another in a respectful manner, and introduce new topics and ideas related to the text (Montes & Au, 2003; Goatley, Brock, & Raphael, 1995; Kong & Fitch, 2003; Raphael & McMahon, 1994). They gain a clear idea about the qualities of a good conversation about books in terms of social and interactional skills as well as the substance of ideas.

Furthermore, studies document substantial improvements in students' attitudes toward reading. Raphael and McMahon (1994) found that Book Club students could recall and talk about at least 9 of the 16 books they had read during the previous year. These results were far superior to those shown by students who had been in a commercial reading program, who could not remember the titles or authors of the stories that had been the subject of instruction. In Montes's classroom, before they began participating in Book Club, 60% of the students had not considered themselves to be readers (Montes & Au, 2003). At the end of the year, 85% thought of themselves as readers.

In all of the studies cited earlier, students demonstrated increased engagement with reading through their willingness and eagerness to participate in book clubs. A dramatic example of students' commitment to book clubs was seen in a fifth-grade classroom with students of diverse backgrounds (Padilla, 2003). These students expressed disappointment that their teacher, Aurene Padilla, was not planning to have them start new book clubs because only 8 days remained before vacation. Because of the students' interest, Padilla decided to proceed with another set of book clubs, despite the short time. She selected five books, and students signed up for their new book clubs. Padilla (2003) described what happened next:

> Once the book clubs were established, the students set out to determine their nightly reading and response homework for their own group. Students were asked to submit a plan to me for approval. As I reviewed my students' plan for their book clubs, I was surprised that one group had assigned themselves 30 pages of reading a night. I met with this group and asked them whether they would like to switch to a book that was shorter in length so that their homework wouldn't be so lengthy. To my astonishment, the students were actually excited about the possibility of finishing the book and discussing it together in their book club. As we began our third book club, I was excited to see my students engaging in the "work" without complaining and with a high level of excitement and energy. I believe that my students had finally gained ownership of learning because I had given them voice and choice. (pp. 36–37)

The results in terms of students' growth in strategies and skills, or the parts of reading and writing, are encouraging as well. Raphael and McMahon (1994) found that students in Book Club and Book Club *Plus* classrooms receive scores on state, district, and standardized tests that are equal to those of students in traditional programs. This is a significant finding, because students in Book Club and Book Club *Plus* classrooms were able to experience the benefits of literature-based instruction, while continuing to perform in a satisfactory manner on skill-oriented tests. Students in comparison classrooms in which teachers tended to focus on skills did not show superior test results. At the same time, students in traditional classrooms were denied the intellectual and attitudinal benefits associated with literature-based instruction. In fact, research generally shows that students of diverse backgrounds in literature-based programs outperform comparison groups on all measures of reading and writing except the standardized test (Morrow, 1992; Morrow, Pressley, Smith, & Smith, 1997).

Kong and Fitch (2003) reported results on the Slosson Oral Reading Test (SORT) and the Meta-comprehension Strategy Index (Schmitt, 1990), administered to Fitch's fifth-grade students at the beginning and end of the school year. Although Fitch had not focused on word identification, students showed an average gain of 37.2 words on the SORT, for an average increase of 43%. All but 1 of the 19 students showed more than a year's growth in vocabulary. The Meta-comprehension Strategy Index assesses students' awareness of reading as a strategic process. Students respond to 25 questions about strategies used before, during, and after reading. The results showed that students gained knowledge of all the comprehension strategies assessed, with improvement particularly in predicting and verifying, self-questioning, drawing from background knowledge, and summarizing and applying repair strategies.

In short, there is strong evidence that students of diverse backgrounds benefit as literacy learners from Book Club and Book Club *Plus,* which I have discussed as examples of a readers' workshop approach. I now turn to the general principles illustrated in Book Club *Plus.* Following these principles will help teachers to improve the literacy learning of students of diverse backgrounds, regardless of the particular reading program favored in their schools.

GENERAL PRINCIPLES FOR STRENGTHENING LITERACY INSTRUCTION

In outlining the general principles for strengthening literacy instruction illustrated in Book Club *Plus,* I draw on Gee's (1994) work on acquisition of the primary discourse. The first principle is that of embodied action. Gee wrote, "The learning of a new complex system is most efficacious when it is initially backed up by and based on embodied action" (p. 335). This is the idea that we have referred to as learning by doing reading and writing, or by engaging in the full processes of reading and writing. In Book Club *Plus,* students are motivated to read and write for a real purpose. They are eager to have ideas to share with the members of their book club and with the whole class. One of the strengths of Book Club *Plus* is that all students engage in reading, writing, and book club discussions, including second language learners and students in special education (Goatley, Brock, & Raphael, 1995). Teachers devise means to give students access to grade-appropriate text through partner reading, read-alouds, or audiotapes. Involving all students is vitally important. Raphael et al. (2001) commented as follows:

As things currently stand, low-achieving readers may conceivably go through school never engaging with challenging texts appropriate for their age level, texts that require higher order thinking and interpretation skills. Moreover, these struggling readers do not have the opportunity to talk with peers about such materials and the ideas they contain. Further, in such circumstances the classroom becomes stratified. It is difficult in that setting, if not impossible, for the low-achieving readers to join or for the teacher to create a functioning community of learners. (p. 599)

I call the second principle suggested by Gee (1994) *learning in two directions*. Gee (1994) noted that most learners use both top-down and bottom-up strategies when trying to understand a complex new domain, such as literacy and the secondary discourse of the school. To support learners best, teachers should provide both experiences with the "whole" and instruction in the "bits and pieces." Book Club *Plus* instantiates this principle by having two components: Book club and Literacy Block. Book club provides students with experience with the whole of reading and writing, or the full processes, including discussions of literature with peers. Literacy Block gives students the chance to study the bits and pieces or parts of reading and writing. The principle of learning in two directions recognizes that most students of diverse backgrounds require both kinds of opportunities to reach high levels of literacy achievement in school.

The third principle suggested by Gee (1994) may be labeled *scaffolding*. We have discussed the idea of apprenticeship and how students need to be apprenticed to the teacher, another adult, or a peer who can serve as a more knowledgeable other. Gee (1994) stated, "Efficacious learning of a new complex system is a process involving socially supported and scaffolded insertion into an activity that one does not yet understand" (p. 336). In Book Club *Plus*, students start to participate in book clubs before they are able to have successful literature discussions. In the beginning, unless they have previously participated in book clubs, students do not yet understand what they should do. Of course, teachers take certain steps to prepare students in advance, such as conducting whole-class discussions of literature and building students' comprehension strategies. However, the only way for students to learn to engage in productive conversations about literature is by giving it a try. This is what Gee meant by insertion—students must actually be placed in book clubs and given a chance to struggle with the activity.

What allows students eventually to conduct good conversations about literature is that their involvement in book clubs is scaffolded. Scaffolding, as Wood, Bruner, and Ross (1976) suggested, is social support that is tailored to the learners' needs but also temporary in nature. Social support is adjusted and gradually removed as students gain competence. Teachers in Book Club *Plus* provide scaffolding in the ways described earlier: They monitor the discussions, provide feedback to groups, show videotapes, conduct fishbowls, and give students time to reflect in small groups and with the whole class. Students receive social support or scaffolding not only from the teacher but from their peers. Recall the book club excerpt in which Crystal asked questions and invited other students into the conversation.

The fourth principle may be termed *routine*. Here is what Gee (1994) had to say about this principle: "Early insertion into an activity one does not yet understand requires that the activity be to a certain extent repeated and routinized or ritualized. Rituals "freeze" meaning for the learner's observation" (p. 336). Much has been written about the benefits of routine and ritual in workshop approaches to the teaching of reading and writing (Atwell, 1987; Calkins, 1994). The idea of routines is that a certain plan of action is regularly followed. The idea of rituals is that there are certain ways of enacting certain activities. Classroom routines and rituals are especially helpful to students of diverse backgrounds, whose primary discourse may differ substantially from the secondary discourse of the school. Learning to read and write well in school, which means gaining proficiency in a secondary discourse, is made easier for students of diverse backgrounds when classroom activities become predictable and understandable. Book Club *Plus* follows a set routine, with a regular weekly schedule and a consistent flow of activities each day, whether the focus is book club or Literacy Block (Raphael, Florio-Ruane, & George, 2001). Teachers carry out the components of book club and Literacy Block, such as community share and guided reading, in a consistent manner. Students of diverse backgrounds can more easily learn about the secondary discourse of the school because of the regularity provided by these routines and rituals. Gee wrote of meaning being "frozen" for the learner to observe. What this means is that, because routines and rituals occur day after day, students can observe and experience the same events and activities again and again. Over time they learn what to expect, and they have multiple opportunities to improve their performance. If they were unable to perform well in a certain ritual—such as writing in response to literature—the day before, they have a chance to improve their performance the following day. Their proficiency in literacy and the secondary discourse of the school improves through a process of successive approximation (Holdaway, 1979) supported by the routines and rituals of workshop approaches. Successive approximation refers to a gradual movement toward proficiency through repeated attempts at a particular activity.

The principles of embodied action, learning in two directions, scaffold-ing, and routine—drawn from Gee's (1990, 1994) analysis of primary discourse acquisition—are foundational to workshop and literature-based approaches, such as Book Club *Plus*. Many different sets of principles for guiding literacy learning in classrooms with students of diverse back-grounds may be formulated (e.g., Au, 1998; Nieto, 1999). The principles discussed earlier are recommended because they have clear practical impli-cations as well as strong theoretical and empirical support.

SUMMARY

In this chapter, you learned that the real challenge faced by teachers who wish to improve the literacy achievement of students of diverse back-grounds is to help them learn the secondary discourse of the school. Read-ing and writing—not just words and letters but the values, beliefs, and be-haviors associated with classroom literacy—are part of this secondary discourse. Based on Gee's (1994) theory of primary discourse acquisition, it can be seen that students need opportunities both for learning by engag-ing with the full processes of reading and writing as well as for learning by studying the parts of reading and writing. Learning by engaging with the full processes must come first, followed by studying the parts. Workshop ap-proaches to literacy instruction—the writers' workshop and the readers' workshop—allow the teacher to provide students with both types of oppor-tunities. The Book Club *Plus* program was discussed as an example of a lit-erature-based, readers' workshop approach, tested and found effective across a wide range of classrooms. Following four general principles of in-struction drawn from workshop approaches may help teachers to improve the literacy instruction of students of diverse backgrounds.

5

Ownership and Building
a Classroom Community

In chapter 4, you learned about workshop approaches, such as Book Club *Plus*. One of the benefits of workshop approaches is that they foster students' ownership of literacy. In the beginning of this chapter, I explain the concept of ownership and discuss why students of diverse backgrounds often do not show ownership, or the motivation to become excellent readers and writers, in school. To explain the typical situation, in which students of diverse backgrounds appear to teachers to be unmotivated to learn to read and write well in school, I turn to the thinking of three anthropologists: Ogbu, Erickson, and D'Amato. Then I discuss steps teachers can take to win students' respect and trust and to foster the classroom as a literate community.

OWNERSHIP OF LITERACY

Ownership involves students' valuing of literacy (Au, 1997). Students with ownership have positive attitudes toward literacy and willingly use literacy for their own purposes. Teachers in classrooms with many students of diverse backgrounds often observe that students seem uninterested in literacy in school. As discussed in chapter 3, part of the reason may be that students of diverse backgrounds often participate in one set of literacy practices in the home and community, whereas they are asked to engage in another set of literacy practices in school. Students may show ownership of literacy at home but not at school because school literacy practices are unfamiliar and unrewarding or do not appear useful.

What does it look like when students show ownership of literacy in school? The following behaviors, reflecting ownership of literacy, were captured during videotaping of the sixth-grade classroom of Pat Nakanishi, a teacher in a Hawaii school with students of many different cultural backgrounds. Students in this classroom participated eagerly in a small-group, teacher-led discussion of *A Wrinkle in Time* (L'Engle, 1962). They presented "think questions" for their classmates to discuss, and they criticized the ending of the novel. In individual interviews, students stated that they enjoyed these discussions because they liked hearing other students' ideas about the novel. During sustained silent reading, students quickly became absorbed in their books. The taping captured a group of six students participating in a discussion about the books they had read independently. One of the girls enjoyed books in the Cirque du Freak series (e.g., Shan, 2002) and was passing them on to one of the boys. (The teacher had received a note from this boy's father describing his astonishment when his son, a sports fan, wanted to stay up late to read a book.) Another girl described how a friend had introduced her to the "series of unfortunate events" books by Lemony Snicket (1999).

These students showed ownership in their love of books and reading and in their willingness to share ideas about novels with their classmates and to recommend favorite books to others. The students' positive attitudes toward literacy, and the support they showed for one another's reading, indicated that the teacher had succeeded in turning this classroom into a literate community. I describe the classroom as a *community*—or more precisely, a *community of practice*—in the sense discussed by Wenger (1998). In communities of practice, members of a group work within a framework of shared understandings toward common goals; in this case, those related to literacy learning.

Ownership of literacy, including behaviors such as those just described, should be the overarching goal of the classroom language arts program for students of diverse backgrounds. True, ownership is important for all students, including those of mainstream backgrounds. However, as I explain in this chapter, ownership is an essential consideration if we are to bring students of diverse backgrounds to high levels of literacy.

Most teachers take pleasure in instructing students who sincerely want to learn to read and write well, even when those students are struggling learners. The difficulty arises when teachers find themselves confronted by students who do not seem to value reading and writing in school. I have heard comments along these lines from many teachers: "My students don't care about reading and writing. If I could get them to care, I could teach them all the strategies and skills they need." Overcoming the indifference or resistance to classroom literacy activities shown by many students of diverse backgrounds is often the key to improving their literacy achievement, and this is why a focus on ownership is vital.

You may be wondering if it is necessary for students to become proficient at reading and writing first, before they can experience ownership of literacy. The answer to this question is no. Students can have ownership of literacy without being proficient readers and writers. Consider the case of Kalani, a Hawaiian student in a second-grade classroom. Kalani struggled with reading and writing and had to work hard to keep up with the other students in his class. For example, by the time most of the other students had written and published three books, Kalani had only completed one. However, his teacher observed that Kalani took books home from school every day to read to his younger sister. When his parents saw how interested he was in books, they built him a bookcase that they filled with books purchased from the Goodwill store. As the year progressed, his teacher reported that, because he was always willing to try his best, Kalani was making steady gains. Kalani is an example of a student whose ownership of literacy supported his gradual development of proficiency as a reader and writer.

Ownership of literacy and proficiency in reading and writing are mutually reinforcing. On one hand, students with ownership of literacy will want to improve their reading and writing abilities, because they recognize the importance of literacy in their everyday lives. In this way, ownership can lead to proficiency. On the other hand, students who are proficient at reading and writing can carry out literacy activities easily and successfully. As a result of these rewarding experiences with literacy, these students may well develop ownership.

Anthropological Perspectives

Ogbu and Involuntary Minorities. As some students of diverse backgrounds move up the grades, it may appear that they are actively resisting their teachers' efforts to improve their reading and writing. Why is it often so difficult for teachers to gain students' commitment to, and active involvement in, literacy learning in the classroom? To answer these questions, let's look at insights that can be gained about students' motivation and ownership of literacy from anthropological research.

Our starting point in addressing these complex issues is the work of John Ogbu. The assumptions in Ogbu's work are those of critical theory, mentioned in chapter 2. This perspective begins with the notion that, in every society, there are basically two groups: (a) the haves or the people in power, known as the dominant group; and (b) the have-nots, known as the subordinate group. The dominant group and subordinate group exist in a complex relation to one another. However, the basis for critical theory is the idea that the dominant group tends to act to reinforce or reproduce the conditions that sustain its position. The dominant group maintains its power, in part, by controlling the society's major institutions, including the schools. For this reason, schooling generally serves as a process of reproducing the existing social order, to the benefit of students who are members of the dominant group. This line of reasoning suggests that schooling is unlikely to involve the processes of social change necessary to provide subordinate-group students with an excellent education.

Ogbu (1990, 1993) proposed the idea that subordinate-group students fall into two categories: (a) castelike or involuntary minorities, and (b) immigrant or voluntary minorities. Members of involuntary minority groups were forced to become part of a larger society through processes of enslavement, conquest, or colonization. In the United States, examples of such groups are African Americans and native Hawaiians. In contrast, members of voluntary minority groups willingly joined the larger society because they saw opportunities for improving their lot in life in social, economic, or political terms. Certain Asian American groups, such as Korean Americans, are frequently cited as examples of voluntary minority groups in the United States

Ogbu (1993) developed a theory to explain why students from involuntary minority groups tend to perform poorly in school, whereas students from voluntary minority groups generally find success. He argued that students from involuntary minority groups, in general, are far less motivated to overcome barriers to school success than voluntary minorities. I discuss critiques of Ogbu's theory later, but for now, let us look at the research that supports his argument.

In research conducted in Stockton, California, Ogbu (1981) found that one possible source for students' lack of motivation was the absence of an economic incentive for pursuing education. He noted, with few exceptions, that no matter how much education African Americans had obtained, they were not hired in any but the lowest paying, lowest status jobs. This phenomenon is known as a job ceiling. In comparison, European Americans were generally hired for jobs commensurate with their level of education; in this case, more education led to a better job. Ogbu's research demonstrated that, due to discrimination, education did not yield the same benefits for African Americans as it did for European Americans.

In interviews, African American parents spoke of how important education was to their children's success in life. However, Ogbu (1981) concluded that parents did not really believe that their children had the same chance to succeed as European Americans. This was a realistic view on the part of parents, given the existence of the job ceiling. Many parents in Ogbu's study did not see a good reason for lending strong support to their children's academic efforts and pushing their children to succeed in school.

Ogbu (1981) noted as well that some parents did not think that inner-city public schools could provide their children with a proper education. This distrust had its basis in reality, including historical conditions of inequality that led to inner-city schools in poor repair, with inexperienced teachers, out-of-date textbooks, and other factors described in the inferior education explanation, presented in chapter 2. These parents thought that public schools were run for the benefit of mainstream children, not their own children, and they did not feel that past conditions of discrimination had been, or were likely to be, corrected.

In these discouraging circumstances, Ogbu (1981) argued, involuntary minorities do not see education as the pathway to success that voluntary minorities or mainstream individuals believe it to be. The result is what Ogbu (1993) called *cultural inversion*. Involuntary minorities invert or act in opposition to the practices of success favored by the mainstream culture, because those practices have not paid off for family members or acquaintances within their cultural group. Failing to do well in school, including an unwillingness to develop ownership of literacy in school, is an example of cultural inversion among involuntary minority students.

Two major criticisms of Ogbu's (1981, 1993) work should be noted. First, because his focus was on the macrolevel, Ogbu's research does not address the human interactions taking place on a daily basis, the microinteractions, that sustain macropatterns of inequality. Educators might be able to change these human interactions, even if there is little they can do to affect the societal forces operating at the macrolevel. A second criticism of Ogbu's research is that it does not account for within-group variability. Ogbu's theory addresses the failure of many involuntary minority students, but it does not explain how certain students from involuntary minority groups manage to succeed in school (Achor & Morales, 1990).

Erickson and Face-to-Face Interactions. As discussed in chapter 2, to gain a complete picture of issues related to the literacy achievement of students of diverse backgrounds, both the macrolevels and microlevels of analysis need to be considered. Within the context provided by the macroview, educators can turn to the microview, because this level of analysis generally addresses patterns that educators may be able to change.

Frederick Erickson (1993; Erickson & Mohatt, 1982) pioneered the microlevel of analysis through the close study of videotaped classroom interactions. He argued that the school success or failure of students of diverse backgrounds is not simply predetermined by broad societal factors but results as well from the face-to-face interactions of students and teachers in the classroom. This view is consistent with a social constructivist perspective, which emphasizes the daily actions taken by human beings that lead to success or failure in school. Erickson suggested that students will be motivated to learn in school if teachers use communication patterns responsive to or compatible with the norms, beliefs, and values of students' home cultures. Engaging in classroom activities consistent with their cultural values allows students of diverse backgrounds to achieve academic success without having to leave behind, or act counter to, beliefs brought from the home. The use of such communication patterns is one form of culturally responsive instruction (Au & Kawakami, 1994; Erickson, 1993; Ladson-Billings, 1995), discussed in chapter 7.

Talk Story and Hawaiian Children. An example of cultural responsiveness in face-to-face interaction is seen in studies of interaction in reading lessons with young children of native Hawaiian ancestry. Native Hawaiians fit Ogbu's (1993) characterization of involuntary minorities. Beginning in the 1820s, a system of common schools was established in the Kingdom of Hawaii under the influence of American missionaries from New England. In the early years, instruction was conducted exclusively in the Hawaiian language, and all the teachers were native Hawaiians. However, the curriculum was always that dictated by the missionaries and other Westerners, who had the goal of using schooling to proselytize their religion and to Westernize the thinking and ways of life of the Hawaiian people. Gradually, more non-Hawaiians entered the teaching force and the language of instruction shifted to English (Au, 2000). Following the overthrow of the monarchy in 1893, Hawaii ceased to be an independent kingdom and was soon annexed to the United States. The curriculum and instruction experienced by Hawaiian children during the latter part of the 19th century, and throughout the 20th century, reflected the beliefs and practices of the American mainstream. The consequences have not been positive. As a group, Hawaiian students in public schools in the state of Hawaii score in the bottom quartile on standardized tests of reading achievement (Kamehameha Schools Office of Program Evaluation and Planning, 1993). Not surprisingly, they often exhibit negative attitudes toward reading and writing in the classroom.

However, some teachers have been able to create classrooms in which Hawaiian students show positive attitudes and meet grade-level benchmarks for literacy (Au & Carroll, 1997). Among other factors, teachers effective in bringing Hawaiian students to high levels of literacy are adept at using talk story-like participation structures, a form of culturally responsive instruction.

Au and Mason (1981, 1983) compared the lessons given by two teachers, Teacher HC and Teacher LC, who had similar professional backgrounds and years of teaching experience. The difference was that Teacher HC had previously taught Hawaiian children, whereas Teacher LC had not. Both teachers taught two lessons on reading comprehension to the same group of six Hawaiian second graders over the course of 4 days. Teacher HC followed rules for interaction similar to those in talk story, a Hawaiian community speech event (Watson, 1974). In talk story, speakers collaborate to produce a narrative. They speak in rhythmic alternation, and there is a great deal of overlapping speech. Most of the time, Teacher HC did not call on children to speak one at a time. Instead, she allowed the children to determine when they would speak. When Teacher HC did call on a particular child, she did not prevent others from adding to that child's response. In other words, the lesson flowed like a normal conversation in which individuals contribute when they feel they have something to say. The high degree of collaboration in the lessons reflected the value given to cooperation, as opposed to competition, in many Hawaiian families.

Teacher LC, who had not taught Hawaiian children before, conducted her lessons following rules for interaction frequently observed in mainstream classrooms. These rules are part of the initiation–response–evaluation (IRE) pattern (Cazden, 1988; Mehan, 1979). In this pattern, the teacher initiates the topic, usually by asking a question. Students who know the answer raise their hands, and the teacher calls on one of them to respond. The student selected by the teacher is the only one who has the right to speak. The role of the other students is to listen attentively and remain silent. After the chosen student has presented a response, the teacher evaluates the answer, indicating whether it is right or wrong. Although the IRE structure is familiar to mainstream students, I do not recommend its use with these students because other structures are likely to be much more effective in promoting thoughtful, lively discussion.

Nevertheless, the IRE pattern for structuring interaction is the usual means of managing recitation in mainstream classrooms. However, it proved ineffective in Teacher LC's lessons with Hawaiian children. Whenever Teacher LC called on a single child to respond, others spoke up to add their ideas. Teacher LC tried repeatedly but without success to keep these other children quiet. As a result, she had to focus her lesson on management, rather than on reading instruction. The rules for the IRE pattern did not fit the children's idea of interaction in lessons. They did not want to remain silent when they had information to add.

Looking at the values underlying the IRE pattern helps us to understand the children's reactions. When teachers use the IRE pattern, they single out individual students to answer. When the teacher spotlight shines on them, students have the opportunity to win approval, and, through their superior knowledge, to put themselves ahead of the other students. The IRE pattern works when students come from mainstream backgrounds in which they have learned to value competition, one-upmanship, and individual achievement. The value of competition may be less prized by students of diverse backgrounds, such as many native Hawaiian students, a point emphasized later in D'Amato's (1988) research.

Au and Mason (1981) found that Hawaiian students exhibited much higher levels of attention and engagement in lessons conducted with culturally responsive, talk story-like participation structures than in lessons with the IRE structure. In addition, students discussed many more text ideas and made more logical inferences during the talk story-like reading lessons. In comparison to lessons conducted in a mainstream manner, culturally responsive reading lessons were related to better academic performance by Hawaiian children.

Why should an adaptation as simple as changing the rules for interaction in a lesson make so much of a difference in the motivation and academic learning of students of diverse backgrounds? Erickson (1993) suggested that these adaptations may reduce the cultural shock in the classroom, because students discover that they can use familiar ways of speaking in an otherwise unfamiliar setting. By accepting students' norms for interaction, the teacher communicates a sense of regard for the students and their cultural backgrounds. Students may sense this regard and feel more comfortable and confident about participating in the classroom.

Resistance to Schooling.   Students are always learning, in school and out, Erickson (1993) noted. To say that students are "not learning" in school means that they are not learning the academic content being presented by teachers. A distinction must be made between the formal curriculum, which teachers plan and intend to teach, and the hidden curriculum, which includes the messages actually communicated to students (Bennett & LeCompte, 1990). When teachers teach using mainstream patterns of interaction exclusively and do not attempt to teach in culturally responsive ways, they may be sending students of diverse backgrounds the message that the ways of speaking and knowledge they have brought from the home are not valued in school. In this situation, Erickson observed, students may show resistance to teachers and to schooling. Students may choose not to learn in the classroom because they have decided to oppose the negative messages of the hidden curriculum. Clearly, students are not going to develop ownership of literacy in school under these conditions.

Teachers must be alert to signs that students are showing resistance to classroom literacy learning activities. This resistance may develop because students do not trust teachers to exercise authority in a fair and understandable way. For example, Teacher LC spent much of the time in her reading lessons insisting that only one child speak at a time. Teacher LC finally gained the children's compliance, but she did not win the children over in this effort. In effect, Teacher LC and the students became involved in reciprocal distancing, as discussed in chapter 2. The teacher maintained her distance from the children by requiring them to follow mainstream rules for interaction. The children kept their distance from the teacher by continuing to follow their preferred, talk story-like rules for interaction.

Rationales for Schooling.   John D'Amato (1988) studied classrooms of young Hawaiian children in which contrasting situations were illustrated. In a few classrooms, teachers were able to build students' ownership of literacy and teach them to read and write well. In many classrooms, however, teachers struggled with classroom management and failed to interact with students in ways that contributed to literacy learning. Resistance was a common phenomenon in this second set of classrooms. D'Amato looked at why teachers in some classrooms succeeded in developing students' ownership of literacy, whereas teachers in other classrooms failed.

D'Amato (1988) pointed out that students of diverse backgrounds often lack a structural rationale for doing well in school. That is, unlike mainstream students, students of diverse backgrounds typically do not know how schooling fits within the structure of the society and adds to one's life opportunities. Mainstream students know that they must graduate from high school to go on to college, and that they must graduate from college to obtain a good job. Students of diverse backgrounds may not have this same knowledge, or they may not believe that education will benefit them in the same ways. As Ogbu (1990) suggested, these students often have not seen the connection between doing well in school and obtaining a good job illustrated in the history of their own families. Because they lack a structural rationale for doing well in school, students of diverse backgrounds may see little reason for cooperating with teachers. Teachers may experience management difficulties because students do not fear the consequences of poor academic achievement or disruptive behavior.

When a structural rationale is unavailable to students, D'Amato (1988) argued, teachers must provide a situational rationale. That is, they must give students good reasons, within the immediate situation of the classroom, for cooperating and gaining proficiency in literacy content and strategies. A situational rationale is provided through culturally responsive instruction that makes classroom activities immediately rewarding to students. In common with Erickson (1993), D'Amato saw talk story-like reading lessons as a good example of such instruction. However, D'Amato's analysis about why talk story-like reading lessons work so well has to do with peer group dynamics. He argued that teachers effective in working with Hawaiian children know how to teach in ways that support harmonious relationships in the classroom and that do not pit children against one another.

Rivalry in Peer Groups. D'Amato (1988) studied the phenomenon of "acting" among Hawaiian students in elementary classrooms. "Acting" involves challenges to the teacher's authority and can begin within minutes of the start of school. D'Amato (1988) explained the term as follows:

> The origins of this term lie in Hawaiian children's home experiences. Hawaiian adults use the desist, "No act," to warn and to reprimand children whose behavior has the appearance of defiance; they use the same desist to indicate affection, approval, and amusement when children's behavior is imaginatively and harmlessly mischievous. From this labeling of behavior, Hawaiian children learn to use the idea and forms of "acting" both to combat and to come to terms with adult authority. (p. 530)

Hawaiian children carry "acting" into the classroom. In the classroom of a successful teacher, "acting" may involve nothing more than teasing or playful challenges, with even these minor transgressions quickly disappearing. In the classroom of a new or less skillful teacher, "acting" may escalate into open defiance and resistance that last all year.

What accounts for the difference is the teacher's ability to organize the classroom in ways that support rivalry versus competition among Hawaiian children. According to D'Amato's (1988) analysis, members of a social network are always engaged in some kind of contention for the regard of others. The form of contention that Hawaiian children show in their peer networks is rivalry. Rivalry is not unique to Hawaiian children; it has been shown to be the form of contention preferred by peer networks of African American children as well (Goodwin, 1982).

In rivalry, players have two tasks. First, they must prove that they are equal to their peers, by matching their peers' performances. Second, they must establish some position of advantage over their peers. D'Amato (1988) wrote the following: "The theory of social order implicit in rivalry is that processes of contention among equals generate self-regulating symmetries of respect and affection" (p. 533). Hawaiian children engage in games of chase and tetherball; in teasing, joking, and arguing; and in mock fighting to show that they are just as good as their peers. The intention is not to dominate, but to establish one's position as an equal.

Rivalry differs from competition, in which players seek to win the game and show that they are superior to others. Competition requires the participation of a superior, someone who is in a position to judge the players' performances and declare a winner. In the classroom, this superior is the teacher, and most teachers expect to serve in this role in orchestrating interactions among students. Rivalry, however, does not provide a place for a superior to judge the players' performances. One of the rules of rivalry is that players must use their own ingenuity and personal resources to earn the respect of their peers. For example, Malia has won a game of tetherball and the right to play against the next challenger. However, the other children refuse to acknowledge Malia's victory. If competition is the basis for contention, Malia can appeal to the teacher for help. If rivalry is the basis for contention, Malia must manage the situation on her own, such as by refusing to budge and by insisting that the other children recognize her victory. Children who are easily intimidated and who do not defend their rights, preferably by verbal means but by fighting if necessary, quickly lose the regard of their peers.

As you can see, the rules of rivalry create many potentially volatile situations. Hawaiian children must know how to minimize the possibility of fist fights and other harmful responses created by rivalry, or they run the risk of destroying the social network itself. D'Amato (1988) discovered that, to move situations along smoothly, Hawaiian children depend on a specific strategy of self-presentation. They try to convey to others that they are both "tough" and "nice." They must show "toughness" to command respect and suggest that they are willing to fight back. They must show "niceness" to indicate that they are generous, friendly, and humble, accepting of others, and willing to keep contention framed as a harmless yet entertaining game.

When instances of "acting" occur in the classroom, teachers of Hawaiian children should be aware that they are witnessing the effects of rivalry. Children engage in "acting" to demonstrate their "toughness" in the face of sanctions that may be issued by teachers. "Acting" is an expected part of peer group dynamics and reflects the children's need to earn the regard of their friends.

Teachers successful in bringing Hawaiian students to high levels of literacy know how to diminish "acting" and win students over to academic activities. They do this by structuring literacy activities to give students the opportunity to participate without creating a highly competitive situation in which some students come away as winners, whereas others are dubbed losers. Using talk story-like participation structures is one way of allowing students to make many small contributions. If a student makes a response that is incorrect, others will chime in quickly. The student does not suffer the humiliation of having performed poorly, and he or she can soon have another try. The teacher orchestrates the discussion with the entire group, without having to pass judgment on individual students.

Difficulties With Competition.   In contrast, the IRE pattern puts the teacher in the role of superior and changes the rules from rivalry to those of competition. Students are no longer able to gain small advantages and to keep even with one another. When the teacher calls on a student, that student alone is supposed to answer. Students who answer correctly set themselves far above their peers. Students who answer incorrectly fall far below them. In effect, competition creates large differences among students and violates the basis for rivalry. In rivalry, students simply want to show that they are equal to their peers, no better and no worse. D'Amato (1988) stated:

> Owing to the differences between competition and rivalry, classrooms organized on a competitive basis tend to generate continual affronts to Hawaiian children's values, identity concerns, and relationships. Lesson processes that produce sharp and distinct differences in merit among children run exactly counter to Hawaiian schoolchildren's concerns with staying even with one another. (pp. 537–538)

Because the teacher has tight control over the situation, the students cannot use any of the strategies normally available to bring their status into equilibrium again, such as joking, making a quick retort, or leaving the area.

In creating a competitive situation and depriving the students of all of their familiar means for controlling contention, the teacher violates the students' sense of fair play, of right and wrong. Furthermore, when teachers serve as judges in competitive situations, they make themselves highly visible targets for the resentments they have created by allowing some students to be seen as winners and others as losers. These resentments may cause students to join together against the teacher, and it is in these classrooms that "acting" and resistance continue throughout the year.

Creating a Literate Classroom Community

The anthropological research discussed earlier leads us to four recommendations about what teachers can do to create a literate classroom community, using culturally responsive instruction and avoiding the pitfalls that an overly competitive situation might create for some students of diverse backgrounds. Although teachers must certainly lead the development of the classroom as a literate community, they should be aware of drawing the students into roles of responsibility as quickly as possible. Ownership of literacy develops in school when the community is shaped by students' contributions, not just the teacher's.

Project a Teacher Presence That Communicates Both "Toughness" and "Niceness." D'Amato (1986) discovered that Hawaiian students value the same combination of "toughness" and "niceness" in their teachers as they value in their friends. D'Amato called this manner of self-presentation and classroom management the "smile with teeth."

Teachers must communicate "toughness" and a sense of authority if they are to win students' respect and willingness to participate in classroom literacy activities. This "toughness" extends to having high expectations for students' literacy learning, a point noted by Ladson-Billings (1994) in her study of successful teachers of African American students. Leroy Lovelace, an African American teacher in an inner-city school in Chicago, advised teachers to make demands on students:

The one thing that black students don't need is teachers who let them get away with saying, "I can't do this, I can't do that"—teachers who feel sympathetic because the students are black, or they are from the inner city, teachers who let them get away with doing nothing. Teachers have to realize that black students—or all students, but I'm talking about black students now—are very clever, especially with white teachers. Too many black students have learned to play the game, to play on a teacher's sympathy in order to get away with doing nothing. Teachers have to demand from black urban students the same as they would demand from privileged white students, and they have to be consistent. Urban black students can do the work, and in the hands of skilled teachers they *will* do it. (Foster, 1997, pp. 47–48)

In terms of literacy learning in school, teachers must inform students that reading and writing well is an expectation, not an option. In chapter 10, we discuss how teachers can use "I Can" statements and rubrics so that students know exactly what they are expected to do and receive the needed instructional support along the way.

One way that teachers can communicate "toughness" is by stating directly and explicitly what they want students to do. Delpit (1988) pointed out that making indirect requests, such as through questions, is ineffective with many African American students. For example, if the teacher wants students to complete their work quickly, she should say in a firm tone of voice, "You have 2 minutes to finish your work" or "I want you to be finished in 2 minutes." She should not ask, "Do you think you could finish your work soon?" or "I wonder if you could finish your work soon?" Students are likely to interpret these indirect requests as offering them the option of not finishing quickly, or as signs that the teacher is not serious about wanting them to finish quickly.

In addition, teachers who want to communicate "toughness" must be willing to follow through with the appropriate consequences if students break the rules or fail to comply with their requests. Because "acting" happens so often in classrooms with Hawaiian children, experienced teachers are prepared in advance to respond quickly to instances of "acting" at the beginning of the year. A veteran first-grade teacher of Hawaiian ancestry, who teaches in a school in a low-income Hawaiian community, described the first student to be caught "acting" as the sacrificial lamb. She knew that she would have to make an example of this student to prevent "acting" from escalating. On the second day of school, after twice warning an offending student, she stopped the reading aloud of a story to reprimand him in front of the class. He was sent back to his seat in tears. At recess, the teacher took the time to speak to the boy individually to express her concern for his well-being, and she asked him to help her with some tasks around the classroom. Having repaired the relationship, the teacher made an effort to praise the boy's efforts often during the days that followed. He did not engage in any other instances of "acting," and neither did the other children in the class.

The manner in which this veteran teacher interacted with her student illustrates the necessary balance between "toughness" and "niceness." The "toughness," represented by the teeth in D'Amato's (1986) metaphor, must always be balanced by "niceness," represented by the smile. This teacher demonstrated "toughness" by taking charge of the situation and making it clear to the whole class that the student's behavior was unacceptable. However, she was equally decisive in mending the relationship, recognizing the student's competence by having him serve as a helper, and praising him often over the next few days. Having asserted her authority, she showed kindness and generosity by quickly restoring the student to a position of respect in her eyes and in the eyes of his classmates. "Toughness" alone, without an adequate dose of "niceness," causes teachers to be perceived as unfair and to lose students' respect and goodwill.

Teachers must learn how to develop positive, caring relationships with students, consistent with the idea of fictive kinship understood by many African American students, as discussed in chapter 2. The importance of teachers' expressing concern for students' well-being and of showing knowledge of their families has been documented as well in studies of classrooms with Mexican American and Yu'pik Eskimo students, among other groups (Carrasco, Vera, & Cazden, 1981; Lipka, Mohatt, & the Ciulistet Group, 1998).

This sense of caring must be communicated to all students, not just some. To win students' regard, teachers must demonstrate that they will treat all students equally and that their kindness and generosity are available to all. In D'Amato's (1988) observations, Hawaiian students were extremely sensitive to indications that the teacher favored some students over others. Teachers who showed signs of favoritism elevated some students above others, inadvertently violating the rules of rivalry, and soon became the targets of group resistance in the classroom.

Successful teachers know that building a literate classroom community depends on the participation of each and every student. Divisions in the classroom, including those created by peer dynamics, must be set aside by both the teacher and students if the classroom is to function as a community of learners in which everyone can blossom as a reader and writer. The teacher's show of kindness, generosity, and fairness is not simply for the purpose of establishing order in the classroom. These demonstrations are intended as well to set the proper tone for the development of the classroom as a literate community.

Create Numerous Opportunities for Students to Gain Recognition.   To build the classroom as a literate community, without fostering an undesirable degree of competition, teachers must give students many little ways to win recognition for their contributions. Contributions to be recognized may include presenting a good idea during a discussion, producing an insightful written response to literature, giving a book talk, sharing a book with a friend, publishing a personal narrative or research report, and helping a classmate during a peer writing conference.

Teachers can certainly recognize students' contributions with praise. Praise should be brief and include a specific description of the students' contribution, for example, "Brandon just wrote an excellent written response in the form of a letter to the main character." In most cases, praise should not be extensive or cause the student to be singled out for an extended period of time. With older students, who may not want to be praised by name, teachers can make positive comments about the performance of a small group or of those working in a particular area of the room, or mention the contribution without naming the student.

Teachers can allow students to win recognition by presenting or displaying their work in the classroom. Many teachers have students share their drafts or published pieces in the Author's Chair (Graves & Hansen, 1983). If students have produced books, these are placed in the classroom library. These books may include a page for comments by readers, including members of the author's family. Other teachers provide each student with space on a bulletin board where students display a recent example of their best work. A second-grade teacher in a school in a low-income Hawaiian community had an authors' bulletin board. A photograph of each student appeared next to a list of the books that he or she had published that year. Other teachers display bookworms made of circles, one for each book a student has completed reading independently.

Displays of students' work serve two functions. First, they allow the students to win recognition for their accomplishments as readers and writers. These displays work best when there is space for each student's work, or when students have an equal opportunity to be recognized, for example, when the bulletin board features a different student author every week. Second, the displays provide students with visible reminders of the importance of their contributions to the classroom as a literate community. When their work can be seen around the room, students take pride in their accomplishments and grow in their ownership of literacy.

Other adults in the school or visitors to the classroom, including parents, can serve as an appreciative audience for students' contributions as readers and writers, adding to the opportunities they receive to win recognition. Other adults in the school and parents may serve as an audience when students read aloud, present their portfolios, or share a recently published piece. Students may serve as guides for visitors to the classroom, describing the functions of different features of the classroom, such as the library or editing table, as well as sharing their work.

For any of these approaches to work effectively, the teacher must be aware of spreading opportunities for praise and recognition evenly across the whole group of students. The teacher who takes the approach of limiting praise and recognition to a handful of students runs the risk of alienating the rest of the class and of being accused of favoritism. In many classrooms with students of diverse backgrounds, teachers must take care to preserve the equality among students, rather than using praise and recognition to foster competition.

Emphasize the Value of Supporting the Literacy Development of Others. In developing the classroom as a literate community, the teacher clearly takes the leadership role. However, the teacher cannot form the community without the full involvement of the students. Assessment results indicate that, in classrooms with many Hawaiian students, all tend to develop ownership of literacy once the teacher is successful in establishing a classroom community (Au, 1994). Although all students may not choose to become full-fledged members of the literate community at the outset, the teacher makes it clear that membership in the community is open to all and that everyone is expected to participate. Students join the community by contributing to its literacy resources, not only by growing as readers and writers themselves but also by supporting the literacy growth of others.

Here are some ways that teachers can encourage students to support one another's progress as readers. During the readers' workshop, the teacher can have students engage in partner reading. In some instances, partner reading may involve two students with similar degrees of reading proficiency. In others, a stronger reader may be asked to assist a struggling reader. Teachers should take the time to teach student tutors how to provide hints about unknown words rather than simply telling the word. During fishbowls conducted to improve students' discussions during book clubs, teachers can call attention to approaches for inviting others into the conversation. These approaches include posing open-ended or interpretive questions, asking another student to share his or her opinion, and reminding talkative students to give quieter students a chance to speak. Teachers can help students to support one another's independent reading by modeling book talks and having students give book talks to small groups or to the whole class. If the teacher has two copies of a book, he or she can ask if two friends would like to read the books, so they can discuss the book as they go along.

The teacher can also show students how to support one another's writing. During the writers' workshop, teachers can ask students to share the topics they have chosen to write about, so that other students can gain new ideas. Teachers can coach students in peer conferences, so they learn to give one another ideas for revision. Students who have strong skills of spelling, punctuation, and grammar may be encouraged to assist others with editing. Finally, teachers can give students ideas about specific, positive comments to be offered when their classmates read their pieces aloud in the Author's Chair. Few things boost the confidence of student authors more than knowing that their classmates, and not just the teacher, have appreciated their writing.

Organize Students to Work in Small Groups. Much has been written about the value of cooperative learning (e.g., Johnson, Johnson, & Holubec, 1994), especially in small groups, and those virtues need not be reiterated here. However, a few words should be said about the central role of small groups in developing students' ownership of literacy and in creating a literate classroom community. As D'Amato's (1988) work implies, small groups may allow teachers to foster a classroom community in part by reducing the time spent in whole-class lessons that foster competition as opposed to rivalry as a form of contention. In addition, small groups provide students with numerous opportunities to win the recognition of their peers and of the teacher, especially through supporting the literacy development of others. Small groups supply students with an audience that can appreciate their literacy performances. At the same time, students run little risk when they display inadequate performance or make a miscue while in a small group, as compared to a whole-class lesson. Participating in small groups allows students more opportunities to contribute and to extend their literacy abilities.

A special role is played by student-directed small groups, such as the book clubs described in chapter 4. Of course, when teachers organize students in small groups of classmates, they must support students' learning in these settings, for example, by making expectations clear, by requiring students to complete specific tasks, and by involving them in self-evaluation. When teachers organize small groups effectively, they can send the message that they recognize students' competence and trust them to begin taking responsibility for their own literacy learning. Many students of diverse backgrounds interpret this sharing of responsibility as a sign that the teacher has respect for their abilities and trusts them to use their time and energies wisely. This sharing of responsibility is welcomed especially by students of diverse backgrounds who are accustomed to making significant contributions to their families, for example, by looking after their siblings (Gallimore, Boggs, & Jordan, 1974), by doing the cooking, or by fishing and hunting (Lipka et al., 1998). Thus, the sharing of responsibility that results through the skillful management of small, student-directed groups can help to cement the positive relationship between teacher and students. This positive relationship is vital to the teacher's ability to foster the classroom as a literate community and to promote students' ownership of literacy in school.

SUMMARY

Students of diverse backgrounds are motivated to become good readers and writers in classrooms that have become literate communities. The teachers in these successful classrooms focus on promoting students' ownership of literacy in school. To create a literate classroom community, teachers must know how to win students' trust and respect. Ogbu's research explained the apparent lack of motivation of some students of diverse backgrounds to do well in school. While Ogbu's research addressed a macrolevel of analysis, Erickson's work looked at a microlevel, emphasizing the role of face-to-face interactions among teachers and students in fostering resistance to schooling. Culturally responsive instruction, in which teachers draw on interactional patterns familiar to students from the home, reduces resistance and helps students to feel comfortable about participating in classroom literacy activities. D'Amato's research took the analysis of cultural responsiveness a step further, by looking at the role of peer group dynamics. Teachers' ability to foster positive relationships with students may depend in part on their ability to work with these dynamics, in particular, to structure literacy activities in a manner consistent with the rules of rivalry versus competition. Drawing on this research base, I presented four recommendations that teachers can follow to build the classroom community and promote ownership of literacy among students of diverse backgrounds.

6

Providing Instruction in Reading Comprehension Strategies

The purpose of this chapter is to explore the why, when, what, and how of instruction in reading comprehension strategies for students of diverse backgrounds. The questions to be addressed include the following: Why should teachers emphasize higher level thinking and comprehension strategies with students of diverse backgrounds? When in the busy school day can strategy instruction occur? What comprehension strategies should be addressed? How can these strategies best be taught? I explain why students of diverse backgrounds are often deprived of adequate time for comprehension strategy instruction and how this situation can be corrected. I recommend a focus on six strategies for reading comprehension and outline an instructional model teachers can follow to ensure that students develop independence in applying comprehension strategies when reading. In each section, I alert teachers to challenges that may arise in teaching comprehension strategies to students of diverse backgrounds and how these challenges can be met.

IMPORTANCE OF HIGHER LEVEL THINKING

In chapter 1, I discussed globalization as the impetus for higher standards for literacy achievement. I argued that educators must be aware of preparing students of diverse backgrounds to meet these higher standards, so that they have the opportunity to go on to college and to pursue a range of employment opportunities, as well as to contribute to their families, communities, and the larger society. In chapter 2, I discussed the bias in schools that leads to a heavy emphasis on instruction in lower level skills, rather than higher level thinking, for students of diverse backgrounds. In chapter 3, I explained the concept of discourse and how dominant-group discourse may lead to a stereotyping of students of diverse backgrounds and their families. The discourse of the larger society reinforces the view that students from privileged backgrounds have the intellectual capacity, motivation, and family support that will enable them to benefit from instruction focused on higher level thinking. This same discourse tends to promote the view that students of diverse backgrounds somehow lack the intellectual capacity, motivation, and family support that will enable them to benefit from the same kind of instruction. For example, newspapers publish test results suggesting that students in low-income communities are not making satisfactory academic gains. Such accounts often give the impression that students of diverse backgrounds cannot learn from the challenging instruction typically emphasized with mainstream students who are judged to be academically talented.

Unfortunately, this situation is made worse if educators hold negative attitudes about the intellectual abilities of students of diverse backgrounds (Oakes & Guiton, 1995), as well as about their families (Compton-Lilly, 2003). As discussed in chapter 3, these negative attitudes are a reflection of the dominant-group discourse that permeates the larger society. Such attitudes can lead some educators to favor a "dumbing down" of the curriculum for students of diverse backgrounds. In these curricula, goals for higher level thinking with text, specifically strategies of reading comprehension, are downplayed or eliminated, in favor of lower level skills. (A strategy may be defined as a plan of action, and a skill as a specific routine or bit of knowledge.) These curricula may include comprehension as well as word identification, but comprehension activities focus on lower level skills of literal recall rather than on strategic, critical, and evaluative thinking. Typically, these curricula include scripted lessons in which the teacher reads off questions with answers that require little thought. These rote learning activities do not encourage teachers to stretch students' minds and to challenge them intellectually. These curricula may have the additional negative effect of disempowering teachers, who are denied opportunities to develop and exercise professional judgment (Shannon, 1989).

Note that attending to higher level thinking does not mean neglecting lower level skills, such as phonics. As discussed in chapter 9, skills such as word identification and spelling are vitally important for students of diverse backgrounds. The danger arises when the literacy curriculum becomes un-balanced, and lower level skills become the sole or main focus of instruc-tion. The danger in these cases is that students receive the mistaken impres-sion that the point of reading is accurate word calling, not understanding (Turner, 1995), and never develop into excellent readers. To avoid this pit-fall, higher level thinking with text and comprehension strategy instruction must have a prominent place in the literacy curriculum, even in the primary grades.

When Should Comprehension Strategies Be Taught?

In chapter 4, I described workshop approaches to the teaching of literacy, specifically a model called Book Club *Plus*. In workshop and similar ap-proaches, teachers should provide comprehension strategy instruction in two language arts settings. First, if the strategy is likely to be valuable to all students, the teacher conducts a whole-class lesson. In Book Club *Plus,* these lessons occur during community share, the whole-class times at the beginning and end of a session. Second, if the comprehension strategy is needed by some students but not the whole class, the teacher provides small-group lessons during the Literacy Block. These lessons may serve as a supplement to and reinforcement for the full lessons conducted earlier, or they can be focused to meet the needs of struggling readers, without taking the time of the whole class. The teacher can have the small group work with easier texts, and he or she can devote more time to modeling, guided prac-tice, and coaching (as described later).

Because comprehension strategies need to be applied not only to fiction but to nonfiction texts read in the content areas, such as math, science, and social studies, some lessons should occur outside the time allotted for lan-guage arts instruction. In fact, some teachers may prefer introducing com-prehension strategy instruction through the content areas. The reason is that content area texts, such as those for science and social studies, tend to be packed with ideas. This feature makes these texts ideal for introducing comprehension strategies such as determining importance, as illustrated later in this chapter.

Regardless of when comprehension strategy instruction is introduced, during the language arts period or during the time set aside for another sub-ject, teachers must be aware of showing students when and how compre-hension strategies can be used throughout the school day. Most learners do not easily see how the strategies they have learned in one area, such as language arts, can be applied to another, such as science (Brown, Collins, & Duguid, 1989). Furthermore, teachers should show students how comprehension strategies may need to be applied somewhat differently depending on the characteristics, structures, or genres of the texts to be read. For example, when reading a story or narrative, the reader who wants to determine importance will look for story elements, such as character, setting, and problem. When determining importance in a science passage, the reader does not look for story elements but instead seeks to separate the key scientific concepts from the supporting details.

Certain situations common in schools tend to deprive students of diverse backgrounds of opportunities to participate in lessons focused on comprehension strategies. I discuss these situations and indicate how each can be adjusted to increase the access of students of diverse backgrounds to instruction in comprehension strategies and higher level thinking.

First, elementary and secondary schools with large numbers of students of diverse backgrounds may adopt scripted programs focused on lower level skills. These programs may cause instruction in lower level skills to be overemphasized for all students, to the neglect of instruction in higher level thinking. The answer for these schools is to supplement the adopted reading program with lessons on comprehension strategies, including all of the steps described later in this chapter.

Second, in elementary schools, students of diverse backgrounds may be placed in the bottom reading group within a classroom. These students typically experience a limited curriculum focusing on lower level skills (Allington, 1983), whereas an enriched curriculum featuring higher level thinking may be available to other students. In this situation, part of the answer is for the teacher to provide whole-class instruction on comprehension strategies. In addition, the teacher makes certain that lessons taught to struggling readers center on review and reinforcement of the comprehension strategies taught to the whole class. During small-group lessons, these comprehension strategies may be applied to texts at the struggling readers' instructional level, which is often significantly below the level of the texts used in whole-class lessons.

Third, students of diverse backgrounds often are removed from the classroom for pull-out programs, such as those for remedial readers, second language learners, or special education students. The instruction they receive in these pull-out programs tends to focus on lower level skills (e.g., Fitzgerald, 1995). Furthermore, during their time away from the classroom, students often miss the higher level thinking activities that the teacher may have presented during the readers' and writers' workshops, and they can easily fail to become full-fledged members of the classroom as a literate community. A common way of addressing this problem is to have the students remain in the general education classroom on most days, and to have the resource teacher come into the classroom to assist them in completing comprehension tasks successfully. For this arrangement to work well, there must be a high degree of collaboration and communication between the classroom teacher and the resource teacher.

Fourth, in secondary schools, students of diverse backgrounds frequently are tracked to take courses with few academic demands, designed specifically for those whose formal education is expected to end with high school. The AVID program (Mehan, Hubbard, & Villanueva, 1994), described in chapter 2, suggests alternatives to tracking that help students of diverse backgrounds to develop higher level thinking strategies and rich content knowledge and to reach levels of academic performance that enable them to advance to college. These alternatives include enrollment in college-prep classes, peer tutoring, and social scaffolding.

Educators will want to be aware of these four patterns that limit students' access to comprehension strategy instruction and of how to put positive patterns in their place. Once the time for comprehension strategy instruction has been found, teachers are ready to address the question of what strategies to teach.

What Comprehension Strategies Should Be Taught?

Higher level thinking with text involves reading comprehension, or the understanding of what is read, particularly when that understanding extends beyond the literal level. Nearly three decades of research supports the use of systematic instruction for promoting students' reading comprehension (e.g., Dole, Duffy, Roehler, & Pearson, 1991; Duke & Pearson, 2002). This research emphasizes instruction in strategies for reading comprehension. A comprehension strategy, as opposed to a skill, is a deliberate plan for constructing an understanding of the text. In contrast, a skill is a routine that can be applied unconsciously and automatically (Dole et al., 1991). Summarization is an example of a comprehension strategy, whereas sequence of events is an example of a comprehension skill. This is not to say that it is easy to teach students to recognize the sequence of events, especially in kindergarten and first grade. But once students learn how to recognize the sequence of events, they will be able to apply this skill easily (except, perhaps, when the author is using flashbacks or otherwise presenting events out of order). Summarization, however, almost always requires thought and reflection, and it can be exceedingly difficult if the text is packed with ideas.

I recommend that teachers provide students of diverse backgrounds with instruction in the following six comprehension strategies: predicting, drawing inferences, determining importance, summarizing information, generating questions, and monitoring comprehension. My recommendations are based on the review of research by Dole et al. (1991). The strategies they highlight can all be taught, and all of them improve students' reading comprehension. Prediction, the only strategy on my list not addressed by Dole et al., is recommended in other reviews (e.g., Duke & Pearson, 2002).

Predicting. Predicting is a good starting point for instruction in comprehension strategies. Good readers are constantly making predictions, and predicting is a strategy that can be carried out even by kindergarten children. A prediction is the reader's hypothesis or educated guess about the information likely to be presented later in the text. Most students, even those in the primary grades, find it quite easy to formulate these hypotheses. The more difficult part of predicting for students is providing a justification for their hypotheses. Justifying a prediction requires that students identify the text information, prior knowledge, or combination of the two that supports their hypotheses. In addition to justification, predicting requires validation. Validating a prediction means being able to verify that the prediction has been confirmed or disconfirmed. Predicting is actually a cycle in which the reader is constantly developing hypotheses, confirming or disconfirming them, and developing new hypotheses. By engaging in this cycle, the reader moves forward through the text in a purposeful manner.

When working with students of diverse backgrounds, teachers will want to remember that predicting always depends to some degree on prior knowledge. As a result, students of diverse backgrounds may occasionally make predictions that are unexpected or that even seem nonsensical to teachers from outside their culture. Because these predictions usually grow from students' own cultural perspectives, teachers may gain insights when they take the time to have students explain their thoughts.

In this example, set in a first-grade classroom with many Hawaiian students, the teacher was leading a small group reading lesson. An illustration in the story showed several tools, including a saw, and the teacher expected the children to make predictions about building or repairing. Instead, one of the boys predicted that the family would be making charcoal. Puzzled, the teacher asked the child to explain his prediction. The boy described how his family made charcoal from logs obtained by cutting trees down with a saw. Although this prediction was not validated by the text, the teacher could praise the child for making a logical prediction on the basis of his own prior knowledge.

Drawing Inferences.   Drawing inferences (also called inferring or inferencing) involves "reading between the lines." Text would be incredibly long and boring if the author had to spell out every last detail for the reader. Instead, the author expects the reader to draw on prior knowledge to construct meaning from the text (Anderson & Pearson, 1984). As capable readers, we draw inferences so quickly and effortlessly that we tend to be insensitive to the importance of these inferences to our ability to comprehend.

As with predictions, differences in prior knowledge may affect the inferences made by students of diverse backgrounds. For example, consider the sentence, "Ray heard the crack of the bat and headed for home." Most mainstream students will quickly infer that "home" in this case refers to the home plate of a baseball diamond, not to Ray's place of residence. However, such an inference would be difficult for a student who was unfamiliar with baseball or who was just learning English and did not know the different meanings of "home." Before having students read about an unfamiliar topic, teachers will want to build students' background knowledge, because taking this step will give students the information they need to make appropriate inferences. Depending on the age of the students, background knowledge may be built through such approaches as read-alouds of picture story books; field trips; guest speakers; television programs, videotapes, and DVDs; or Internet research.

Determining Importance.   Determining importance requires that readers distinguish the key points from the minor details. Making these distinctions is far from easy and requires considerable judgment on the part of the reader. In particular, students need to be taught the difference between reader-based and author-based importance (Dole et al., 1991). Reader-based importance is what the reader thinks is significant, from a personal point of view. Author-based importance refers to the main points the author is trying to convey, in the eyes of most readers. On most occasions when students are asked to determine importance, they are expected to identify the author's key ideas, not the ideas they themselves think important.

Determining importance can be challenging for any reader when the text contains many new and different ideas. This difficulty is exacerbated for students of diverse backgrounds, because many of the texts they read will be written from a mainstream cultural perspective. If students have a different cultural perspective, their notions of importance may differ from those of most mainstream readers, including the teacher. Several experimental studies show how readers' cultural backgrounds lead them to differing interpretations of the same text (e.g., Reynolds, Taylor, Steffensen, Shirey, & Anderson, 1977).

In the following example, a first-grade teacher, in a school in a Hawaiian community, was conducting guided reading lessons based on "The Little Red Hen" with a small group of students. She asked the children to write in response to the question, "What was the problem in the story?" The teacher expected the children to write about how the dog, the cat, and the pig failed to help the Little Red Hen do the work required to produce the loaf of bread. Most of the children did write responses along this line. However, one of the boys, who was of Hawaiian ancestry, wrote the following: "The problem was that the Little Red Hen did not want to share." In a follow-up discussion, the teacher discovered that this child had been taught the importance of sharing whatever one has with others. From his point of view, the important idea in the story was the Little Red Hen's selfishness or failure to share.

As this anecdote implies, the teaching of comprehension strategies to students of diverse backgrounds may, in part, involve familiarizing them with mainstream discourse and the interpretations that seem logical to mainstream readers. Exposing students to a mainstream interpretive perspective may be important, because students' responses on high stakes tests and in gatekeeping situations are likely to be judged from this perspective. At the same time, teachers must be aware of communicating the value of the responses constructed from students' own cultural perspectives, because it is these responses that make texts meaningful to students. Teachers will want to praise students for the logic followed in their responses, while modeling the types of responses that would be typical for many mainstream readers (for example, through think-alouds, as described later in this chapter).

Summarizing Information. Summarizing is a complex strategy involving multiple steps (Taylor, 1982). Summarizing encompasses determining importance, because to create a summary, students must first identify the key ideas in the text. After that, students must condense, reorder, and paraphrase the key ideas. Then these ideas must be organized and blended together to form a coherent new text, including a topic sentence. Given all of these requirements, it is easy to see why so many students find it difficult to summarize the texts they read.

For students of diverse backgrounds, summarizing may be particularly challenging. Students may experience difficulty determining importance, as discussed earlier. Second language learners may find it difficult to paraphrase the text, because they may not be familiar with the English words, such as superordinates, that can be substituted for the sake of brevity (for example, wild animals might be substituted for lions, tigers, and bears). Furthermore, the issue of reader-based versus author-based summaries presents the same difficulties as those discussed for reader-based versus author-based importance. For all of these reasons, teachers will want to be aware of taking ample time to teach summarization when working with students of diverse backgrounds. Allowing repeated opportunities for coaching, as described later, gives students the chance to wrestle with the steps of summarizing with a partner or small group, before having to attempt this challenging task on their own.

Generating Questions. Generating questions is a comprehension strategy that reverses the roles typically played by teacher and student. Generating questions improves comprehension because students have to think more deeply about the text if they are the ones asking, rather than simply answering, the questions.

Question–answer relationships (QARs; Raphael, 1982, 1986) provide a useful starting point for instruction in generating questions. In this approach, students are taught to think about questions and the source of their answers. The first step students must take is to decide whether the answer for the question comes from "in the book" or "in my head." If the answer is to be found in the book, it may be "right there" or explicitly stated in one or two adjoining sentences. However, sometimes the answer requires students to "think and search" because the information for the answer must be inferred or gathered from several places in the text. If the question falls into the "in my head" category, it may be one the reader can answer "on my own" without reference to the text. Or the question may require the reader to link information from the text with prior knowledge, a category termed "author and me."

Teaching students about QARs gives them ideas about the kinds of questions they can create. However, knowing what question you want to ask, and being able to find the proper wording for that question, are two different things. Teachers of students of diverse backgrounds should be aware that they may need to spend time teaching students to formulate questions in standard English. For example, reciprocal teaching is a widely applied, research-based approach that teaches students four comprehension strategies, including generating questions (Palincsar & Brown, 1984). When reciprocal teaching was implemented in a school with many Hawaiian children, teachers reported that the children seemed to be progressing well in learning all of the strategies except generating questions. Observations revealed the reason. The children spoke Hawaii Creole English (HCE) as their primary language. In HCE, a question usually is not marked by subject–verb inversion. Furthermore, HCE features copula deletion (that is, it does not require use of the verb "to be"). For example, a student might say, "Ellen Ochoa born when?" or "When Ellen Ochoa born?" for the standard English question, "When was Ellen Ochoa born?" Once teachers understood the language issues, they were able to recognize students' efforts to ask questions, praise those efforts, and extend students' knowledge by modeling standard English forms of questioning.

Monitoring Comprehension.   Good readers are constantly monitoring their understanding of the text as they read (Wagoner, 1983). They know when they have a clear understanding of the text and when their understanding has broken down. As soon as good readers become aware of a failure to comprehend, they use strategies to repair the situation (Dole et al., 1991). Repair or fix-it strategies include rereading or looking back, reading ahead, pausing and reflecting on one's understanding up to that point, and figuring out the meaning of unfamiliar vocabulary.

Researchers recommend that monitoring comprehension be taught in two stages (Dole et al., 1991). First, students are taught to recognize when they have encountered a problem with comprehending the text. Second, students are taught the repair strategies they can use at these times.

I worked with a group of primary grade teachers in Hawaii who discovered another problem typical of young, struggling readers. They found that their students were insensitive to breakdowns in comprehension. Students thought of reading as accurate word calling, and they did not have the expectation that the text should make sense. These teachers found that they first needed to work with their students on visualization. They had the students read simple sentences that presented easily visualized situations, such as the following: "Mary wore her red dress. It was a bright, sunny day as she walked to school." The teachers had students discuss the image that these words called to mind. After listening to students' responses, teachers pointed out that students should have a clear picture like this whenever they were reading. If the picture in their minds was fuzzy, or if there was no picture at all, they needed to stop and take the time to make the picture clear. One teacher experienced success in conveying this idea when she compared a breakdown in comprehension to the poor television reception that results when cable service is unavailable. Once students grasped the difference between a clear versus fuzzy or nonexistent mental picture, they saw the purpose for learning repair strategies.

Although recommending these six strategies, I am not proposing that all six should be taught at once. In my experience, teachers can find success with comprehension strategy instruction if they focus on only a small number of strategies during the course of a semester, with the aim of teaching those strategies well. Teachers working with struggling readers may want to focus on just a couple of these strategies during the course of a semester. Comprehension strategies are interrelated, and this means that learning one strategy well leads students to learn about other strategies at the same time. For example, teaching students to generate questions almost always leads them to think about the important ideas in the text. As a result, although the teacher may be targeting the strategy of generating questions, he or she will have the opportunity to teach students the strategy of determining importance as well.

How Should Comprehension Strategies Be Taught?

Now that you have an idea of what to teach or which comprehension strategies to target, I turn to the question of how to provide effective instruction in these strategies. Each comprehension strategy should be taught thoroughly, following a six-step process (based on Au & Raphael, 1998). Students are guided to independence in the use of each strategy following the six steps, so that the gradual release of responsibility can be achieved (Pearson & Gallagher, 1983). In the gradual release of responsibility, the teacher bears the burden of executing the strategy in the beginning. The teacher guides students through the steps, systematically decreasing the support he or she provides for students' performance. As students gain knowledge of and proficiency in the strategy, they assume responsibility for carrying out the strategy on their own.

Explicit Explanation. In explicit explanation, the teacher tells the students exactly what they are to learn and why. Explicit explanation involves making the purpose of the lesson clear to students, including connecting the lessons to standards and goals for learning. The teacher makes certain that the students understand which strategy they are about to learn and why that strategy is important in terms of helping them to become good readers. For example, suppose that the teacher wants to focus on the comprehension strategy of determining importance with her fifth-grade students. The teacher can begin the lesson by stating the following:

> Today we're going to be learning the comprehension strategy of determining importance. This lesson will help you with one of our I Can statements, "I can determine the important ideas when I read." Someone who can determine the important ideas can tell the main ideas from the supporting details. In fifth grade and the grades above, you'll be doing a lot of reading, so much that you won't be able to remember everything. You'll need to have a way of sorting out the important ideas, the parts that you should remember.
>
> Let's look at the three levels in the rubric and consider what you have to do to meet the benchmark (refers to the chart with the rubric). You'll notice three items under the *meets* column: (1) reads a fifth grade text independently, (2) chooses the few words that tell the main idea, and (3) gives a good reason for this choice. At the end of the lesson, you'll be assessing your own performance to see how well you did on each of these items.
>
> To learn how to determine the important ideas, we're going to be reading a science article about wolves. For each paragraph, we'll be choosing the sentence or part of the sentence that tells what the whole paragraph is about. We'll see if we can figure out which part tells us the important or main idea, as opposed to the supporting details.

Notice that the teacher begins by setting the purpose for the lesson and naming the comprehension strategy for the students. He or she relates the comprehension strategy to the "I Can" statements, which are standards or benchmarks worded in student-friendly language (for more about standards, benchmarks, and "I Can" statements, see chapter 10). The teacher goes on to explain to the students how this particular strategy can help them. He or she explains the rubric to students as a way of making expectations clear to them and lets the students know that they will need to assess their performance in terms of this rubric. Finally, the teacher introduces the text students will be reading, and he or she outlines the procedure they will follow to determine importance.

For the sake of giving students a clear introduction to the strategy of determining importance, the teacher has adopted a somewhat artificial approach, requiring the students to select just one sentence from each paragraph. The goal is to teach the students to be selective, because the teacher noticed that students had a tendency to underline nearly every sentence on a page. Obviously, this approach does not work in cases where a paragraph contains two sentences with ideas of equal importance, or in cases where a paragraph contains no important ideas. However, if either of these cases occurs during a lesson, the teacher has an excellent opportunity to discuss the limitations of the approach and to extend students' thinking about how to determine importance.

Modeling. After the students have been introduced to the strategy through explicit explanation, the teacher proceeds to modeling. Modeling or demonstrating requires that the teacher show the students how the strategy is carried out. Because reading comprehension is an invisible mental process, the teacher needs to find a way to make this process visible to the students. Making the invisible, visible can be accomplished through a think-aloud (Schunk & Zimmerman, 1997). During a think-aloud, the teacher verbalizes the thoughts that go through the mind of a proficient reader when seeking to comprehend a text, and specifically in this case, to determine the important ideas. Think-alouds are easy to do if the teacher makes an overhead transparency of the text. During the think-aloud, the teacher reads the text aloud and points to the sentences, verbalizing the thoughts that come to mind. As mentioned earlier, in classrooms with students of diverse backgrounds, think-alouds can give the teacher the chance to show how readers with a mainstream perspective typically approach a certain text.

The opening paragraph of an article about wolves follows. Shown in italics are the comments the teacher might make during the think-aloud:

In many ways, wolves are like dogs and lions; yet wolves have a bad reputation, unlike dogs and lions. *(I never thought of wolves as being like dogs and lions. I think wolves are scary. They do have a bad reputation.)* Dogs are our "best friends," but all the dogs in the world are descended from wolves that were domesticated more than ten thousand years ago. *(I think I might have read that dogs were descended from wolves, but I never thought about it.)* And most of the things people like about dogs are also true about wolves. *(I don't agree with this statement, because I don't understand how wolves could be anything like dogs—especially the nice dog I have for a pet.)* (text from Simon, 1996, p. 131)

The teacher is modeling for students how a good reader thinks actively about the text. Some teachers hesitate to do think-alouds, because they think the comments they make as they go along have to be profound or insightful. These teachers need not worry. It is enough during a think-aloud for the teacher simply to share the ordinary thoughts that come to mind. In this case, the teacher has expressed both agreement and disagreement with the text and made a personal connection to his or her own dog.

After going through the text once, the teacher returns to the text to continue the think-aloud, reading the sentences quickly and modeling for the students how he or she determines importance. In this case, the teacher might continue the think-aloud in the following manner:

> Now I'm going to reread this paragraph to determine the important idea. I see that the first sentence is comparing wolves to dogs and lions. The second sentence is telling me that dogs are descended from wolves. The last sentence is saying that wolves have good features, just like dogs. O.K., my choice of the important idea in this paragraph is going to be the part of the first sentence that says "wolves are like dogs." I'm choosing that part because the author keeps comparing wolves and dogs. Let me underline just those words.

The teacher shows the students that they will probably need to read the paragraph more than once to determine importance. The teacher reviews what each sentence is about and then makes a choice. The teacher gives students the reason for this choice, modeling how a good reason might be stated. The teacher shows students that underlining should take place only as the last step.

In this example, for the sake of brevity, I am showing the teacher modeling the strategy by thinking aloud with just a single paragraph. In practice, especially if the comprehension strategy is new to the students, the teacher will probably want to do think-alouds with two or three paragraphs. This more extensive modeling will give students a better chance to see how the strategy works.

Guided Practice. After the students have seen the strategy modeled, they are ready to try using the strategy under the teacher's guidance. During guided practice, the teacher has students try out the strategy but with a great deal of scaffolding. The teacher proceeds by saying the following:

> Now that I've shown you what I do to determine the important idea, it's time for you to try to do the same. Let's read the next paragraph together.

Continuing with our example, here is the next paragraph in the article about wolves:

> Like dogs, wolves are very loyal to other wolves in their family. Wolves raised by people become loyal to those people as well. Dogs are friendly and intelli-

gent, and those traits too come from wolves. Wolves in a pack are playful with each other. They are among the most intelligent animals in nature. (Simon, 1996, p. 131)

When the group has read the paragraph together, the teacher says the following:

Don't say anything yet. Reread the paragraph silently to yourself and decide which sentence, or part of a sentence, you think tells the important information. Be prepared to explain why you made that choice. You may even find that none of the sentences is right and that you want to write your own sentence with the important idea.

Notice that the teacher encourages the students to reread and to be clear about the reasons for their choices.

During comprehension strategy lessons, the teacher should focus on the quality of students' thinking, rather than on a single right answer. This approach makes sense (in fact, is necessary) because there is often more than one reasonable response, even for a task as seemingly straightforward as choosing the sentence that tells the most important idea. For example, when I have used the earlier paragraph with groups of teachers, some have chosen the second sentence, about how dogs are friendly and intelligent, with these traits having come from wolves. Others have decided that none of the sentences works well and have written their own sentence, such as "Wolves are loyal and intelligent."

Because even mature readers may well have different opinions about the important ideas in a particular paragraph, the teacher should be prepared to accept any answer a student provides, as long as it is supported by a strong rationale. The teacher should be sure to point out to students that more than one answer may be accepted, by making statements similar to the following:

I'm really glad that this situation came up, where Lani suggested one sentence and Ryan another. They both gave good reasons, too. Often, good readers will have more than one opinion about what is important in their reading, and there won't be just one right answer. In that case, you just have to decide what you think is important and have a good reason to back up your decision.

The foremost consideration is that the students are working actively to understand the text and apply the targeted comprehension strategy. As with modeling, this phase of instruction may require the use of several paragraphs or examples before the students are ready to move on.

Coaching. During coaching, the teacher continues with the gradual release of responsibility. Students work in pairs or small groups to apply the comprehension strategy. The students read the next paragraph and discuss their choices with their partner or group members. For example, here is what the teacher might say to initiate the coaching phase:

> We worked together as a whole class to determine the important ideas in the first few paragraphs of our science article. Now you're going to choose a partner. You and your partner will work together to determine the important idea in the next paragraph. Read and discuss the paragraph together. Then decide on the sentence, or part of a sentence, that you think contains the important information. Remember that you also have the option of making up your own sentence.

The teacher monitors the discussions the students are having in pairs or small groups and provides assistance as necessary. Students receive some teacher guidance but less than during guided practice with the whole group. When the pairs or small groups have arrived at their decisions, the teacher calls the class back together and has students share their responses, again encouraging them to provide reasons for their choices.

As with all of the previous steps in instruction, students may need to work through several text examples in pairs or small groups, with teacher coaching, before they are ready to move on. Teachers will want to use their judgment in deciding when students should proceed to independent application. In some cases, students may not have developed enough strength in the targeted comprehension strategy to move to independent application after only a single lesson. They may need to develop more knowledge of and experience with the strategy through teacher modeling, guided practice, and coaching.

In my observations, coaching appears to be the step most often neglected in the reading instruction of students of diverse backgrounds. In many reading programs, lessons skip from guided practice with the whole class straight to independent application. This skipping poses a problem, especially for struggling readers who need the additional scaffolding provided by coaching.

Furthermore, coaching, in conjunction with having students work with a partner, works well in classrooms in which students are oriented toward rivalry rather than competition, as discussed in chapter 5. Partner work, in common with talk story-like reading lessons, allows students many opportunities to make a contribution and keep even with their peers. Engaging in joint problem solving and giving help in this context, often with an audience of one, allows students to gain a degree of recognition by supporting the literacy learning of their classmates. Errors made are easily overlooked because students' actions are not being witnessed by the whole class. While students are working with their partners, the teacher can customize coaching to meet individual needs. For example, the teacher might cue one student about using headings to locate information, while reminding another to highlight only the most important ideas. Finally, coaching has the advantage of reducing the teacher's visibility as a target for acting and other misbehavior (D'Amato, 1988), because students are interacting with one another and not just the teacher.

Independent Application.   During independent application, students attempt to carry out the targeted comprehension strategy on their own, without any help from the teacher or other students. To set up the independent application phase of the lesson, the teacher might say the following:

> You did a good job of determining the important ideas when you had a chance to work with a partner. Now it's time to see how well you can determine importance when you read on your own. Do your best to read the next three paragraphs and determine the important ideas by yourself. Be sure to think of a good reason to justify your choice. We'll get back together to discuss our choices in a few minutes.

During the time for independent application, the teacher gathers assessment information by observing the students as they work. If some students are not yet able to use the strategy on their own, the teacher plans to have them meet later for a small-group lesson.

Self-Assessment and Goal Setting.   When the students have completed the assignment, the teacher calls the whole class together for a discussion. Students are encouraged to share their thoughts about the important ideas in the paragraphs, along with reasons for their choices.

After the discussion, the teacher refers students back to the "I Can" statement, "I can determine the important ideas when I read," as well as to the three items in the rubric. He or she leads the students to engage in self-assessment by saying words to this effect:

Now it's time for self-assessment. I want you to assess how well you did today with our new comprehension strategy of determining important ideas. On your self-assessment sheet, write down the I Can statement. Then look at the three items in the *meets* column of the rubric. First, the article we read about wolves was written at the fifth grade level. Were you able to read the paragraphs on your own? Decide if your answer is yes or no. Second, were you able to find the few words that showed the important idea? This could be a sentence from the paragraph, or part of a sentence, or you could have written your own sentence. Third, were you able to give a good reason for the sentence you chose? Which of these three things could you do? Which ones do you need to keep working on? The items you need to keep working on are your goals for the next time we have a lesson on determining the important ideas. There's space at the bottom of the sheet where you can write down your goals.

In future lessons on this same comprehension strategy, the teacher will begin by having students review their goals from the previous lesson. At the end of the lesson, students will again engage in self-assessment, comparing their most recent performance to the earlier one, and setting new goals. Involving students of diverse backgrounds in self-assessment and goal setting builds their ownership of and engagement with comprehension strategy learning. Learning moves forward more quickly when students have recognized their strengths and weaknesses and set goals for themselves, rather than having to work on goals imposed by the teacher. This point is discussed as well in chapter 10.

SUMMARY

In this chapter, I discussed the importance of providing students of diverse backgrounds with ample instruction in reading comprehension strategies. I highlighted times within workshop approaches, such as Book Club *Plus*, when strategy instruction should occur. Students should be taught reading comprehension strategies with nonfiction, as well as with fiction, because the majority of texts they read in the upper elementary grades and above are nonfiction. Four arrangements that commonly limit students' access to strategy instruction were discussed, along with suggestions about how these arrangements can be adjusted to increase access. I recommended that teachers focus on six comprehension strategies, all amenable to instruction and all shown to improve students' ability to understand text. Challenges that often arise in teaching these strategies to students of diverse backgrounds were discussed, along with responses to these challenges. Finally, I illustrated the application of a six-step process for teaching a comprehension strategy well, following the gradual release of responsibility. This six-step process includes engaging students in self-assessment of their progress in learning strategies. As teachers move students of diverse backgrounds toward independence in applying comprehension strategies across a range of texts, they increase students' chances for attaining high levels of literacy and academic success.

7

Culturally Responsive Instruction in Multiethnic Classrooms

My focus in this chapter is on the complex yet common situation in which teachers are working in classrooms with students of many different cultural and linguistic backgrounds. I begin by discussing the key characteristics of culturally responsive instruction and responding to three frequently asked questions. I briefly discuss ways of changing curriculum to include content relevant to students' cultural backgrounds. Then I address issues of social process or how teachers can structure interaction to promote students' active participation in literacy activities. The idea is that the best approach is for teachers to offer students opportunities to participate in structures consistent with a diverse worldview, as well as with a mainstream worldview.

KEY CHARACTERISTICS OF CULTURALLY RESPONSIVE INSTRUCTION

You may have noticed that researchers use somewhat different terms for what we are calling culturally responsive instruction. These terms include *culturally congruent instruction* (Au & Kawakami, 1994), *culturally relevant pedagogy* (Ladson-Billings, 1995; Osborne, 1996), and *culturally responsive teaching* (Gay, 2000). Rather than discussing the nuances of difference among these terms, I highlight the assumptions and key characteristics that appear to unite researchers concerned with building on students' cultural strengths in the classroom.

First, culturally responsive instruction resides firmly within a pluralist vision of society, as discussed in chapter 1. As Gay (2000) stated, "It acknowledges the legitimacy of the cultural heritages of different ethnic groups, both as legacies that affect students' dispositions, attitudes and approaches to learning and as worthy content to be taught in the formal curriculum" (p. 29). Teachers who use culturally responsive instruction begin with a high regard for the competence of students of diverse backgrounds and their families and recognize the likely differences between literacy demands in school and the community, as discussed in chapter 3.

Second, culturally responsive instruction aims at school success for students of diverse backgrounds, acknowledging that a disproportionate number of these students typically experience failure in school. As noted in Osborne's (1996) research, this failure is an international phenomenon. Exactly what constitutes school success for students of diverse backgrounds is a topic open to discussion. However, as highlighted in chapter 1, in the era of globalization, all students must be able to engage in higher level thinking with text. The emphasis in this chapter is on culturally responsive instruction that can bring students to high levels of achievement and close the literacy achievement gap. Connections are made to chapter 4 and workshop approaches, as well as to chapter 6, where I discussed the teaching of reading comprehension strategies.

Third, to improve the school success of students of diverse backgrounds, culturally responsive instruction seeks to build bridges between students' experiences at home and at school. In some cases, as in Moll's (1992) research on funds of knowledge held by Mexican American families, the effect is to change the content of the curriculum so that topics relevant to students' lives become central to classroom lessons. In other cases, as in my research on talk story-like participation structures (discussed in chapter 5), the effect is to change the social processes in the classroom, or the manner in which teachers interact with students. This second area of change is the focus of this chapter.

Fourth, culturally responsive instruction supports students in building, or at least maintaining, their competence in the home culture and language (issues of language receive further attention in chapter 8). The home culture and language do not simply serve as vehicles that educators can use to give students access to mainstream school processes and content. Rather, the home culture and language are valued for their own sake.

Finally, culturally responsive instruction fosters social justice through an emphasis on equality of educational outcomes and the celebration of diversity. Culturally responsive instruction is aimed at righting the wrongs inherent in the present educational system, which produces a layering of test scores in favor of dominant-group students, as shown in the NAEP results in chapter 1. But this equality is not to be achieved by pitting one group against another. Rather, culturally responsive instruction seeks to move away from a mentality of educational winners and losers toward a future in which students from all groups achieve at high levels, and diversity is celebrated and not merely tolerated.

Responses to Frequently Asked Questions

As a result of discussing the topic of culturally responsive instruction with many educators, I know that certain questions arise again and again. Here are responses to the three questions that I am most often asked by teachers.

I Teach in an Urban School, and My Students Come From a Dozen or More Different Cultural and Linguistic Backgrounds. Can Teachers in a Multiethnic Setting Like Mine Still Use Culturally Responsive Instruction?   The answer to this question is yes, although the implementation of culturally responsive instruction will require considerable thought. This question grows from the fact that much of the research on culturally responsive instruction has been conducted in classrooms in which the majority of students are from one particular ethnic group. For example, many of the studies I have discussed—such as the work by D'Amato (1988) on "acting" cited in chapter 5—were conducted in classrooms where most of the students were native Hawaiians. Ladson-Billings's (1994) research was conducted in classrooms where nearly all the students were African American. Philips's (1983) classic research was conducted in classrooms on the Warm Springs Reservation with students who were Native Americans.

Many teachers puzzle over how to apply the results of this research, because these studies seem to point to the need for a precise match between instructional practices and students' cultural backgrounds. These teachers feel quite rightly that they cannot achieve such a match, because they teach in settings in which students come from many different cultural backgrounds. In short, although culturally responsive instruction sounds like a promising idea, it may appear impractical in the multiethnic, multilingual classroom.

Certainly, one way of looking at research on culturally responsive instruction is to emphasize the relation between the instructional innovation and the cultural background of the students, for example, linking the use of talk story-like participation structures to improved reading performance in Hawaiian children (Au & Mason, 1981). However, there is another way of applying research on culturally responsive instruction to multiethnic, multilingual settings. This approach involves identifying patterns of instruction consistent with a diverse worldview that resonates with the cultural values of many nonmainstream groups (cf. Spindler & Spindler, 1990). Teachers in multiethnic classrooms can implement culturally responsive instruction by making sure that there are times during the school day when lessons and activities are organized according to this diverse worldview, as discussed later.

One of the themes running through this volume is that educators must be able to recognize negative patterns that characterize the ways we usually "do school" with students of diverse backgrounds and that routinely hinder literacy achievement. Next, educators must put in place new, positive patterns that will foster students' literacy learning in school. Research on culturally responsive instruction is an important source of information about these positive patterns, consistent with a diverse worldview. A number of research reviews on culturally responsive instruction have been published, including Au and Kawakami (1994), Osborne (1996), and Gay (2000). In the sections that follow, I draw on the effective patterns of instruction noted in these reviews.

It is important to understand that culturally responsive instruction does not involve duplicating home and community settings in the classroom. Classroom and home settings should remain distinct and different from one another, so that teachers can carry out classroom activities in a manner that promotes academic achievement, and families can carry out their lives in a manner consistent with their own goals.

Instead of duplication, culturally responsive instruction entails hybridity or hybrid events (Au, 2001; Manyak, 2001). Hybridity refers to the creative combining of elements from students' home cultures with elements typical of the classroom and academic learning. A talk story-like reading lesson is a hybrid literacy event, as is the daily news in Ms. Page's second-grade classroom, described in chapter 2. In culturally responsive instruction, the teacher is creating hybrid settings with two features: (a) they foster the academic goals that students of diverse backgrounds, like all other students, should meet to do well in school and in later life; and (b) they create a comfortable and understandable environment in which students can meet these goals. Hybrid settings depart from familiar ways of doing school while maintaining a rigorous academic focus.

Can Mainstream Teachers Who Are Outsiders to the Students' Cultures Still Implement Culturally Responsive Instruction? Again, the answer is yes. A finding common to all the research reviews is that teachers of mainstream backgrounds, as well as teachers of diverse backgrounds, can successfully use culturally responsive instruction and teach students of diverse backgrounds (e.g., Osborne, 1996). In my study of talk story-like reading lessons, one of the teachers, Teacher LC, was a mainstream teacher. Although initially unsuccessful in conducting reading lessons with young Hawaiian students, Teacher LC learned after a year to use talk story-like participation structures and to link her lessons to students' interests. In a related vein, Ladson-Billings's (1994) study of teachers effective in promoting the literacy of African American students included five African Americans and three European Americans. Ladson-Billings found that the three European American teachers followed the same general principles in their teaching as the African American teachers. One of the European American teachers had gone to school in the community, but the others had not. Nevertheless, all three of these teachers connected the content of their lessons to the concerns of the community and the students. They made an effort to understand their students' interests and lives outside of school and to establish positive, caring relationships with their students. They encouraged the development of a family-like feeling in the classroom and provided students with many opportunities to work cooperatively, as discussed later in this chapter. Although teachers who share their students' cultural backgrounds may have an advantage in establishing positive relationships and providing students with effective instruction, other teachers can definitely learn to adjust their teaching to become more effective. It is important to remember also that teachers who share the ethnicity of their students may not share their social class background, and that this difference may create barriers to understanding.

Differences between the cultural backgrounds of students and teachers are increasingly common. Although the student population in the United States is growing in diversity, the population of teachers has remained much more uniform (Au & Raphael, 2000). Although many studies demonstrate the positive contributions made by teachers of diverse backgrounds (King, 1993), the reality is that many students of diverse backgrounds, now and in the foreseeable future, will be taught by mainstream teachers. These shifts in population lend increased significance to the finding that teachers of mainstream backgrounds can and do learn to use culturally responsive instruction effectively.

Isn't Culturally Responsive Instruction Just Good Teaching, and Shouldn't Good Teaching Be the Same in Every Setting? This time the answer is no. This question is a bit complicated to tackle, but let's begin with this quotation from Gay (2000):

> Many educators still believe that good teaching transcends place, people, time, and context. They contend it has nothing to do with the class, race, gender, ethnicity, or culture of students and teachers. This attitude is manifested in the expression "Good teachers anywhere are good teachers everywhere." Individuals who subscribe to this belief fail to realize that their standards of "goodness" in teaching and learning are culturally determined and are not the same for all ethnic groups. The structures, assumptions, substance, and operations of conventional educational enterprises are European American cultural icons. . . . (p. 22)

In other words, to advocate a universal concept of good teaching may actually amount to advocating teaching from a European American or mainstream perspective. It is true that certain general principles of good teaching seem to be widely applicable. Examples of such principles include building on students' prior knowledge and establishing positive relationships with students. However, the way these principles are instantiated may well differ depending on the cultural backgrounds of the students. For example, in chapter 5, I discussed how teachers can go about establishing positive relationships with students of diverse backgrounds. I noted that, although teachers can successfully use competition as the basis for establishing a positive classroom environment with students of mainstream backgrounds, this approach can prove disastrous in some classrooms with students of diverse backgrounds.

To gain a fresh perspective on these matters, consider the following point. The way we usually "do school" is itself a form of culturally responsive instruction, in this case, instruction responsive to the cultural backgrounds of mainstream students. These students generally perform well in school because instruction has been adapted to their cultural backgrounds, in terms of both the content of the curriculum and the social processes of the classroom. For example, when it comes to the content of the curriculum, most mainstream students can easily make connections to the literature typically read in the classroom, including familiar stories such as "The Little Red Hen." When it comes to social processes, mainstream students are usually comfortable with the IRE structure (Mehan, 1979), as described in chapter 5.

From this perspective, it becomes apparent that the concept of culturally responsive instruction is applicable to all students, those of mainstream as well as diverse backgrounds. In both cases, the idea is that students have a better chance of experiencing academic success and of reaching high levels of literacy when instruction is responsive to their cultural backgrounds. The difference is that instruction consistent with the ways we usually "do school" is responsive to the cultural backgrounds of mainstream students, but not to the cultural backgrounds of students of diverse backgrounds. Cultural responsiveness in instruction for mainstream students, but not for students of diverse backgrounds, may help to explain the vast differences in academic performance shown in the NAEP reading results, presented in chapter 1.

Gollnick and Chinn (2002) identified individualism and freedom as paramount values of the dominant group, a conclusion supported in research by Spindler and Spindler (1990). These are the values privileged in school, values that underlie the way the dominant society believes schooling should be conducted. The dominant or mainstream point of view assumes that people can control the outcomes in their lives through their own individual efforts. Individuals are believed to advance in society through their own hard work, determination, and perseverance. Competition is viewed as a healthy process that ensures the survival of the fittest, and success is measured in material terms, such as through the acquisition of money and material goods. Self-reliance and independence from others are emphasized. People are seen as separate from nature and as having the right to control nature and use its resources for their own ends.

Although a belief in individualism and freedom can be held to varying degrees by members of subordinate or nonmainstream groups, different values may be preferred (e.g., Howard, 1974; Spindler & Spindler, 1990). These different values contribute to what I have called a *diverse worldview*. As this diverse worldview is outlined, notice that the situation is not one of right or wrong, of either-or.

Consider a diverse worldview based on the following beliefs. People's lives may be influenced by factors beyond their control, making it best to tackle life's challenges with the support of family, friends, and colleagues. By working in concert, the whole group—family, friends, community, or another social network—can move ahead together. Cooperation allows challenges to be met more easily, as members of the group all bring their thoughts and efforts to bear. What is important is the well-being of the group, especially the family, extended family, or kinship network. Success is measured in terms of positive relationships with others, as well as of spiritual growth, rather than in terms of material wealth. People are not separate from nature, and the natural world is viewed with a sense of wonder for its beauty, power, and the gifts it has to offer. People must respect and care for the environment if nature is to continue to provide for future generations. As you can see, although different from the values typically reflected in schools, the diverse worldview has many positive features. In the classroom, students are likely to benefit from a hybrid environment in which they have experiences with both kinds of values.

Conflicts may develop in the classroom when the teacher and students are unknowingly operating according to two different worldviews, similar to those contrasted earlier. Events in these classrooms show the effects of culture differences, as discussed in chapter 1. Recall the example of the teacher who chastised a Hawaiian student for seeking help from other children. Culturally responsive instruction should involve giving students experiences with cooperation as well as competition, with working for the good of the team as well as for one's own benefit. Times when individual achievement is emphasized should certainly be present. However, teachers should be aware that "doing school" only according to the privileged, dominant worldview may put students of diverse backgrounds at a serious disadvantage in classroom learning situations.

Curriculum Content

Certainly, implementing culturally responsive instruction should involve making students' home or heritage cultures central to the literacy curriculum. Research suggests that there are several different approaches to centering the curriculum on content related to students' cultural backgrounds (Banks, 1995). In my view, all approaches should involve the use of multicultural literature to connect students to their own culture and the cultures of others. Although it is beyond the scope of this chapter to discuss specific works of multicultural literature, readers are referred to the comprehensive annotated bibliographies published by the National Council of Teachers of English (NCTE), including Bishop (1994), Barrera, Thompson, and Dressman (1997), Yokota (2001), and Hansen-Krening, Aoki, and Mizokawa (2003).

One approach to making students' cultures central to the content of the literacy curriculum is for the teacher to develop units focused on the history, traditions, customs, and beliefs of particular cultural groups. In the United States, the best known examples of this approach have been described by educators concerned with the quality of education of African American students (e.g., Shujaa & Afrik, 1996). Similarly, I have worked with teachers in Hawaiian communities interested in developing Hawaiian studies units. In my observations, these units can be highly effective in strengthening the knowledge of non-Hawaiian students about Hawaiian culture, as well as in fostering the pride of native Hawaiian students in their heritage. However, there is surprisingly little research on the academic and attitudinal benefits of such units and an absence of detailed descriptions of the teacher's role in teaching such units successfully (Banks, 1995). Research does suggest that teachers need to be aware of the feelings of students whose cultural backgrounds are not reflected in the units, and of the feelings of American-born versus immigrant students (Ulichny, 1996). Understandably, teachers may be reluctant to pursue this particular approach if they do not possess the deep knowledge of the culture necessary for development of a successful unit.

Another approach is for the teacher to invite parents or other community members to bring culturally relevant content into the classroom, or to teach this content collaboratively with these more knowledgeable others (see chapter 8 for an example). This approach has the advantage of involving those with an inside view of the culture, which the teacher may not be able to impart. In common with the first approach, this approach may become impractical when students are from many different cultural backgrounds and not all groups are represented in the curriculum.

The third approach to making culturally relevant content central to the curriculum may be the most practical for teachers whose students come from many different cultural backgrounds. In this approach, used in Book Club *Plus* and mentioned in chapter 4, the teacher involves students in projects that encourage them to bring aspects of their culture into the classroom. Third-grade teacher Marianne George used this approach when teaching the Family Stories unit within the overarching theme of "Our Storied Lives." As a culminating project for this unit, George had her students prepare oral retellings of family stories based on artifacts that had meaning to their families (Raphael, Florio-Ruane, & George, 2001). For example, Nathan interviewed his grandfather and learned the story of how his great-grandfather had come to America from Ireland by hiding in a pickle barrel and stowing away on a ship. Nathan and his father made a model of a pickle barrel to go along with his oral retelling of this story. Other students told stories revolving around artifacts such as a silver teapot, military uniforms and medals, a kerosene lamp, and a butler's tray, representing the experiences of their ancestors from China, Germany, Iraq, Italy, Macedonia, Mexico, Poland, Sweden, and other countries. Some students shared photos and newspaper clippings referring to their grandparents' participation in events in the United States, including a steel workers' strike and minor league baseball games.

This approach has the obvious advantage of making space in the curriculum for the differing cultural experiences of all students, so no student or group is left out. Families become involved as they help the students select artifacts and provide information for the stories students will present in class. Because students work with their families, parents can direct students to information they feel comfortable sharing, and sensitive topics can be avoided. Invariably, students learn more about their own families and cultural backgrounds and develop a greater appreciation for their own heritage. They also have the opportunity to learn about their classmates' backgrounds in a manner that centers on families' varied experiences and does not promote stereotyping. Furthermore, teachers can implement this approach without having extensive knowledge of students' many cultures and can gradually become better informed through their interactions with students and their families.

Social Processes in the Classroom

I turn now from the content of the curriculum to social processes in the classroom. In this section, I provide specific suggestions about what teachers can do to implement culturally responsive instruction through the use of different groupings and structures for participation. Some of these structures for participation are consistent with a worldview oriented toward individual achievement and competition, whereas others are consistent with a worldview oriented toward group well-being and cooperation (the diverse worldview discussed earlier). The teacher will carefully observe students' performances across the different structures to make certain that every student is comfortably engaged with literacy learning during at least one structure for participation. This point should be emphasized: Every student must feel "at home" in the classroom during some time in the school day. Especially in the upper elementary grades and above, students of diverse backgrounds quickly become disaffected with school. Teachers must take action from the very first day of school to build positive relationships with students and provide them all with successful literacy learning experiences.

Culturally responsive instruction is never intended to limit students' learning only to structures for participation that they find comfortable. Teachers must also take responsibility for giving students the ability to engage successfully in structures for participation that may initially be uncomfortable. Teachers in multiethnic classrooms act as mediators in helping students of diverse backgrounds acculturate to structures for participation consistent with mainstream values and expectations. Teachers accomplish this task by explaining the rules for participating in different lessons and activities, by modeling appropriate behaviors, by having other students serve as models, and by encouraging students to participate as best they can.

This process of acculturation requires time, patience, and persistence on the part of both teachers and students. However, if the teacher is consistent in establishing routines, most students will gain knowledge of and comfort with most, if not all, of the structures for participation that occur in the classroom (for more about routines, see chapters 4 and 8). In this chapter, I highlight the importance of routines in encouraging the acculturation of students of diverse backgrounds to a range of classroom structures for participation, especially for the purposes of developing strategies of higher level thinking with text.

Let's look at the different structures for participation that teachers in multiethnic classrooms should try to include during a school day. For each structure, I discuss (a) consistency with the two worldviews highlighted earlier, (b) how the structure can be used to promote higher level thinking with text, and (c) research findings teachers should consider when implementing the structure.

Whole-Class Lessons.   Many teachers feel that it is most convenient and efficient to keep the whole class together and have all students do the same thing at the same time. Whole-class instruction is typically conducted according to the teacher initiation, student response, teacher evaluation (IRE) structure, as discussed in chapter 5. The IRE structure is consistent with a mainstream worldview oriented toward individual achievement and competition. However, whole-class lessons can draw on elements of a worldview oriented toward the well-being of the group and cooperation. This can happen if the teacher uses whole-class lessons as a time to bring the students together as a community of learners, as in the community share component of Book Club *Plus* (Raphael & Goatley, 1997).

In general, teachers should reserve whole-class literacy lessons for content, strategies, and skills needed by all students. For example, as discussed in chapter 6, teachers can use whole-class lessons to provide instruction in reading comprehension strategies. Teachers can make effective use of this time by giving explicit explanations, modeling strategies, providing guided practice, and giving feedback about performance to the whole class.

Many teachers make use of whole-class lessons particularly at the beginning of the year, to acquaint students with the routines to be followed. For example, Pat Nakanishi, a sixth-grade teacher in a multiethnic classroom in Hawaii, launches the readers' workshop in her classroom by reading a novel aloud to the students (Nakanishi, 2002). She teaches students to compose different kinds of written responses to literature after each chapter is read aloud. Written responses taught include making personal connections, expressing one's feelings about the text, and walking in the character's shoes (imagining what it would be like to be the character). In addition to teacher modeling, whole-class lessons give the teacher an opportunity to present students with examples of other students' work, which can serve as positive examples. Nakanishi's students are prepared through whole-class instruction to complete written responses independently, an ability they will need when they move into book clubs, each reading a different novel.

Whole-class lessons usually require students to learn at the same pace and to conform to the same expectations for behavior. These expectations for conformity mean that teachers tend to rely on the IRE pattern to keep the students under tight control. As noted in chapter 5, the IRE pattern may create management problems for the teacher in classrooms in which students have been taught at home to value cooperation and working for the benefit of the group. In classrooms with many African American or Native Hawaiian students, for example, use of the IRE participation structure during whole-class lessons often leads to difficulty, because teachers make themselves visible targets for acting and other forms of disruptive behavior (D'Amato, 1988). Rather than serving as the most easily managed structure for participation, whole-class lessons may actually turn out to be the most difficult to manage, especially for novice teachers.

The solution in many classrooms with students of diverse backgrounds is to use whole-class instruction judiciously, such as for minilessons lasting about 10 to 15 min (Routman, 2000). During this time, teachers provide instruction in new content, strategies, and skills, and set the tone and focus for the readers' or writers' workshop. Teachers then move students into small-group instruction, where there are usually many more opportunities for instruction and for students to participate productively.

Many skillful and experienced teachers can use whole-class instruction effectively in classrooms with many African American students, native Hawaiian students, and others. These teachers take a number of factors into consideration. One factor is the pace of interaction. Teachers in some classrooms—notably, with many African American students—find that a brisk, rhythmic pace, including choral responding, works well (Hollins, 1982).

Teachers in other classrooms, such as those with many Native American students, find that speaking in a slower, measured manner is effective (Erickson & Mohatt, 1982).

Another factor is the means by which students obtain turns at speaking. Students from some cultural backgrounds are very comfortable with raising their hands and eager to be chosen. Students from other cultural backgrounds are reluctant to volunteer to speak, even when they have many ideas to share (Boggs, 1972). These students may believe that responding in front of the whole class is a form of showing off, bragging, or putting oneself above others. In these situations, to involve all students, teachers may want to vary the participation structure. Specifically, instead of relying on students to volunteer, the teacher may have each student in turn give a brief response.

Another factor relates to whether students have had time to prepare their responses to teachers' questions. Students from some cultural groups are taught at home to rehearse, practice, and otherwise prepare themselves before displaying their knowledge (Philips, 1983). Students from some cultural groups may be especially hesitant about sharing their responses when questions require interpretation or speculation rather than factual answers, because they have been taught to provide the answers expected by the teacher. To get around this problem, teachers can pose a question and have students discuss their ideas with a partner or a small group of three or four. A representative of each pair or small group then shares a key idea or answer with the whole class. This approach has the advantage of involving all students in discussion, without the pressures of speaking in front of the whole class.

Teacher-Led Small-Group Lessons. By small groups, I mean groups of no more than about six students. In my experience, groups larger than six do not work as well because some students find it easy to avoid contributing. In groups of six or fewer, everyone usually feels obliged to make a contribution, and a lack of participation on the part of any student is readily noticed.

As mentioned in chapter 5, teacher-led small-group lessons provide students with many opportunities to respond and to receive recognition for their efforts from both the teacher and peers. Small-group lessons can be times when the students work together, under the teacher's guidance, to construct the theme of the text and to make their own personal connections to literature (Au, 1992). Small-group lessons often provide teachers with the most valuable instructional time, both to promote language and literacy development and to establish positive relationships with students. In a large group, the teacher must try to involve many students, so each student's response is usually quite brief. In small-group lessons, the teacher can ask questions that allow students to speak at length, and students can express more complex ideas in these extended responses. This time for students to develop ideas in a deeper and more thoughtful manner is especially important for promoting higher level thinking with text. Furthermore, these extended responses make up an ever-increasing part of assessments designed to tap students' reading comprehension.

Once they know what students are thinking, teachers can promote higher level thinking about text through responsive questioning (Au, 1992). In responsive questioning, teachers ask questions based on the students' answers, rather than working through a preset list of questions. Successful teachers in classrooms with native Hawaiian children have described small-group lessons to me as a time when they can "stretch" students' minds, an obvious reference to promoting higher level thinking.

With students of diverse backgrounds, teachers will find it effective to structure small-group lessons following the experience–text–relationship (ETR) approach. In this approach, teachers help students to draw on prior knowledge or experiences related to the text, guide students point-by-point through reading of the text, and then have students draw relations between text ideas and their own experiences (Au, Carroll, & Scheu, 2001). Through these lessons, students of diverse backgrounds come to see that literature contains lessons relevant to their own lives. This message is particularly important for students whose families engage in forms of literacy that do not include the reading of books, as discussed in chapter 3. During small-group lessons, teachers have the chance to help students make personal connections to books and literature.

Teachers may also use small-group lessons to promote the application of comprehension strategies introduced in whole-class lessons, as described in chapter 6. Taylor, Pearson, Clark, and Walpole (2000) discovered that effective teachers in schools in low-income communities do not just provide students with explicit instruction in strategies. Rather, these teachers cue students to apply the strategies during real reading. During small-group lessons, teachers can observe students' reading performance closely and spot opportunities when students should be using comprehension strategies. They can cue students to apply these strategies, until students are able to do so consistently on their own. As noted in chapter 6, this is an important step in the gradual release of responsibility.

As in whole-class lessons, teachers must continue to attend to issues of turn-taking and pacing. If the teacher allows students to speak when they have something to say, instead of tightly controlling turn-taking, small-group lessons become consistent with a worldview oriented toward the well-being of the group and cooperation. To establish a collaborative tone to the lessons, teachers must avoid the IRE pattern and allow students to determine when they will speak. Some students have ideas to offer but do not know how to enter the conversation on their own, particularly if it is fast-paced. If the teacher sees that a student wants to speak but has not been able to enter the conversation, the teacher can make a space by quieting the group. For example, the teacher might say, "Excuse me, let's stop for a moment to see if Cheryl has anything to add. Cheryl, do you have an idea to share?" Students such as Cheryl realize that their contributions are valued, and over time they will gain the confidence and skill to jump into the discussion.

Small-group discussions may proceed at a brisk pace, as in talk story-like reading lessons, or the pace may need to be more leisurely. Teachers should watch students for clues about their comfort with the pace of the lesson and make adjustments accordingly. For example, research suggests that teachers in classrooms with Native American students may need to wait an extra moment to be sure students have finished speaking and do not feel interrupted (Vogt, Jordan, & Tharp, 1987).

Student-Led Small Groups. An example of student-led small groups is seen in the book clubs in Book Club *Plus*, described in chapter 4. Student-led small groups can be organized in a manner consistent with a worldview oriented toward the well-being of the group and cooperation. This view is reinforced if the teacher guides students to set the ground rules to be followed during these small-group discussions. For example, the fourth graders in Torry Montes's class agreed that everyone should participate and that shy students would be invited to join the conversation (Montes & Au, 2003). Rules such as these promote collaboration rather than competition among students within the group.

Student-led small groups in the form of book clubs can be used to promote higher level thinking about text, as shown in chapter 4. Teachers can take a number of steps to enhance students' ability to engage in thoughtful discussions about novels and so make good use of the time in book clubs. Teachers should make sure all students have access to the text, for example, by having struggling readers engage in partner reading or giving them access to a listening center where they can hear the book on audiotape or CD. Teachers need to make sure students know how to prepare written responses, by providing whole-class instruction along the lines followed by Pat Nakanishi. In general, teachers should model the kinds of comments students might make about the text, such as offering interpretations or making personal connections, as well as giving students help with learning how to ask open-ended questions. Teachers can have students observe and comment on live or videotaped book club discussions, so that students see the difference between productive and unproductive conversations about literature. Some groups of students, such as the African American students observed by Florio-Ruane (personal communication, October 4, 2004), may have the skills to engage in discussions of literature with little or no teacher guidance.

Another valuable use of student-led small groups involves having students work together to complete a project. The project should involve students in making the knowledge or insights they have acquired available to the whole class. For example, when students have finished reading a novel, they may think of a way of sharing the novel with the whole class, such as through a dramatization of key scenes. Small groups may also be used to have students conduct research, pull together information from a number of different sources, and summarize their information in a report to be presented to the whole class. For example, the teacher may compile a list of scientific breakthroughs, such as the invention of television, and allow students to conduct research on the scientists who contributed to these discoveries.

Teachers need to be aware of the role of instruction in ensuring that students' experiences with these projects will contribute to literacy learning. The teachers' guidance is particularly important in multiethnic classrooms, where there may be a significant number of students who struggle as readers and writers. Teachers must be sure to prepare students with the reading and writing strategies and skills needed. For example, if students are going to dramatize scenes from a novel, the teacher should help students learn how to prepare a script by rereading the relevant sections of the novel and drafting the parts to be spoken by the characters. If students are going to prepare a report using information from several sources, teachers need to help students learn to take notes, rather than copying the information exactly as it appears.

In some cases, as in classrooms with many native Hawaiian students, teachers should not assign roles for members of the student-led groups but let students work out these roles on their own. Native Hawaiian students, for example, often have considerable experience working with their siblings and cousins to accomplish tasks, and so know how to organize a small group to reach a common goal. In other cases, small groups may function more smoothly if the teacher assigns students roles, such as recorder or reporter. This approach may be necessary if students prefer to work on their own, are not accustomed to working with their peers, or come from cultural backgrounds with an orientation toward individual accomplishment.

Pairs, Partners, and Peer Tutoring. Having students work in pairs builds on a worldview oriented toward group well-being and cooperation, if the teacher makes it clear that the goal is to learn together, not to show that one knows more than another. Having students work in pairs provides them with another structure for participating in literacy activities. Children in the primary grades can discuss with a partner a story read aloud by the teacher. Older students can discuss chapters in a novel with a partner. As Cole (2003) pointed out, it is easy to enter a discussion of literature when the only competition is one other person. Teachers can also use partner work to build students' independence in the use of comprehension strategies, as described in chapter 6.

Pair or partner work has an important place in the gradual release of responsibility. Too often, teachers provide lessons in strategies and skills and then expect students to use the strategy on their own. For teachers in all classrooms, and especially multiethnic ones, this can be an unrealistic expectation, especially for struggling readers and writers. When students work with partners, they can discuss the strategy and how it is to be applied, and they can learn together. After completing a number of tasks with partners, students will be better prepared to work on their own.

Teachers in multiethnic classrooms should adopt the attitude that the room is filled with teachers. Not only other adults, but each student in the class is a potential teacher. This attitude is important in multiethnic classrooms in which there are many struggling readers and writers, because the teacher will never have enough time to provide each of these learners with all the help needed. Some of that help must come from other students. Teachers sometimes wonder whether peer tutoring may be detrimental to the academic progress of capable students. Studies suggest that peer tutoring is beneficial to the learning of both the tutor and the target student (Cohen, Kulik, & Kulik, 1982). Peer tutoring helps to build the community of learners, by showing students that they can and should contribute to the progress of others as readers and writers. A caution is that teachers must also give capable students ample opportunity to engage with challenging texts and literacy tasks.

Individual or Independent Work Time. Obviously, if students of diverse backgrounds are to be successful in school, they need to learn to work on their own. The ability to complete academic tasks independently is valued in school settings oriented toward individual achievement and competition and that emphasize standardized or state tests. As with the previous four structures for participation, teachers should discuss the expectations and rules for participating appropriately with students. For example, in a primary-grade classroom, the teacher might explain the situation to students in the following way:

> I'm going to be giving you a piece of paper with a short story on it. Your job is to read the story on your own and then write the answers to the three questions about the story. We're going to be doing this work in a different way. Usually, if you need help, you can ask someone at your table. With this work, you cannot ask anyone at your table. If you need help, you will raise your hand and wait for me to come over to you. The reason we're doing things this way is so that I can see the kind of reading you can do on your own. This information will help me teach you to become a better reader. Do you have any questions about what we're going to be doing now?

In this explanation, the teacher has made the rules for participation explicit for the students. This new structure for participation has been contrasted to the structure with which students are familiar. The teacher has given the students the reason that this structure for participation is being used. However, despite the teacher's clear explanation, it may not be easy for students to engage successfully in this new participation structure on the first few tries. To support students' learning of these new rules for participation, the teacher should take a few minutes at the end of the lesson for a whole-class discussion. During this discussion, the teacher has the students evaluate their performance during the activity and provide suggestions about how they might improve their performance the next time. The teacher should give the discussion a positive tone and avoid expressing disappointment or scolding students. It takes time for students of diverse backgrounds to learn to participate appropriately in new structures, particularly if those structures reflect an individualistic, competitive worldview.

Teachers in multiethnic classrooms must be careful about making assumptions, even about independent activities that seem to involve straightforward procedures, such as sustained silent reading (SSR). SSR has the purpose of promoting students' interest in reading. During SSR, students read books of their own choosing. However, teachers may not be aware that many students of diverse backgrounds have not had the opportunity to develop their tastes and interests as readers and do not know how to find books they will enjoy reading. For example, a native Hawaiian fifth-grade student told me during an interview that he would go to the library and "grab any book." Similarly, Reyes (1991) observed that two girls with Southeast Asian backgrounds did not know how to choose books and consequently did not benefit from the time set aside for SSR, because they received no guidance from the teacher in solving this problem. Teachers can help students find books they will enjoy by conducting an interest inventory, by giving book talks and encouraging students to do the same, and by showing students how to find books they will enjoy. Teachers in multiethnic classrooms who want to make a strong impression on reluctant readers should consider lending these students books to read from their own personal collection. Students appreciate such thoughtful gestures that show their teachers have their best interests as literacy learners at heart.

A final insight about individual work time is provided by Philips (1983). Philips observed that Native American students used this time to approach the teacher for help with their work. These students preferred to receive assistance from the teacher individually and in private, rather than during whole-class or small-group lessons. This study suggests that teachers in multiethnic classrooms may want to make themselves available for individual conferences with students at some time during the school day. The teacher may have students sign up for these conferences in advance, as during the writers' workshop, or students may simply come over to the teacher's desk when no other student is there.

In short, teachers in multiethnic classrooms have the challenge of organizing to create a place for these five structures over the course of a week, if not a day. These five structures are whole-class lessons, teacher-led small-group lessons, student-led small groups, partner work, and individual work time. This variety of structures for participation is necessary if students of diverse cultural backgrounds are to engage successfully in literacy learning, at least part of the time, from the beginning of the school year. As the year goes on, teachers enable students to participate effectively in structures that may initially have been unfamiliar or uncomfortable. Teachers achieve this goal by explaining the rules for different structures, giving students reasons why these structures are being used, modeling appropriate behaviors, and coaching students in the use of these behaviors. The opportunities for literacy learning available to students of diverse backgrounds increase as they begin to engage successfully in all the structures for participation commonly found in school; those consistent with a worldview oriented toward competition as well as with a worldview oriented toward cooperation.

SUMMARY

In this chapter, I addressed culturally responsive instruction, especially as this approach might be implemented in multiethnic classrooms. Culturally responsive instruction does not require a one-to-one match between characteristics of students' home cultures and classroom practices. Rather, teachers in multiethnic classrooms should be aware of two contrasting worldviews, one oriented toward competition and individual achievement, and the other toward cooperation and the well-being of the group. The first worldview is reflected in the way we usually "do school" and makes typical schooling responsive to the culture of mainstream students but not to the culture of many students of diverse backgrounds. Implementation of culturally responsive instruction requires changes to both the content of the curriculum and to the social processes in the classroom. I focused on the latter by discussing five different structures for participation. One of the keys to the successful implementation of culturally responsive instruction in multiethnic classrooms is the teacher's purposeful inclusion of structures for participation consistent with a worldview oriented toward cooperation and group well-being.

8

Second Language Learners, Multiliteracy, and the Language of Power

This chapter deals with issues of linguistic diversity. I begin by discussing the two categories of second language learners and issues of language and power. I look at what research has to say about the conditions that best promote the school literacy learning of students who speak a home language other than the language of power, the standard language of the larger society. In the rest of the chapter, I focus on effective literacy instruction in the multilingual classroom, where teachers are working with students who speak many different home languages. I describe ways that teachers can promote multiliteracy in the classroom, as well as ways that teachers can build students' proficiency in the language of power. I highlight strategies teachers can use during both the readers' workshop and the writers' workshop. As in chapter 7, I offer a range of suggestions, with the understanding that teachers must use professional judgment to meet the literacy learning needs of students of diverse backgrounds.

ENGLISH LANGUAGE LEARNERS

Throughout this book, I use the term *English Language Learners* (ELLs) to describe students in the United States whose primary language, first language, or home language is not the language of power, which is the language of the dominant group and the larger society. Growing up speaking a primary language other than the language of power does not mean that students have no familiarity with the language of power. Some students have the opportunity at home to learn two or more languages, including the language of power. In the United States, where television is ubiquitous, most children will have heard the language of power, standard American English, even if they do not speak it themselves.

For ELLs, learning the language of power means learning the secondary discourse of the school, as discussed in chapter 4. Learning the secondary discourse of the school often goes far beyond learning a new linguistic code. For students of diverse backgrounds, it is also a matter of learning a new worldview (see chapter 7) and a new set of cultural practices. As pointed out in chapter 4, to gain proficiency in the kind of literacy favored by the school and the larger society, students must have opportunities to engage in the full processes of reading and writing in standard English. They must also have opportunities to study parts of reading and writing in standard English. Workshop approaches to the teaching of literacy are especially effective, because they can provide students with both types of opportunities.

The dominant-group discourse that pervades many schools may give some teachers a negative attitude toward students who speak a primary language other than the language of power. In these instances, students' ability to speak AAVE or Spanish is seen as a problem, and teachers perceive these students as less capable in language and literacy than students who enter school with the ability to speak the language of power.

It is important at the outset for teachers to understand that students' speaking a primary language other than the language of power does not in itself constitute a barrier to achieving high levels of literacy in school. For example, consider the situation of the Nisei, the second-generation Japanese Americans in Hawaii studied by Tamura (1994):

> Among their peers the Nisei either spoke some level of Japanese or Hawaii Creole English. In the first decade of the twentieth century Japanese was the common language among playmates, but by 1920, Hawaii Creole English dominated. By learning Standard English at school, many became bilingual or trilingual—speaking various levels of Japanese, Hawaii Creole English, and Standard English. (p. 200)

Opportunities to gain proficiency in standard English varied, with access easier for Nisei students enrolled in schools in urban areas than for those attending schools in rural areas. Tamura noted that teachers played a major role in the Nisei's development of standard English proficiency, but that this influence could be negative as well as positive. A few teachers discouraged students through sarcastic comments that denigrated Hawaii Creole

English (HCE). Many teachers, however, helped students learn standard English by making the differences between the two languages clear and by explicitly teaching standard English grammar and vocabulary. As they progressed through school, many Nisei developed a command of standard English, and this command of the language helped them gain success in the larger society. For these Japanese Americans, including U.S. Senators Daniel Inouye and Spark Matsunaga, both law school graduates, speaking HCE as a primary language did not constitute an insurmountable barrier to success in school and later life. However, as Tamura observed, speaking standard English did not lead the Nisei to abandon HCE. Most Nisei continued to speak HCE with their friends and family as a mark of cultural identity, and this practice was sustained by their descendants.

Why does speaking a primary language other than the standard language so often appear to become a barrier to literacy learning and school success? As implied earlier, the problem may begin when teachers do not show respect for students' primary languages and do not know how to build on students' language strengths, by extending those strengths and using them as a means to foster proficiency in the standard language. When teachers do not show respect for students' primary languages, students may decide to resist using the standard language so that they can maintain their cultural identity. An example of such resistance was described in chapter 3. In this example, two boys, who felt a lack of positive regard from their English-speaking classmates, spoke together in Spanish (Lopez, 1999). The researcher noted that these interactions reinforced the students' sense of cultural identity but simultaneously served to cut them off from their mainstream classmates and opportunities for academic learning.

The term *second language learners*, as used here, encompasses students who fall into two different categories based on the relationship of their primary language to the language of power. In the United States, for example, the language of power is standard American English. Students in the first category are those who speak a primary language other than English, such as Spanish, Vietnamese, Hmong, and so on. Students in the second category speak a nonmainstream variety of English as their primary language. These students include speakers of AAVE and HCE. The literacy learning opportunities of both groups of students are affected by issues of ethnicity and social class, as well as primary language. However, the languages of students in the first category are in a less ambiguous political situation than the languages of students in the second category.

Table 8.1 lists the top 25 languages spoken by U.S. students in the first category of second language learners, those who speak a primary language

TABLE 8.1
Top 25 Languages Spoken by English Language Learners
in U.S. Classrooms (Kindler, 2002)

Language	Number of Speakers
1. Spanish	3,598,451
2. Vietnamese	88,906
3. Hmong	70,768
4. Chinese, Cantonese	46,466
5. Korean	43,969
6. Haitian Creole	42,236
7. Arabic	41,279
8. Russian	37,157
9. Tagalog	34,133
10. Navajo	27,029
11. Khmer	26,815
12. Chinese, Mandarin	22,374
13. Portuguese	20,787
14. Urdu	18,649
15. Serbo-Croatian	17,163
16. Lao	15,549
17. Japanese	15,453
18. Chuukese	15,194
19. Chamorro	14,354
20. Marshallese	13,808
21. Punjabi	13,200
22. Armenian	13,044
23. Polish	11,847
24. French	11,328
25. Hindi	10,697

other than English, and shows as well the number of speakers of each language (Kindler, 2002). Spanish is the primary language of about 3.6 million or 79% of the more than 4.5 million ELLs in the United States. Ranked a distant second is Vietnamese, spoken by just under 2% of ELLs. Students who speak Hmong as their home language account for about 1.5% of ELLs. Languages with between 40,000 to 50,000 speakers are Cantonese Chinese, Korean, Haitian Creole, and Arabic. Languages with between 30,000 to 40,000 speakers are Russian and Tagalog. Languages with between 20,000 to 30,000 speakers are Navajo, Khmer, Mandarin Chinese, and Portuguese. Overall, state reports indicate that students in U.S. classrooms speak over 433 non-English primary languages.

The U.S. government does not collect data on nonmainstream varieties of English and the number of students who speak them. However, if even half of African American students speak AAVE as a primary language, the number of students who speak nonmainstream varieties of English in U.S.

classrooms can conservatively be estimated at 3.9 million. This suggests that the number of students who speak nonmainstream varieties of English at home is probably equal to, or perhaps greater than, the number who speak primary languages other than English, such as Spanish and Vietnamese. Overall, it is safe to conclude that perhaps 20% or more of students in U.S. classrooms speak a primary language other than standard English.

In their work with second language learners, teachers must be aware of how issues of power affect attitudes about language in the larger society. In chapter 3, I discussed how dominant-group discourse can be used to devalue or render invisible the literacy abilities shown by students of diverse backgrounds and their families in the community. In a parallel fashion, dominant-group discourse can be used to devalue the language proficiency of students and their families. This devaluing has been particularly evident in the case of AAVE and other nonmainstream varieties of English, which generally are not even recognized as languages by dominant-group institutions. For example, although students who speak AAVE as their home language likely outnumber students who speak Spanish, AAVE does not appear on the list of languages recognized in the U.S. government's survey, as shown in Table 8.1. Similarly, the Hawaii State Department of Education does not recognize HCE as a language. These omissions continue despite decades of research, including hundreds of linguistic studies documenting the history, rules, current usage, and evolution of these languages (e.g., Baugh, 1999; Sato, 1985).

Dominant-group discourse has led many—including some educators, as well as nearly all students and their parents—to believe that AAVE and HCE are forms of "broken English" spoken by individuals who lack the education or ability to speak English properly. For example, Richardson (2003) described the negative attitudes about AAVE held by African American college students before taking her course that put African American rhetoric and literature at the heart of the curriculum:

> Some students mentioned that they didn't believe African American English was a reality. They mentioned that prior to taking the course, they knew it to be "Broken English" or "a joke." This points to the way that oppression and racism influence the ways that people know. These students showed that what they knew was discredited knowledge. To put it another way, if something that is distinctly African American does exist, it is worthless. Educators must work against this type of oppression. (p. 112)

Richardson's students had accepted the misconceptions about AAVE, their primary language, promoted through dominant-group discourse.

It is important for educators to understand that AAVE, HCE, and other nonmainstream varieties of English are languages with the same potential for expressing complex ideas as standard English (e.g., Labov, 1969) or any other language. The extent to which one language is considered superior to another is determined not by its expressive potential but by the status of its speakers. The power of its speakers determines the extent to which a language is held in high regard in the larger society. AAVE, HCE, and other nonmainstream varieties of English have been positioned by dominant-group discourse as inferior forms of language because they are typically spoken by members of subordinate groups.

RESEARCH FINDINGS

In the United States, many students who speak a primary language other than English are immigrants or the children of immigrants. Studies of the ideas expressed in speeches by members of the U.S. congress and in newspaper editorials and letters to the editor show the widespread fear that immigrants and their children are not learning English (Tse, 2001). This fear underlies legislation aimed at abolishing bilingual education and making English the official language of the United States and the only language used in schools (e.g., Proposition 227 passed in California in 1998).

Tse (2001) presented considerable evidence to show that this fear is groundless. Census data indicate that immigrants constituted a higher percentage of the U.S. population in 1900 than in 1999; 13.6% versus 10.6%. Yet in this earlier period, the higher percentage of immigrants did not cause English to lose its status as the language of power in the United States. In the era of globalization, Tse observed, immigrants have even stronger reasons for becoming proficient in English. One hundred years ago many people could still earn a living by working on a farm or in a trade, without a high school diploma and a high level of English literacy. With the dominance of the knowledge and service economy in the era of globalization, immigrants readily recognize the difficulty of earning a living without these qualifications. Considerable research suggests that both adult immigrants and their children are learning English at a rapid rate (Tse, 2001). Rong and Preissle (1998) found that over 85% of foreign-born students indicated that they could speak English "well" or "very well," although more than half had been in the United States for fewer than 5 years.

Tse (2001) argued that educators, policymakers, and the general public may be focusing on the wrong issue. The problem is not that immigrant students are failing to learn English. Instead, the problem is that these students are rapidly losing the ability to speak their heritage languages. Furthermore, of those who maintain an oral proficiency, many never develop the ability to read and write in their heritage languages. If the educational system in the United States were as rigorous with regard to language learning as the educational systems in other developed nations, all American students would be required to gain proficiency in one or two other languages, in addition to standard English. In other words, the goal would not just be literacy in English but biliteracy or multiliteracy.

Research suggests that gaining proficiency in a second language should follow an additive process (Lambert, 1987), in which the second language is added onto the foundation formed by the primary language. The contrast is a subtractive process in which the first language is ignored or denigrated in the process of learning the second language. Bilingual education in the United States is based on the concept of an additive process; submersion English-only education generally reflects a subtractive process.

In a typical bilingual program, students who enter kindergarten from Spanish-speaking homes learn to read and write in Spanish first. In about the third grade, having already become good readers and writers in Spanish, these students start learning to read and write in English. Studies show that students only need to learn to read and write once, because many aspects of literacy can be transferred from one language to another (Snow, 1990). Reading comprehension strategies such as predicting and making inferences can be transferred, as can writing strategies such as planning and revising. If the languages are related, such as English and Spanish, some decoding skills can be transferred, as well as knowledge of cognates (words related in origin, such as *telephone* and *teléfono*).

This model of having students first learn to read and write in the primary language is the one followed in many bilingual education programs in the United States. However, from the point of view taken here, the weakness in many of these programs is that, once instruction in English begins, little is done to promote continued growth in students' literacy in the primary or heritage language. The goal of many bilingual education programs often is not biliteracy, but literacy in English. Students' strength in the home language is used primarily to help them make the transition to becoming successful students in an English-language environment.

If the goal is biliteracy, then two-way immersion programs offer a strong model (Howard & Christian, 2002). In these programs, students are provided from the start with instruction in both their primary language and a second language, for example, Spanish and English. The same classroom includes some students who speak Spanish as their primary language, and others who speak English as their primary language, preferably with about the same number of speakers of both languages.

In two-way immersion programs in the 50/50 model, students spend half the day (50% of the time) with a teacher who provides instruction in Spanish, and the other half with a teacher who provides instruction in English. This approach teaches students both languages simultaneously. In programs in the 90/10 model, students start by spending 90% of the time receiving instruction in Spanish (the minority or heritage language) with 10% of their instruction in English (the majority language or language of power). This approach teaches literacy in the minority language first. After first grade, the percentage of time in the minority language gradually decreases, until it has dropped to 50% in the fourth grade. The logic behind the 90/10 model is that an extra effort must be made to promote the minority language if students are to develop and maintain their proficiency in it. Because the pull of the majority language is so strong in the larger society, there may be limited opportunities for students to use and to see the value of the minority language.

Lindholm-Leary (2001) conducted research on the academic performance of a large number of students in kindergarten through Grade 8 enrolled in five different types of programs: (a) 90/10 model with a low number of low-income, minority students; (b) 90/10 model with a high number of low-income, minority students; (c) 50/50 model; (d) transitional bilingual education; and (e) English only. Overall, 61% of the students spoke Spanish as their primary language, and 64% qualified for free or reduced-price lunch.

The results showed both the 90/10 and 50/50 models to be effective in promoting students' proficiency in English as well as Spanish (Lindholm-Leary, 2001). Students in both models reached the same levels of proficiency in English. This was even true of students whose primary language was Spanish and who were enrolled in 90/10 programs. These students reached the same level of proficiency in English as their peers enrolled in 50/50 programs. However, students whose primary language was English and who were enrolled in 90/10 programs achieved higher levels of proficiency in Spanish than their peers enrolled in 50/50 programs. The 90/10 model was required to give English-speaking students adequate opportunity to develop their proficiency in Spanish.

Students in two-way programs obtained reading test scores similar to those of peers with the same language backgrounds, according to test norms in California (Lindholm-Leary, 2001). English speakers who began English reading instruction in Grade 3 performed as well on reading tests as

English speakers who had received instruction exclusively in English. Higher levels of bilingual proficiency were related to higher levels of reading achievement. The test results of students in two-way immersion programs showed a trend of improved achievement from Grade 3 to Grade 7, and these students outscored students of comparable backgrounds not enrolled in two-way programs.

In short, a two-way immersion approach for language and literacy learning can be very successful. The question is how teachers in classrooms with students of many different language backgrounds can replicate some of the advantages of this approach. A major limitation is the fact that teachers may be monolingual. Even if teachers speak several languages, they usually are not fluent in all of the children's primary languages. In the rest of this chapter, I discuss ways that teachers can work around these limitations.

Two-Pronged Approach

Our focus in this chapter is on the multilingual classroom, in which the teacher is likely to have students from both categories of second language learners: those whose primary languages are officially recognized and those whose primary languages are nonmainstream varieties of English. I recommend a two-pronged approach to issues of linguistic diversity. First, the teacher should recognize and respect the language strengths that students bring from the home and seek to foster multiliteracy in the classroom. Second, at the same time, the teacher should work consistently and systematically to improve students' ability to read and write in the language of power, as well as to listen and speak in this language. This dual approach gives students the message that their primary language is valued, while fostering proficiency in the language of power.

FOSTERING A MULTILITERATE CLASSROOM ENVIRONMENT

Teachers can serve as models of multiliteracy even if they are fluent only in one language. To start, Schwarzer, Haywood, and Lorenzen (2003) suggested that monolingual teachers investigate their own cultural backgrounds and heritage languages. They can interview family members and construct a family language use tree to show the different languages spoken, read, and written across the generations. They can learn how to write their names in the writing system of the heritage language, and they can master simple phrases, such as "good morning," "good afternoon," "What is your name?" "My name is ___," "thank you," and "good job." The point is that teachers who wish to promote multiliteracy in their students must face some of the same language learning challenges themselves, so that they can share their own experiences with students and better understand students' struggles.

Alexia Haywood promoted the multiliteracy development of students in her prekindergarten classroom (Schwarzer, Haywood, & Lorenzen, 2003). Haywood's class included six Korean speakers, four Chinese speakers, three Spanish speakers, two native English speakers, and one Turkish speaker. Haywood and her colleagues emphasized that teachers are not the only ones who can teach in the classroom. To create a multiliteracy learning community, teachers should draw on the help of students, parents, siblings, clergy, elders, and other community members.

Teachers can start on the road toward multiliteracy by introducing simple phrases in the students' heritage languages (Schwarzer, Lorenzen, & Haywood, 2003). The teacher can make a chart listing the phrases, beginning with standard English and including all the languages spoken by the students, as well as the teacher's own heritage language. Students who are able to write these languages can help with the chart, or parents and other adults can be enlisted to do the writing. The teacher can lead students in reading the phrases on the chart in all the different languages, and after a time students can lead the class in this activity. Students who speak these languages can serve as resources to the teacher and other students by helping them to pronounce the phrases correctly. Throughout the school day, as appropriate, the teacher can use these phrases when interacting with students, and students can use these phrases when addressing each other.

In principle, phrases in AAVE or other nonmainstream varieties of English should be included on the chart, but teachers should be sure to check with other educators, parents, and community members to determine their attitudes toward seeing these phrases in writing. Attitudes about nonmainstream varieties of English will differ depending on the history of language issues in the school and community (cf. Baugh, 2002). Some of these complexities were tackled by Delpit (1995). She wrote that parents

> . . . want to ensure that the school provides their children with discourse patterns, interactional styles, and spoken and written language codes that will allow them success in the larger society.
>
> It was the lack of attention to this concern that created such a negative outcry in the black community when well-intentioned white liberal educators introduced "dialect readers." These were seen as a plot to prevent the schools from teaching the linguistic aspects of the culture of power, thus dooming

black children to a permanent outsider caste. As one parent demanded, "My kids know how to be black—you all teach them how to be successful in the white man's world." (pp. 28–29)

Some languages do not have a written form or are seldom seen in print. For example, relatively few speakers of HCE have ever seen this language in print. A handful of published authors do write in HCE (e.g., Lum, 1990), but they do not follow a uniform system for spelling. Students who speak HCE as their home language are generally discouraged from writing it, except perhaps as dialogue in narratives. In some settings, AAVE, HCE, and other nonmainstream varieties of English may have fallen to such a low status that even parents and community members who speak these languages think it inappropriate to see their primary language displayed in written form in the classroom. Teachers should respect these feelings, while continuing to convey their positive regard for the language abilities of all children, including those who speak stigmatized primary languages.

In some cases, there may actually be good reasons for encouraging students to use a culturally familiar discourse style in their writing. Smitherman (2000) found that African American students who used a black discourse style in their writing received higher NAEP writing scores than students who did not. Elements of a black discourse style identified by Smitherman included rhythmic and dramatic language, the incorporation of proverbs or other Biblical references, a tone resembling those of sermons in the tradition of the Black church, and a conversational style in which the reader is addressed directly.

As a result of these findings, Smitherman made the following recommendations to classroom teachers. First, encourage students to draw upon their knowledge of African American cultural discourse to strengthen their writing. For example, the teacher could read students poetry by Langston Hughes and encourage them to write with a similar sense of rhythm and drama. Second, help students to take a field-dependent perspective, that is, to put themselves in the center of the situation being described in their writing, in contrast to distancing themselves from the situation. Third, begin with narratives, a mode of writing in which many African American student writers may excel. Have students analyze the features of effective writing in this mode, and then have students transfer these effective features to other modes, such as essays or research reports. Fourth, do not overemphasize standard English grammar by highlighting students' grammatical miscues that may result from differences between standard English and AAVE. Smitherman (2000) warned that "overconcentration on these forms frequently suppresses the production of African American discourse and its rich, expressive style" (p. 186).

To express a valuing of multiliteracy, Cary (2000) recommended using students as language teachers. These students consult with their parents about which language to teach. Most second language learners select their primary language. Native speakers of English may focus on a heritage language, even one that has not been spoken as the family's first language for several generations. Nguyet, a Vietnamese girl, served as the student language teacher in a kindergarten through first-grade classroom observed by Cary. At the start of the school day, as her classmates entered the room, Nguyet greeted each classmate with *Xin chào* (hello). Vietnamese was the language of the week, and Nguyet's teacher planned to have her teach the class to say "please" and "thank you." Nguyet's grandmother was scheduled to come to class the next day to teach the children a song in Vietnamese. The teacher prepared the children for this experience by making a tape of the song available in the listening center. Cary wrote the following:

> Nguyet was the classroom's sixth language teacher this year. Other students had taught the three-phrase set in Japanese, Spanish, Mandarin, Tagalog, and German. Like Nguyet, each student who wanted would play the language teacher role at some point during the year. Language teachers taught the three phrases informally for a week. Dolores [the teacher] encouraged kids to use the classroom's ever-growing stock of language phrases whenever and wherever they wished. Kids primarily used a phrase set during the week it was introduced, but a few phrases had exceptionally strong legs—like "arigato" and "shieh shieh," thank you in Japanese and Mandarin—and traveled with the students week after week. (p. 100)

Haywood created a multiliteracy print environment with simple changes, such as labeling students' cubbies with their names in English, Spanish, and Chinese or Korean (Schwarzer, Haywood, & Lorenzen, 2003). These Asian languages were included to show students that not all writing systems are based on the Roman alphabet. Haywood asked parents to find posters that showed the alphabets or writing systems of the different languages represented in the classroom. Parents can also be asked to contribute other print materials in the child's primary language for display in the classroom. These include newspapers, magazines, labels from cans or bottles, and notices.

Schwarzer, Haywood, and Lorenzen (2003) recommended having older siblings, parents, or other adults read aloud books in the primary language. These books can be read to the whole class or just to the students who speak that language. They suggest including books in students' primary languages in the classroom library, so that students can read these books during sustained silent reading or refer to them when conducting research. To the degree possible, written communications from the school to parents should be translated into the students' primary languages. The message that students' primary languages are valued is reinforced if the school and classrooms have signs written in different languages, including "exit," "principal's office," and "welcome" (Schwarzer, Haywood, & Lorenzen, 2003). School displays can celebrate students' language backgrounds, for example, by showing the different primary languages spoken by students in each classroom.

Seeing print materials in their primary languages displayed in the school and classroom signals to students that their languages have a place. Furthermore, when students see the languages of their classmates in print, they begin to take an interest in these languages and in becoming multiliterate.

Teachers who show a respect for and interest in students' heritage languages can make a strong positive impression on students, especially older students who may previously have experienced a devaluing or ignoring of their languages in school. A positive impression can be made on parents, too. Parents can see that they have knowledge that is valued in the classroom, and the teacher has an authentic purpose for calling on them to help. As suggested earlier, the activities incorporating students' heritage languages do not have to be elaborate. The main point is that the teacher has put forth a sincere effort to make these languages part of classroom life.

ASSESSING STUDENTS' LITERACY IN THE PRIMARY LANGUAGE AND IN ENGLISH

Teachers will want to learn if students can read and write in their primary languages, so that they can design lessons that build on this background. If students are literate in their primary language, teachers may be able to make reading materials available to help students at least maintain their literacy in this language. Teachers can create some writing assignments that allow students to compose in the primary language. Teachers can also make use of students' literacy in the primary language to promote their literacy in English. As mentioned earlier, strategies and skills of reading and writing in these languages can be transferred to English.

Teachers may be fortunate enough to find staff members at the school or community members who can help them assess students' literacy in the native language. However, as Schwarzer, Haywood, and Lorenzen (2003) pointed out, teachers do not need to know students' primary languages to do a general assessment of their literacy in these languages. Teachers can ask students or parents about students' literacy in the primary language. Teachers may be able to determine if a student is reading fluently and with expression, or reading haltingly and stumbling over many words, while reading a text in the primary language. Teachers might make use of texts translated from English, such as familiar folk tales or favorites such as *Brown Bear, Brown Bear, What Do You See?* (Martin, 1983). To assess students' reading comprehension, teachers can ask them to represent text ideas using a combination of drawing and writing. Older students may display their proficiency through the use of dictionaries that enable them to translate words from English into their native languages and vice versa.

Students' ability to write in the primary language might be assessed by having them create word lists, followed by the English equivalent (Schwarzer, Haywood, & Lorenzen, 2003). These lists can be posted in the class and may also be a reference for the teacher in communicating with the student.

What about assessing students' literacy in English? Here the recommended approaches are the same as those widely used with native speakers of standard English, namely an analysis of oral reading, such as running records (Clay, 1985) or miscue analysis (Goodman, Watson, & Burke, 1987; Wilde, 2000), and informal reading inventories (e.g., Leslie & Caldwell, 2001). Running records or miscue analysis provide appropriate procedures for assessing students' word identification, whereas informal reading inventories provide information about students' reading comprehension. It is beyond the scope of this book to provide an overall explanation of these procedures (which may be found in the references listed earlier in this paragraph). Instead, I focus on considerations in using miscue analysis and informal reading inventories with second language learners.

Miscue analysis and running records employ somewhat different conventions, but both are based on the idea that fluent, accurate reading depends on the balanced use of three cue systems or sources of information. In miscue analysis, these systems are the *graphophonic,* the *syntactic,* and the *semantic.* In running records, the parallel terms are *visual, structural,* and *meaning.* Freeman and Freeman (2000) noted that miscue analysis can be used with texts in students' primary language or in English. If used when the student is reading in English

> . . . miscues are assessed on the basis of the reader's dialect—the usual way the student speaks English. For example, teachers of students who speak one of the Southeast Asian languages, such as Hmong or Lao, will not be surprised if students read "He walks" as "He walk." These students have not made a

reading miscue. They have simply translated the English text into their normal oral language pattern. Since this is how the student would say the sentence in conversation, it is not rated as a miscue. (p. 86)

This same approach should be observed in considering the miscues of speakers of AAVE (Goodman, 1965) and other nonmainstream varieties of English. It is particularly important to note whether the reader is preserving meaning while reading, even as miscues consistent with his or her oral language are occurring. Readers who preserve meaning have the overall concept that reading is the process of constructing meaning from text. In chapter 9, I discuss skill lessons that may be taught to help second language learners with phonics and syntax or grammar.

Students' results on the Qualitative Reading Inventory (QRI; Leslie & Caldwell, 2001) and other informal reading inventories should also be interpreted in the light of possible differences in culture and language. One of the strengths of the QRI is that it starts with an assessment of the students' prior knowledge about the topics covered in the text. The performance of students of diverse backgrounds may well be affected by their differing cultural and linguistic backgrounds. For example, immigrant students may lack the knowledge of American history, traditions, or culture required to understand a particular passage. Teachers who have assessed students' prior knowledge will know this in advance and can take this factor into consideration when interpreting the results. Another difficulty in interpreting informal reading inventory results stems from the fact that many second language learners who speak a primary language other than English are usually able to comprehend much more about the text than they can express in English (Moll & Diaz, 1987), either orally or in writing. For these reasons, the results obtained may underestimate students' reading comprehension.

FOLLOWING CONSISTENT ROUTINES

In chapter 4, I discussed the importance of routines in the readers' workshop, and I pointed out how routines support the literacy acquisition of students of diverse backgrounds. Routines are especially important with second language learners who need to acquire the secondary discourse of the school and to learn to read and write in mainstream ways. For example, Book Club involves four components: community share, reading, writing, and book club discussions. Teachers can support second language learners by establishing a consistent routine incorporating each of these four components. Students are taught systematically to engage effectively in real reading and writing at these times. A similar point can be made about the writers' workshop. The successful teachers I have observed in classrooms with many second language learners follow a regular routine. They try to hold a writers' workshop every day, and they always begin with a whole-class minilesson. This is followed by time for the students to write, with teacher and peer conferences for those who need assistance. Finally, the class gathers for the Author's Chair (Graves & Hansen, 1983).

Second language learners benefit from consistent routines because they have the opportunity to become familiar with the kinds of language and literacy required during each component of the readers' and writers' workshops. Consider the Author's Chair. At the start of the year, teachers model for students what they can say to receive the piece the author has just read aloud. For example, teachers might model language such as the following:

- Your lead got me interested in hearing the rest of your story.
- Your story had a lot of interesting details.
- I liked your story about visiting your grandmother because it reminded me of a time when I went to see my grandmother.

By hearing the teacher's examples, as well as compliments offered by other students, second language learners gain ideas about what they might say to the author. The process of learning the language and literacy practices appropriate to each different situation, such as the Author's Chair or a peer writing conference, takes time. That is why it is important that an activity such as the Author's Chair take place on a regular basis, over and over again. If students' learning is consistently supported by routines, they can devote their full attention to improving as readers, writers, speakers, and listeners of the language of power.

Peers as well as the teacher can help second language learners adapt to routines during the readers' and writers' workshops. For example, in classrooms with Book Club *Plus*, second language learners can participate with other students (Goatley, Brock, & Raphael, 1995). If available, a peer mediator with the same language background can be assigned to the same book club as the target student. The two students can engage in paired reading, with the peer mediator giving the target student access to the text and necessary background knowledge. During book club discussions, the peer mediator can serve as a translator when the target student has ideas to contribute but is not yet able to express these ideas in English.

PROVIDING COMPREHENSIBLE INPUT

For young students who are second language learners, two particularly effective routines for reading instruction are the reading aloud of picture storybooks and shared reading. Many researchers have highlighted the importance to second language learners of what Krashen (1985) termed *comprehensible input* (see Freeman & Freeman, 2001, for an overview of theories of second language acquisition). Teachers need to make certain that second language learners can comprehend the new material being presented. With picture storybooks, illustrations can reinforce the message of the text, and teachers can attach vocabulary words to the objects or situations pictured. In shared reading, the teacher uses a big book or enlarged text to bring the benefits of family storybook reading into the classroom (Holdaway, 1979). The teacher begins by reading the text aloud as the children follow along. Shared reading (e.g., Koskinen et al., 1999) is almost always based on simple texts with a close match between the words and the pictures. Furthermore, shared reading often involves books with predictable or repetitive texts (e.g., "Brown bear, brown bear, what do you see? I see a red bird looking at me. Red bird, red bird, what do you see?"). During shared reading, second language learners can chime in with the rest of the class and practice saying these language patterns, without the pressure of individual performance.

Using multicultural literature can also make input comprehensible to students, because the content of the text is culturally relevant and familiar. For example, because many students in Hawaii are members of large, multiethnic families, they enjoy the picture storybook *Dumpling Soup* (Rattigan, 1998), featuring a young girl named Marisa. This book tells of a New Year's Day gathering at which it is traditional for women to make dumpling soup. With this book as a starting point, teachers in Hawaii can easily lead students in a discussion in which they compare and contrast their own family traditions for celebrating the New Year with those of Marisa and her family. Furthermore, students can be motivated to write about these traditions for a class book.

USING THE PRIMARY LANGUAGE
AS A BRIDGE TO LITERACY

How can teachers support second language learners in gaining proficiency in literacy in the language of power? In the terms used in chapter 4, this means helping students to acquire the secondary discourse of the school. It seems logical to take an additive approach by building on the foundation of students' first language. However, it may not be obvious how teachers can follow an additive approach.

A first step teachers can take is to allow students to begin by expressing their ideas in the home language, and then teaching them how to express those same ideas in the language of power. For example, I have observed many discussions in classrooms in Hawaii where teachers asked questions in standard English and Hawaiian students responded in HCE. Teachers successful in bringing Hawaiian students to high levels of literacy accept students' answers at the level of ideas. However, they then paraphrase students' ideas in standard English, so that students hear the way their ideas would be expressed in the secondary discourse of the school. For example, a student might describe the problem in the story as "Ruby wen copy," using the "wen" marker that designates the past tense in HCE. The teacher replies, "Yes, you're right, the problem in the story is that Ruby copied what other people were doing." In this case, the teacher accepted the student's idea as correct, then used standard English to restate and extend what the student had said. Typically, I see that students immediately begin to incorporate into their oral responses the standard English elements modeled by the teacher.

Rynkofs (1993) observed the same pattern in his study of the writing instruction provided by Ellen Hino (pseudonym), a successful teacher in a second-grade classroom with Hawaiian children who spoke HCE as their primary language. During the writers' workshop, Ellen was speaking to Raoul about his writing when Ginger entered the conversation: "Ginger [speaking softly]: One time, one time my dad cotch one rabbit. Da ting was running in my uncle's yard and my dad cotch it. Ellen: Your dad caught [emphasis] it and?" (Rynkofs, 1993, p. 129). Later, Ellen used the word "caught" again. The next time Ginger spoke, she substituted "caught" for "cotch." Rynkofs found little evidence of HCE in the children's writing. When children wrote with HCE phrases, they usually shifted their words toward standard English in the process of rereading and revising their writing. For example, in her first draft, LaShawn wrote, "My brother was happy because he is scared of any kind dog." That same day, she reread the last part of this sentence as "any kind of dog." The next day, while reading her draft to Ellen, LaShawn changed the end of the sentence to "all kinds of dogs," the appropriate standard English expression. A few children experienced difficulty making these shifts on their own, and in these cases, Ellen modeled how their ideas could be phrased in standard English. For example, when Dwayne said, "I wen fall right off and I wen land," Ellen provided him with a rewording in standard English: "So why don't you tell us here then—I went up the ramp but I fell off the skateboard" (Rynkofs, 1993, p. 199).

Some teachers believe that errors in students' standard English pronunciation and grammar should be called to their attention, and that students should be required to make corrections on the spot. Erickson (1993) commented on an incident reported in Piestrup's (1973) classic study, in which the teacher was having the children read aloud. The teacher repeatedly corrected an African American first-grade child for pronouncing *what* without the final *t*. As noted earlier, researchers do not consider a pronunciation consistent with the child's first language to be an oral reading error. Erickson noted that this teacher deliberately called attention to the child's first language in a negative way, and that this kind of teacher behavior is bound to build students' resistance to school. Piestrup (1973) found that, in classrooms in which teachers negatively sanctioned students' use of AAVE, students did not learn standard English but continued to speak AAVE throughout the year. In contrast, in classrooms in which teachers built on students' ideas and did not humiliate them for speaking AAVE, students made gains in their ability to use standard English and had higher levels of reading achievement. Piestrup observed both African American and European American teachers using positive approaches to the children's language. She found that effective teachers were in tune with the rhythm of the students' language, encouraged high levels of participation, and acknowledged students' responses in a positive manner. They introduced students to standard English vocabulary and pointed out differences in sounds (for example, between "feed" and "feet").

In chapter 5, I discussed issues of ownership and resistance. Teachers must be aware of motivating students to develop proficiency in standard English and of minimizing students' resistance. ELLs in the primary grades, like the speakers of HCE observed by Rynkofs (1993), are often aware of the differences between their first language and the language of power, and older students are certainly aware of these differences.

Teachers must help students to see the value of learning standard English, in addition to the heritage language. This task is best accomplished by making students aware of times when effective communication requires use of one language or the other. In this way, the status and importance of the language of power can be acknowledged without making students feel that there is no place for their primary language. For example, a teacher in a sixth-grade classroom with many Hawaiian students frequently had her students engage in role playing. Sometimes students played roles that required them to use standard English, and sometimes they played roles that required them to use HCE. When the assignment required students to serve as television newscasters, they performed their parts in standard English. On another occasion, the assignment required students to act out scenes in which they had to say no to peers who were trying to persuade them to go surfing instead of going to school. Students performed these skits in HCE. In both cases, the teacher had students discuss which language they had chosen to use and why. These discussions helped students to recognize the importance of using the language that would be most effective in communicating their messages to particular audiences. Sometimes, but not always, that language will be standard English. At other times, that language will be HCE (or in other settings, AAVE, Spanish, Vietnamese, or other languages).

SUMMARY

One of the ideas discussed in this chapter is that there are two categories of ELLs. The primary languages of some ELLs are recognized and acknowledged by the larger society, but the primary languages of others may be stigmatized and go unrecognized. Dominant group discourse is used to position languages with respect to one another and to give the highest status to the dominant language. From an educator's perspective, however, it is important to recognize the expressive potential of all languages, including nonmainstream varieties of English. All students bring language strengths that may be built on in the classroom, especially if the goal is multilingualism and multiliteracy. Suggestions were provided to help teachers create a place in classrooms for recognizing students' heritage languages, as well as for promoting the language of power.

9

Effective Instruction
of Phonics and Other Skills

One of the recurring themes in this book is the need to give students of diverse backgrounds ample opportunity to develop higher level thinking with text and to learn reading comprehension strategies. In this chapter, I discuss how skills such as phonics can and should receive proper attention in the context of classroom approaches oriented toward higher level thinking. I explain why teachers should view skill instruction as a means of helping students learn about the secondary discourse of the school and mainstream culture. Given this perspective, four guidelines are presented to help teachers provide effective skill instruction for students of diverse backgrounds so that they can achieve high levels of literacy.

PERSPECTIVE ON SKILL INSTRUCTION

The answer to the question of exactly how teachers should approach skill instruction for students of diverse backgrounds is necessarily quite complex. While zeroing in on skills, we must always keep in mind that skills are far from being the whole of reading and writing. Skills are not an end in themselves. Rather, we teach skills to enable students to meet their larger purposes as readers and writers. For example, we teach decoding so that students will be able to gain independence as readers and to read interesting books on their own. We teach spelling so that students will be able to put their ideas down quickly, in a fashion easily read by others. Although acknowledging that all students need basic skills to function capably as read-

153

ers and writers, we must simultaneously avoid the dangerous tendency to overemphasize lower level skills and underemphasize higher level thinking with text in classrooms with students of diverse backgrounds.

In chapter 4, I discussed workshop approaches to literacy instruction. Several points made in that chapter provide the basis for understanding the nature and timing of effective skill instruction for students of diverse backgrounds. I pointed out earlier that students of diverse backgrounds need to learn a new discourse, the secondary discourse of the school, to be successful at literacy learning in the classroom. I discussed Gee's (1994) notions of acquisition and learning and established the importance of both processes for mastering a secondary discourse. In the case of literacy learning in school, I equated acquisition with learning by engaging in the full processes of reading and writing and learning with learning by studying parts of reading and writing.

In essence, skill instruction involves helping students become literate through study of the parts of reading and writing. As pointed out in chapter 4, learning by studying parts of reading and writing must be timed correctly to be effective. According to Gee's (1990) theory of Discourse, instruction in the skills or parts of reading and writing will be most beneficial for students of diverse backgrounds if it occurs after students have already gained some experience with the full processes of reading and writing. These experiences with the full processes are necessary to help students of diverse backgrounds gain familiarity with the secondary discourse of the school, including literacy activities common in the school but not necessarily in the home. School literacy activities that may not occur in the homes of many students of diverse backgrounds include the reading aloud of storybooks and responding to known-answer questions (Heath, 1983). Students need to be involved in the readers' and writers' workshops, where they can engage in the full processes of reading and writing, because these apprenticeship experiences help them to understand some of the major purposes of literacy in the classroom. The job of teaching skills becomes much easier when students see how knowing skills will help them to meet purposes such as reading a fascinating book or composing a narrative about an important life event.

Once students of diverse backgrounds have received adequate apprenticeship experiences with the full processes of reading and writing, they are ready for skill instruction, or study of the parts of reading and writing. Delpit (1986) emphasized the importance of ensuring that students of diverse backgrounds learn such basic skills as phonics and standard English grammar. Delpit described these skills as the codes of the culture of power, her term for the secondary discourse of the school and of mainstream society. Students of diverse backgrounds need instruction in these codes if they are to succeed in school and benefit from opportunities offered by the larger society. However, Delpit (1991) warned, it is important not to limit instruction to basic skills alone, because students of diverse backgrounds must be treated as thinkers and leaders, not just workers and followers.

In earlier chapters, I discussed how easy it can be for educators to fall into the trap of underestimating the intellectual abilities of students of diverse backgrounds and lowering expectations for their achievement. An overemphasis on instruction in basic skills often reflects such a lowering of expectations. Clearly, the challenge for educators concerned about the literacy achievement of students of diverse backgrounds is to find the proper balance between instruction in higher level thinking and in basic skills.

Delpit (1988) found that African American college students welcomed explicit instruction in skills related to the secondary discourse of the school and the larger society, because they understood power relations and the importance of being able to demonstrate their knowledge of the secondary discourse. These students were well aware of their need for standard English skills such as grammar, spelling, and punctuation. They showed resentment when mainstream instructors downplayed the importance of such skills in English classes. Delpit noted that mainstream teachers may not be aware of the importance of standard English skills to students of diverse backgrounds, because these teachers have grown up with the codes of the culture of power and did not themselves depend on instruction in school to learn these codes. Although identifying herself as an advocate of the process approach to writing, Delpit also argued for the importance of product. Students will ultimately be judged by their products, such as essays written for admission to college or when applying for a job. Gatekeepers, such as college admissions officers or company interviewers, are likely to make favorable decisions only if students' products reflect a command of the secondary discourse of the school and larger society, including conventional spelling and standard English grammar.

In short, skill instruction is highly important for students of diverse backgrounds, and educators must find ways to keep skill instruction in proper perspective so that it serves as a means of empowering students to use reading and writing effectively. The guidelines discussed later indicate how skills can be taught effectively and efficiently, enabling teachers to maintain an appropriate balance between instruction in lower level skills and higher level thinking.

PROVIDE A MEANINGFUL CONTEXT
FOR SKILL INSTRUCTION

The first guideline involves placing skill instruction in a meaningful context, so that students of diverse backgrounds can understand why these skills are important. If skill instruction, or studying the parts of reading and writing, precedes engagement with the full processes of reading and writing in school, many students of diverse backgrounds may not see the point of this instruction. Teachers need to be sure to begin skill instruction only after students have gained familiarity with school literacy activities and found these activities to be meaningful in their lives. This view is supported by research in emergent literacy showing that young children's literacy learning starts with an understanding of purposes, not skills (Taylor, 1983; Teale, 1987).

The readers' workshop is helpful in this regard because it provides teachers with the opportunity to help students fall in love with books. Through the readers' workshop, students realize just how enjoyable reading can be. They discover that they can gain lessons and information important to their lives from reading books. The writers' workshop is valuable because it allows teachers to teach students to write from the heart about experiences they have found important. Students learn that writing can be a powerful means of self-expression that leads to insights about one's own life (Calkins, 1994).

In the context of the readers' and writers' workshops, it is easy for teachers to provide skill instruction as a means of helping students with the reading and writing tasks they want to carry out. For example, a student eager to read a biography of the film star Jackie Chan will willingly accept help with decoding unfamiliar words. A student preparing a book about an exciting Halloween adventure will willingly accept help with spelling and punctuation. Engagement in meaningful literacy activities gives students of diverse backgrounds the motivation required to learn and apply skills.

Mrs. Benns, a first-grade teacher observed by Diamond and Moore (1995), fostered her students' attention to skills by reading high-interest books aloud. She captured the children's attention through the beautiful language and illustrations in these books. She reinforced children's awareness of and appreciation for the sounds and rhythms of language through spirited choral reading. Here is a lesson that Diamond and Moore (1995) observed:

. . . Mrs. Benns reinforces understanding of the symbol/sound relationships for her first-graders in the choral reading of *Chicka Chicka Boom Boom*, by

Bill Martin and John Archambault [1989]. After chorally reading the story and experiencing the rhythm and magic of language, her students scan their choral reading to find words that begin with certain sounds. If Mrs. Benns asks them to find a word that begins like *button*, for example, students suggest *"Beat* . . . I'll *beat* you to the top of the coconut tree," or *"Boom* . . . Chicka chicka *boom boom!"* Likewise, if she asks them to find a word that begins like *table*, they place their fingers under their example and respond, *"Tangled.* H is *tangled* up with I," or *"Tooth.* It's black-eyed P, Q R S, and loose-*tooth* T." Having the students share their example first reinforces the letter sound; having the students read the word in the context of its sentence reinforces the sound in meaningful text. As her students begin to learn about ending sounds and vowels, she follows the same techniques to reinforce these symbol/sound relationships. (pp. 105–106)

The rhyme, rhythm, and colorful illustrations of *Chicka Chicka Boom Boom* (XXXX, XXX) make this action-packed alphabet book a favorite of many children. Mrs. Benns first created a meaningful context for the enjoyment of literature and then challenged the children to practice skills in this context. Because the children enjoyed the text, they found the skill activity meaningful and participated enthusiastically. As Mrs. Benns named consonants such as "B" and "T," the children eagerly scanned the text and called out words that began with these letters. Everything seemed to make sense to the children, even the nonword "chicka" used to represent the sound of the letters starting to fall from the coconut tree.

A Counterexample

These observations of Mrs. Benns's classroom may be contrasted with observations in a classroom that lacked the vital ingredient of a meaningful context to make reading a rewarding experience for students of diverse backgrounds. Meyer (2002) observed a typical lesson taught by a first-grade teacher named Karen. Karen taught this lesson from a scripted phonics program that had been mandated by her school district in an effort to raise reading test scores. Karen was an experienced teacher, knowledgeable about constructivist forms of teaching, who was trying to do her best within the confines of the scripted program. She worried about the time spent to complete a phonics lesson: 60 min on this particular day, but up to 90 min on others.

Here are Meyer's (2002) observations:

At 10:05, Karen turns towards the marker board and writes *superman*. Two children call out "Superman!" right away. They are precocious readers and volunteer many of the words Karen writes. . . . Karen erases the <n> in *super-man* and puts a <d> at the end to make the nonword *supermad*. Some of the students in Karen's class believe it is a word, and one child suggests that if you are mad at someone, you "are *supermad* at them." Next Karen puts an <n> back in place of the <d> but then places a <n> after the <n> to make *supermand*. The children slowly work to say the nonword. One calls it out, and a few others echo. They look at their teacher: "What is *supermand*?" asks one.

Karen says, "It's not a word."

Karen erases *supermand* and writes *baboon*, which is read by one of the same two precocious readers. Karen changes it to *baboot*. Some of the children say it; others echo it. Some are silent. (p. 6)

Meyer noted that this lesson taught the children that reading requires accurate sounding out, without the need for the word to make sense. The children had to pronounce the sounds that had been strung together simply so the lesson could move on. For a time, they persisted in trying to make sense of the activity, providing a good guess about the possible meaning of "supermad" before being stumped by "supermand." Sadly, the teacher had to inform the class that "supermand" is "not a word." By the time the teacher presented the nonsense word "baboot," the children had stopped trying to make sense of the activity and their interest had diminished. In a larger sense, Meyer noted, lessons such as this one may be teaching children that reading does not have to make sense and that they do not have to be meaning makers. This is the direct opposite of the message students of diverse backgrounds should receive if we want them to advance in using higher level thinking to comprehend complex texts.

Provide Instruction to Address All Three Stages of Word Identification Development

This second guideline relates to instruction in word identification, a key skill area in beginning reading. Citing common findings across studies by a number of different researchers, Stahl (1997) concluded that children go through three broad stages in learning to identify words. He labeled these stages awareness, accuracy, and automaticity.

In the awareness stage, children are developing a conceptual understanding of the nature of written language and its relation to spoken language. This understanding covers four areas: functions of print (knowing purposes for literacy), conventions of print (knowing, for example, that one reads from left to right), forms of print (knowing that writing consists of letters), and phonemic awareness (knowing that spoken words can be broken into separate sounds or phonemes). Stahl (1997) asserted that these four understandings serve as the foundation for children's later development as readers, and that children are likely to have trouble learning to read when any of these understandings is missing.

In the second stage, accuracy, children learn to decode words accurately. They are focused on print and working to identify words correctly. Sulzby (1985) observed that, in this stage, children who had once freely retold stories from familiar books would refuse to do so, stating, "I don't know the words." Children read text aloud in a laborious, choppy, word-by-word fashion, a phenomenon often termed *word calling*. Stahl (1997) noted that this stage is generally short-lived, leading quickly into the third stage, automaticity, in which children come to recognize words automatically. The rapid, automatic recognition of words is necessary to free up information processing capacity so that students can focus on comprehending (and not just decoding) what they are reading.

This overview of the development of word identification ability has important ramifications for the teaching of students of diverse backgrounds, who often receive large doses of phonics instruction beginning in kindergarten and continuing up the grades. The term *phonics* refers to relations between letters and sounds, or more accurately, spelling-to-sound correspondences (Mason et al., 2003). Considerable research supports the value of phonics instruction (Ehri et al., 2001). Phonics instruction is vital because many children of diverse backgrounds have not learned letter–sound correspondences before entering kindergarten. However, Stahl's (1997) analysis suggests that phonics instruction should be emphasized when children are in the accuracy stage, not earlier (when they are in the awareness stage) or later (when they are in the automaticity stage). Phonics plays a crucial but temporary role, and phonics instruction should be properly timed to achieve its optimal effect.

Awareness Stage

Teachers in kindergarten, first-, and even second-grade classrooms may discover through assessment that quite a number of their students are in the awareness stage. These children show signs of emergent literacy (Teale, 1987). They are reading (or making meaning from) pictures rather than print (Ferreiro & Teberosky, 1982); they are still learning concepts about print, such as the difference between a letter and a word (Clay, 1985); and they are not yet tracking print when they read.

As mentioned earlier, students of diverse backgrounds need to learn the functions of literacy in school before they can gain a good understanding of the forms or skills involved in literacy. For this reason, appropriate activities for students in the awareness stage include the morning message (Crowell, Kawakami, & Wong, 1986) and writing time during the writers' workshop, and shared reading (originally called the shared book experience; see Holdaway, 1979) during the readers' workshop. Examples of these activities are discussed in the next section. Phonics or letter–sound relations can certainly be part of the morning message and shared reading. However, it makes little sense to teach phonics in isolation, or to overemphasize the learning of phonics, for children in the awareness stage. Some kindergarten teachers insist on drilling children on letter names and sounds in isolation, a form of teaching that is too abstract for children in the awareness stage. Too much time spent on phonics often leaves too little time for developing the four foundational understandings identified by Stahl (1997), which are crucial if children are to progress from the awareness stage to the accuracy stage.

Accuracy Stage

Through observation and assessment, teachers learn when children are moving from awareness to accuracy. Children who are making the transition to the accuracy stage will attend to print and not just pictures when they read. They will be able to point to each word as they read the text from a big book the teacher has introduced through shared reading. They will use initial consonant sounds with some degree of accuracy to represent words when they write, and they will be able to reread their writing. Often, these children can read perhaps 20 words by sight, including their name and the names of classmates, as well as common words such as "cat" and "red." Children in the accuracy stage are at the point where they can benefit greatly from instruction in phonics.

However, even when working with children in the accuracy stage, teachers must keep phonics in proper perspective. Because of the attention given to phonics by the popular press, it has been easy for some educators, as well as many members of the general public, to gain the mistaken impression that phonics instruction is all that is necessary to help students become effective at identifying words. Research suggests that using phonics or decoding is just one of at least four ways to identify words (Ehri, 1994). Other ways include reading words by sight, by analogy, and by contextual guessing. Proficient readers are able to read almost all the words they encounter by sight, which is the most efficient and least effortful way to read a word. When they come to an unknown word, proficient readers use analogy, comparing parts of the unknown word to similar words they already know. For example, if the unknown word is "paronym," "par-" at the beginning of the word might be compared to "parent," and "-onym" at the end of the word might be compared to "synonym." Proficient readers do not sound words out letter by letter, because reading words by sight and by analogy takes less time and attention than using phonics. Because they can identify words so easily, proficient readers are able to devote nearly all of their attention to comprehending the text. (Space does not permit a full discussion of the teaching of decoding by analogy. For lesson ideas, refer to Gaskins, Gaskins, & Gaskins, 1991; Gaskins, Ehri, Cress, O'Hara, & Donnelly, 1996; Gaskins, Ehri, Cress, O'Hara, & Donnelly, 1997; Wagstaff, 1997.)

Of course, there is a big difference between proficient and beginning readers. Beginning readers cannot read efficiently, using sight and analogy, because they do not yet have the enormous mental word bank that would allow them to recognize an unknown word instantly or to compare it to parts of other words. This is where phonics can help. Phonics allows beginning readers to use the regularities in the English spelling system to identify unknown words (Mason, Stahl, Au, & Herman, 2003). Note that the purpose of phonics instruction cannot be to make students dependent on decoding every word they see in a letter-by-letter fashion. Reading words in such a slow and laborious manner would take up too much of the students' information processing capacity, leaving too little capacity for comprehending the text. Instead, the purpose of phonics instruction should be to help students build up a store of words that they will be able to draw on in the future, to read most words instantly and automatically. Once identified through phonics, the previously unknown word should become part of the students' automatic recognition mechanism for reading (Rayner & Pollatsek, 1989). Ideally, the word should not have to be laboriously decoded through phonics again. As more and more words can be read effortlessly, children are able to devote more attention to comprehension or understanding the meanings of text, which is the larger purpose for reading.

In the accuracy stage, instruction should definitely focus on phonics. Although phonics can be taught in a rote manner, it appears that children may learn phonics just as well, or even better, if they are allowed to engage in reasoning about the relationships between letters and sounds in the English language. A sample lesson using word sorts (Bear, Invernizzi, Templeton, & Johnston, 2000), which involves children in thinking actively about letters and sounds, is presented later in this chapter.

Another effective approach for teaching phonics through reasoning is invented spelling. Some teachers worry that allowing children to invent their own spellings may hinder their movement toward conventional orthography. For example, the concern is that a child who writes "DG" for "dog" will persist in that misspelling. Research suggests that these fears are groundless—provided that teachers use invented spelling as a springboard for further learning. Studies show that children who are allowed to invent their own spellings for words eventually become better spellers than children who have been taught spelling through rote memorization (Ehri, 1987; Wilde, 2000). The reason appears to be that children who are encouraged to experiment with invented spelling have the chance to infer for themselves how the English spelling system works. In general, the understandings gained stay with these students, whereas students who learn spelling through rote memorization soon forget what they have been taught. The opportunity to use invented spelling may be especially valuable for students of diverse backgrounds who may need numerous opportunities actively to explore and gain understandings of how letters go together to form words. These opportunities are readily provided when teachers conduct the writers' workshop on a daily basis.

A question that frequently arises about phonics instruction is what skills should be taught and in what order. Research points to developmental phases in children's learning to read and spell (Mason, Stahl, Au, & Herman, 2003), and these phases should be the basis for the overall sequence of skill instruction. Teachers may refer to any number of resources to gain an idea of how skill instruction should flow, including reviews of research (e.g., Templeton & Morris, 2000), professional books (e.g., Bear, Invernizzi, Templeton, & Johnston, 2000), state standards documents, district curriculum guides, and the teachers' guides of basal reading programs. In general, all of these resources highlight the same general sequence of skills.

However, within this broad flow, there is no exact order of teaching phonics skills that has been demonstrated to be superior with all, or even most, children (Allington, 1997). The preferred course when determining what skills to teach is to follow the suggestion of Bear, Invernizzi, Templeton, and Johnston (2000). They recommend that teachers look at what children "use but confuse" when deciding what skills to teach next. For example, children who can accurately read and write the initial consonants for words soon recognize that some words start with more than one consonant, showing the teacher that they can benefit from instruction in blends and digraphs. [Blends are combinations of two consonants (such as sp in spot) or three consonants (such as spl in splash) in which the individual letter sounds remain distinct. Digraphs are combinations of consonants (such as ch in chair or sh in shout) that represent a sound in which the individual letter sounds no longer remain distinct.]

Automaticity

What are the signs that students are moving from the accuracy stage to the automaticity stage? In my observations in classrooms in Hawaiian communities, I see that most students make this transition sometime between the end of first grade to the end of third grade (cf. Stahl, 1997). Students making this transition can read most words accurately, although they may have some difficulty pronouncing multisyllablic words such as "grueling" or "rations." However, many students moving into the automaticity stage may be reading slowly and laboriously, without expression. These students need to reach the point where they can identify words quickly and with a minimum of effort. As noted earlier, achieving automaticity in word identification is essential to free up information processing capacity for text comprehension.

Little teaching of new word identification skills is required by students in this stage, and teachers can focus instead on activities that help students gain automaticity and fluency. The "Readers' Theater" is perhaps the most engaging way to provide fluency practice. This activity can grow out of the reading of a work of literature, such as *Lon Po Po: A Red Riding Hood Story From China* (Young, 1990), that includes a considerable amount of dialogue in the text (Au, Carroll, & Scheu, 2001). After students have read and discussed the literature, the teacher has them write their own script of the story. Students can start with the dialogue already in the text, revising some lines and adding others of their own. Students gain fluency as they read and reread their parts in preparation for a presentation to the rest of the class. The teacher models fluent, expressive reading for the students as necessary.

Repeated reading, originally introduced by Samuels (1979) as an individual activity, can be used with the whole class or small groups of children as a means of fostering fluency. Rasinski, Padak, and Sturdevant (1994) recommend that teachers select a high-interest passage of 50 to 150 words. Each student receives a copy of the passage and follows along as the teacher reads it aloud to the group, perhaps more than one time. The teacher and students discuss the content of the passage. Students then engage in choral reading. If the passage is a challenging one, the teacher may read each sentence first, with the children echo reading that sentence. Next, students work with a partner. Each individual reads the passage three times while the partner provides assistance and praise. To gain additional practice, students may take the passage home to read aloud to family members.

Of course, the promoting of automaticity cannot involve only activities, such as the Readers' Theater, centered on reading aloud, because automaticity during silent reading is actually the more important outcome. Therefore, wide, independent reading should be the foundational activity for promoting automaticity. In a study of classrooms in Grades 1 through 3, Taylor, Pearson, Clarke, and Walpole (2000) found that effective teachers gave their students more time for independent reading than did ineffective teachers. Teachers should encourage students who are choppy, word-by-word readers to read and reread easy books (Johns & Lenski, 2001). As students gain automaticity, they can proceed to the independent reading of books closer to their instructional level.

While students are building automaticity in identifying words, skill instruction can shift to a focus on vocabulary and word meanings. Early on, most of the words students need to identify are in their oral vocabularies. However, especially from the fourth grade and above, the amount of content area reading increases, and students begin to encounter words previously unheard and unfamiliar in meaning. Vocabulary instruction can begin with what students have already learned about base words and affixes and proceed to Greek and Latin word elements (Bear, Invernizzi, Templeton, & Johnston, 2000).

In short, when it comes to students' learning of word identification skills, phonics must be recognized as an important piece but not seen as the whole picture. In particular, neglecting automaticity and overemphasizing phonics may depress students' achievement. Analyses of the results of the reading assessment of the NAEP suggest that, by the fourth grade, students' progress may be slowed more by a lack of automaticity than an absence of basic reading skills (Campbell & Ashworth, 1995). In a large-scale study of schools in low-income areas, Taylor, Pearson, Peterson, and Rodriguez (2003) found a negative effect between reading achievement and high levels of phonics instruction at Grades 2 through 5. This same relation was not observed at Grade 1. The findings of Taylor et al. suggest that teachers successful in promoting the literacy achievement of students of diverse backgrounds provide intensive phonics instruction in Grade 1, when most students are in the accuracy stage. In Grades 2 and above, when most students are in the automaticity stage, effective teachers no longer dwell on phonics but move on to activities that promote fluency and build reading comprehension. Specifically, Taylor et al. found a positive relation between reading achievement and teachers' use of higher level questioning.

Teach Skills in an Integrated Manner to Strengthen Students' Understandings and Allow Time for Instruction in Comprehension and Higher Level Thinking

The third guideline for the effective skill instruction of students of diverse backgrounds involves teaching skills in an integrated fashion. Often, teachers have several programs and textbooks for the language arts, with the same skills covered in two or more places. For example, fifth-grade teachers at a school in Hawaii, located in a native Hawaiian community, worked with a basal reading program, a language arts textbook (used as the basis for writing skills), a spelling textbook, and a vocabulary workbook. Some skills, such as synonyms and Latin roots, were addressed in all four of these resources. When these teachers made the shift to readers' and writers' workshops, they created a master list of the key skills they wanted to be certain to teach their fifth-grade students. Then they decided on the context in which particular skills might best be introduced. For example, they decided to teach synonyms during the writers' workshop, because they felt students would recognize that using synonyms might make their writing more colorful. They decided to teach Latin roots during the readers' workshop at a time when the students would be reading a science article including terms such as *erupted* and *destructive*. Taking this approach allowed the teachers to introduce specific skills in the writers' workshop and reinforce them in the readers' workshop, and vice versa. Skill instruction that had previously been fragmented and redundant became streamlined and integrated into meaningful contexts for the students. Because these teachers could now teach lower level skills more efficiently, they had ample time to provide students with instruction on reading comprehension strategies and higher level thinking, as described in chapter 6.

The kindergarten teachers at this school went through a similar process of decision making to create an integrated approach to phonics instruction. They decided to introduce initial consonant sounds during the writers' workshop. These teachers modeled writing through the morning message (Crowell, Kawakami, & Wong, 1986), with an emphasis on using initial consonant sounds to compose sentences. Teachers said the words in the message slowly, pausing to encourage the children to help spell the word by naming its first letter. They taught minilessons showing children how to say words slowly and isolate the sounds, so children could draft their own messages. They introduced children to initial consonants by having the children associate letters and sounds with the names of their classmates ("r" for "Ryan") or familiar objects ("d" for "door").

From the very first day of school, during the daily writers' workshop, teachers monitored the children as they drew pictures and attempted to write letters. Gradually, they identified those who were beginning to grasp the concept of letter–sound relations. Through individual writing conferences and small-group lessons, teachers taught these children first to use initial consonants to label their drawings and then to draft short sentences, using invented spelling. By the spring semester, almost all of the children in these classrooms could use initial consonants to compose a short piece of several sentences during the daily writing period.

A girl in one kindergarten classroom was observed while drafting the following sentence: I am popping firecrackers with my friends at home. She used the skills she had been taught, saying each word slowly to isolate its first sound, then writing the letter. In effect, this girl created a series of phonics exercises for herself, reinforcing her knowledge and understanding of the sounds of "p," "f," "m," and so on. She was motivated to apply her knowledge of consonant sounds because she wanted to write about an exciting event in her life.

The kindergarten teacher in this classroom, along with many others, found that teaching phonics (specifically, consonant sounds) in a meaningful context during the writers' workshop was much faster and more effective than teaching phonics in isolation as part of reading instruction. Once students understand the concept of letter–sound correspondences, it is not difficult for teachers to help them apply their understandings of these correspondences to the stories they see in books during the readers' workshop. In this same classroom, the teacher centered the readers' workshop on big books and shared reading. After children had read and reread a big book such as *To Town* (Cowley, 1990), the teacher wrote the text on sentence strips. Because the illustrations were no longer available, students needed to rely on their knowledge of letters and sounds to read the sentences. They could identify words that began with the same letters, or look for a certain letter within or at the end of a word.

In short, children in kindergarten classrooms received most of their instruction in phonics through the writers' workshop, and the knowledge they learned was then applied and reinforced during the readers' workshop. Like the fifth-grade teachers, the kindergarten teachers found that teaching in an integrated manner allowed them to give students a thorough understanding of skills, while removing redundancy and saving time. The kindergarten teachers had more time for the reading aloud of stories when they could introduce students to comprehension strategies through listening. For example, with a story such as *Swimmy* (Lionni, 1991), students could respond to questions requiring them to make inferences. These experiences gave students background in thinking about the meaning of texts, valuable preparation for the instruction on reading comprehension strategies they would be receiving in later grades.

Word Study Approach

Taking a word study approach can guide teachers to integrate the instruction of specific skills, as shown in the earlier examples from fifth grade and kindergarten, in a research-based manner. As described by Bear, Invernizzi, Templeton, and Johnston (2000), word study involves teaching students to examine words closely so that they can discover for themselves the patterns and rules needed to become good readers and spellers. Word study is based on decades of developmental research on the evolving word knowledge of both children and adults (e.g., Henderson & Beers, 1980; Templeton & Morris, 2000).

To teach following a word study approach, teachers must be familiar with the five stages of reading and spelling development that children move through as they learn to read, write, and spell words. Teachers identify what students understand and are able to do so that they can plan instruction effectively. As shown in Table 9.1, these stages are as follows: (a) emergent and emergent, (b) beginning and letter name–alphabetic, (c) transitional and within word patterns, (d) intermediate and syllables and affixes, and (e) advanced and derivational relations. The brief descriptions provided in Table 9.1 for reading stages are from Bear et al. (2000, p. 14) and for spelling stages from Bear et al. (2000, pp. 17, 21, 23, 25, 27). The descriptions for the spelling stages indicate what students can do correctly when they first enter that particular stage (for details about what students can do in the middle and later part of each stage, refer to Bear et al., 2000). The logic of word study is identical to that followed in our earlier discussion of the stages of word identification, with the difference being that word study is more comprehensive. The awareness stage corresponds to what Bear et al. called the emergent stage of reading. The accuracy stage corresponds to the beginning stage and the early part of the transitional stage. The automaticity stage corresponds to the later part of the transitional stage and to the intermediate and advanced stages.

The word study approach allows teachers to follow the broad developmental trends identified in research, while teaching specific skills according to children's needs and interests. For example, Bear et al. (2000) described a first-grade classroom in which the teacher, Mr. Perez, had divided the stu-

TABLE 9.1
Reading and Spelling Stages

Reading Stage	Spelling Stage	Grade Levels
Emergent—Pretend read.	**Emergent**—Writes on the page, holds the writing implement.	Prekindergarten to middle of Grade 1
Beginning—Read aloud, word-by-word, fingerpoint reading.	**Letter Name–Alphabetic**— Represents most salient sounds, usually beginning consonants.	Kindergarten to middle of Grade 2
Transitional—Approaching fluency, some expression in oral reading.	**Within Word Pattern**—Initial and final consonants, consonant blends and digraphs, regular short vowel patterns.	Grade 1 to middle of Grade 4
Intermediate—Reads fluently with expression. Develops a variety of reading styles. Vocabulary grows with experience, reading, and writing.	**Syllables and Affixes**—Initial and final consonants, consonant blends and digraphs, regular short vowel patterns, plus short vowel patterns, most long vowel patterns, (e.g., ed) and most inflections.	Grades 3 to 8
Advanced—Reads fluently with expression. Develops a variety of reading styles. Vocabulary grows with experience, reading, and writing.	**Derivational Relations**— Spells most words correctly.	Grades 5 to 12

Note.   Adapted from Bear, Invernizzi, Templeton, and Johnston, 2000, pp. 14–27.

dents into three groups. Cynthia's group included children who needed help distinguishing between similar-sounding consonants, such as "v" and "f" and "s" and "c." With this group, Mr. Perez had the children sort pictures by beginning sounds. Later, they drew and labeled pictures starting with these same sounds and did word hunts, looking through texts such as big books for words beginning with these sounds. Children in Tony's group understood beginning and ending consonants but needed help with blends, digraphs, and short vowels. Mr. Perez had these children sort words by phonograms (e.g., "-at," "-an"). Children in Maria's group knew how to deal with blends, digraphs, and short vowels in familiar phonograms. Mr. Perez had these children identify short vowel sounds in nonrhyming words (e.g., "fish," "ship").

In short, Mr. Perez was able to customize instruction to meet the needs of different groups of children by assessing their strengths and weaknesses in reading, writing, and spelling. The use of small groups is essential if teachers are to provide students with skill instruction matched to their needs. Taylor (2002) found that highly accomplished primary-grade teachers in effective schools spent more time teaching students reading in small, flexible groups than as a whole class.

A word study approach involves students in reasoning through hands-on activities that help them to see how words work. For example, in word study, students might sort words according to various characteristics. Younger children might sort words by their spelling patterns, placing all the "-at" words in one group and the "-an" words in another. Somewhat older students might sort words according to whether they contain a prefix, suffix, or both. Middle school students might sort words according to their Greek or Latin roots.

In a word study approach, students are actively involved in thinking about words and their spellings and meanings. This active engagement and reasoning are highly beneficial to students of diverse backgrounds. Some package programs, widely used in schools with many students of diverse backgrounds, center on scripted lessons and the rote learning of skills. The motivation of students of diverse backgrounds may wane when they must repeatedly learn about words through rote memorization rather than reasoning. This problem is especially acute if skill instruction (the study of parts of reading and writing) is taking place in the absence of the readers' and writers' workshops, which provide engagement in the full processes of reading and writing.

Teach According to a Six-Step Process That Leads to the Independent Application of Skills

In chapter 6, I outlined a six-step process for teaching comprehension strategies. This same six-step process can be followed in teaching skills to students of diverse backgrounds. Many package programs routinely skip one or more of these steps during lessons. Lessons typically include explicit explanation, modeling, and independent application but neglect guided practice, coaching, and self-assessment. As discussed earlier, including all of these steps together gives students of diverse backgrounds a better chance of gaining the ability to apply skills when reading and writing on their own.

The following is an example of a lesson using word sorting to teach short vowels, adapted from Bear et al. (2000). This lesson will give you an idea of how skills can be taught following the six steps and moving toward the gradual release of responsibility. First, prepare for the lesson by making a set of word cards you can use to model the sorting activity with an overhead projector or a pocket chart. Begin with step number 1, explicit explanation, telling students the purpose of the lesson:

> I've been noticing that you know how to use consonants sounds very well when you read and write. Now you're ready to learn more about vowel sounds, because learning these sounds will help you to read and write words even more accurately. Today's lesson on words with the short *a*, short *e*, and short *i* sounds will help you with two of our I Can statements: I can decode new words when I read, and I can spell new words when I write.

Move on to step number 2, modeling, to show students how the sorting activity works. Here is the procedure recommended by Bear et al.:

> Begin by laying down a well-known word as a header for each vowel. Read each word and isolate the vowel sound by saying something like this: "Here is the word *cap*. Listen, *cap, ap, a*. We will listen for other words that have the same vowel sound in the middle." Repeat for each category.
>
> Pick up a new word such as *fast* and say something like this: "I am going to put this word under *cap*. Listen, *cap, fast*. Continue to model one or two words in each category, reading each new word and comparing it to the header." (p. 158)

Proceed to step number 3, guided practice:

> Invite students to try sorting next. Correct any errors made during the first sort. The final sort might look something like this:

cap	*pig*	*hot*
fast	ship	stop
camp	fish	lock
hat	sit	shop
mad	hill	job
trap	him	not

> After all the words have been sorted, lead a discussion to focus your students' attention on the common features in each word: "How are the words in each column alike?"
>
> Reread the words in each column and then lead the students in sorting a second time. Any mistakes should be left until the end and checked by reading down the columns. (p. 158)

Follow with step number 4, coaching. Divide students into pairs and have partners work together to sort the words by short vowels. Provide students with helpful hints and other assistance as necessary. Then proceed to step number 5, independent application. Give individual students their own sets of words to sort at their seats, and make note of those who can complete the activity easily versus those who need further instruction. In step number 6, self-assessment and goal setting, have students discuss their own performance during this activity and establish goals for improvement in this area, if needed.

Bear et al. (2000) recommended following this activity with buddy sorting, because it is easy for students to sort the word just by matching the vowel letters, without becoming aware of different vowel sounds. In buddy sorting, one student reads the target word aloud, without showing the card to his or her partner. Because the partner cannot see the card, he or she must make a decision about which of the three cards the target word goes under, on the basis of its pronunciation alone.

In general, vowel sounds show much more variability in pronunciation than consonant sounds. For this reason, Bear et al. (2000) suggested introducing the oddball or miscellaneous category when teaching vowels. They stated the following:

> This category will accommodate variations in dialect and spelling. Some children may hear a short-o in *frost*, but others will hear a sound closer to /aw/. Some children hear a different vowel in *pin* and *pen*, but others consider them homophones. Rather than forcing students to doubt their own ear, the oddball category offers an alternative and acknowledges that people do not all speak quite the same way nor does spelling always match pronunciation. (p. 159)

Teachers will want to remember that students of diverse backgrounds may speak varieties of English in which the pronunciation of some words differs from mainstream pronunciation. Before concluding that students have made an error while sorting words according to vowel sounds, teachers should ask students to read the apparently misplaced word aloud. In many cases, teachers find that students have sorted the words correctly in keeping with their own pronunciation.

Research by Taylor et al. (2000, 2003) provides additional insights about the skill instruction provided by teachers at Grades 1 and 2 who are more or less effective in improving the literacy achievement of students of diverse backgrounds. Somewhat surprisingly, these teachers do not differ in terms of providing students with explicit instruction in phonics. What effective teachers do, that ineffective teachers do not, is cue students to apply the skills they have learned across a range of texts and events and not just during workbook exercises. For example, when a child is struggling with a word in a book chosen for independent reading, the teacher might remind the child to think of another word with that same spelling pattern. In short, throughout the school day, effective teachers cue students to apply the reading and writing skills they have been taught.

SUMMARY

Effective skill instruction for students of diverse backgrounds is based on giving students the opportunity to study the parts of reading and writing, but only after they have gained some experience with school purposes for literacy and with the full processes of reading and writing. I argued that skill instruction is highly important for students of diverse backgrounds, because they must master what Delpit (1986) called the codes of the culture of power or the secondary discourse of the school and mainstream society. I suggested four guidelines for making skill instruction highly beneficial to students of diverse backgrounds. First, skills should be taught in a meaningful context, so that students see the point of learning skills and are motivated to do so. Second, instruction should be provided to address all three stages of word identification development, avoiding an imbalance in which students receive extensive instruction in phonics but little or no instruction directed toward building awareness and automaticity. Third, skills should be taught in a well organized, integrated manner that both strengthens students' understandings and leaves time for instruction in comprehension strategies and higher level thinking. Following a word study approach can be very helpful for these purposes. Finally, skill instruction should follow a six-step process that leads to the gradual release of responsibility, including teacher cueing to promote the application of skills across a wide variety of tasks and texts.

10

Schoolwide Change to Improve Literacy Achievement

In other chapters in this volume, I have provided principles and ideas that teachers can put into practice in their own classrooms. This chapter differs in addressing change at the level of the whole school, rather than the classroom, to improve the literacy achievement of students of diverse backgrounds. I begin the chapter by discussing why whole-school change based on standards is needed and why educators should focus on in-depth change for long-lasting results and avoid the temptation of superficial quick fixes. Four characteristics of in-depth change are presented. I then discuss the standards-based change process (SBCP) as an example of a system with these four characteristics. The SBCP centers on a nine-step To-Do List, and each of these steps is described. I close this chapter and the volume with a discussion of the importance of long-lasting change for schools serving students of diverse backgrounds.

THE STAIRCASE CURRICULUM

Chapter 1 presented evidence documenting a literacy achievement gap between students of diverse backgrounds and mainstream students (Grigg, Daane, Jin, & Campbell, 2003). With the sweeping changes brought about by globalization, students of diverse backgrounds need many more opportunities, than they presently receive, to learn comprehension strategies and higher level thinking with text. Efforts undertaken by individual classroom teachers to improve students' literacy achievement, for example, by provid-

173

ing sound instruction in comprehension strategies, can certainly be effective—for that year. As explained in chapter 6, comprehension strategies and higher level thinking involve complex, multistep cognitive processes that take time for students to learn. Clearly, students of diverse backgrounds stand a much better chance of becoming excellent readers when they receive coherent literacy instruction, coordinated across the grades. Coherence in a school's instructional program has been found to be related to improvements in achievement test scores (Newmann, Smith, Allensworth, & Bryk, 2001).

In an effective whole-school change effort in literacy, the goal is to create a staircase or spiral curriculum in which students receive well organized, coordinated instruction that enables them to make consistent progress as they move up the grades (cf. Taba, 1962). The left half of Fig. 10.1 shows such a staircase curriculum. The top step represents the vision of the excellent reader who graduates from that school. Beginning at the bottom of the staircase, each step is intended to move students closer to the achievement of this vision. Figure 10.1 uses the example of an elementary school with students from kindergarten to Grade 5. After gaining a thorough understanding of the vision of the excellent reader who graduates from their school, the kindergarten teachers define the end-of-year literacy outcomes they will help their students attain. These outcomes form the first step. The first-grade teachers define the end-of-year literacy outcomes they want their students to attain, and these outcomes form the second step. This same process continues up the grades. Teachers make the adjustments in end-of-year outcomes necessary to ensure that students can move up the staircase systematically, year after year, to achieve the vision of the excellent reader.

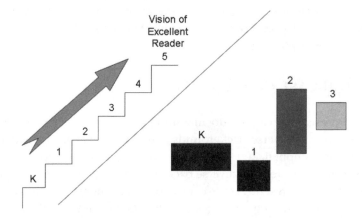

FIG. 10.1.   Staircase versus fragmented curriculum.

Obviously, this kind of coordination in end-of-year outcomes can only be achieved when teachers at different grade levels or departments are communicating with one another on a regular basis.

The right half of Fig. 10.1 shows a fragmented curriculum, the opposite of the staircase curriculum and the situation seen in many schools, including those serving large numbers of students of diverse backgrounds. At the typical school, teachers at different grade levels may well have planned interesting literacy lessons and thematic units for their students. However, although coordinated within the grade level or department, these lessons and units usually are not coordinated across the grade levels or departments. The progress of students of diverse backgrounds, who may struggle with literacy learning in school, is hampered by the gaps between the learning opportunities presented from one grade level to the next.

Research suggests that a coherent curriculum helps students make achievement gains because they have the time to acquire basic skills as well as the strategies needed to tackle challenging tasks (Newmann, Smith, Allensworth, & Bryk, 2001). Students' motivation also appears to improve when there is continuity in instruction within and among classes over time (Pittman, 1998). Success builds on success, because as students gain confidence, they are willing to work harder and can more readily learn.

WHOLE-SCHOOL REFORM MODELS AND PACKAGE PROGRAMS

The approach to building instructional coherence through a staircase literacy curriculum, recommended here, is the SBCP. Before turning to details of the SBCP, I want to address a frequently asked question: Why should the teachers at a school have to develop their own staircase curriculum? Why not just adopt a ready-made, externally developed solution? The answer to this question is that schools enrolling high proportions of students of diverse backgrounds almost always do rely on ready-made, externally developed solutions. Yet this proclivity seems to me to be one of the reasons that so few of these schools ever succeed in bringing students of diverse backgrounds to high levels of literacy.

Two major patterns are observed at many schools that do not succeed in elevating the literacy achievement of students of diverse backgrounds. In the first pattern, the school attempts to work with a variety of initiatives (Newmann et al., 2001). Teachers divide up to attend the workshops and conferences related to each initiative. Over time, it becomes clear that these initiatives have collectively failed to produce improvements in student achievement, and teachers experience feelings of frustration and burnout. Even as failed initiatives are discontinued, the school still adds one new program after another. This "Christmas tree" pattern continues in part because of the positive attention and resources the school receives for undertaking each new initiative (Bryk, Sebring, Kerbow, Rollow, & Easton, 1998). A "Christmas tree" school often looks good in the eyes of outsiders, such as district officials and community members, because of its high level of activity. A "Christmas tree" school does not succeed because it lacks a central focus. Teachers' time and energies are always scattered across several different initiatives, and no new effort ever becomes the focus of sufficient attention to yield positive results in terms of student achievement.

Administrators at schools that follow the second pattern understand that they must avoid the "Christmas tree" problem. They believe they can achieve curricular coherence by focusing on a single externally developed solution, either a whole-school reform model (Newmann et al., 2001) or a package reading program, as a means of pulling the staff together. Whole-school reform models and package programs give the appearance of being a ready-made solution to the problem of coherence in a school's literacy instruction efforts. This choice is made easy for schools because whole-school reform models or package programs are often supported or even mandated by school districts. Furthermore, adopting an established model or program involves less effort and commitment on the part of the teachers than developing a unique, school-based solution.

Yet, all whole-school reform models and package programs prove themselves effective in some schools but ineffective in others (cf. International Reading Association, 1999). Newmann et al. (2001) explained why this is the case. Whole-school reforms may be effective in spurring a school to make improvements or to restructure. However, these reforms may not succeed either in aligning together all of the components (such as school leadership, teachers' professional development, and parent involvement) at a school or in establishing definite links among all of these components and student learning. Whole-school reform models may succeed or fail, not only because of weaknesses in their design, but also because of the manner in which they are implemented at a particular school.

Similar conclusions can be drawn about package reading programs. I followed the achievement results of a number of Hawaii schools that had used the same package reading programs over periods of 3 to 5 years or more. Some schools showed gains in test scores, especially in the first 2 years, with small but steady improvements in later years. In other schools, test scores remained at the same level with no significant gains, whereas in others, scores even declined a bit. The reasons for these differences were often obvious to teachers within the schools, as well as to district officials. Successful schools had principals who provided strong leadership, pulled the school together around the package program, and declined to have the school participate in initiatives that might detract from its focus. Large schools had a strong curriculum coordinator who monitored the details of program implementation that the principal did not have time to pursue. Teachers at successful schools received extensive professional development that gave them the knowledge needed to successfully implement the program. Less successful schools generally lacked strong leadership, curriculum support, and coordinated professional development. In short, it was not the program alone, but the way it was carried out and supported in a particular school, that made the difference. Clearly, factors other than a whole-school reform model or package program come into play to influence a school's success in improving the literacy achievement of students of diverse backgrounds.

DIMENSIONS OF SCHOOL CHANGE

Most policymakers, district leaders, and researchers tend to see change in schools as largely a matter of "scaling up" reform efforts. In the common view, the idea is to identify effective programs and to disseminate these programs to as many schools as possible (e.g., Slavin & Madden, 1994). Some of the problems with this view of educational change have already been discussed, in terms of the potential weaknesses of whole-school reform models and package reading programs. Research by Coburn (2003) presented a different picture of what it means to extend reform efforts. She argued that the strength of reform efforts should be judged not simply on the basis of the number of schools and districts involved, but according to four related dimensions: depth, sustainability, spread, and shift in the ownership of reform.

In terms of depth, Coburn (2003) pointed out that the history of public education is filled with reform efforts that failed to reach into the classroom and affect instruction. Quite naturally, teachers tend to gravitate toward teaching approaches compatible with their existing beliefs and prior practice. Therefore, Coburn suggested, reforms need to bring about "deep and consequential change in classroom practice" (p. 4). In my view, Coburn's notion of depth is particularly significant in schools with many students of diverse backgrounds, because of research pointing to the poor quality of instruction students typically receive (e.g., Darling-Hammond, 1995; Fitzgerald, 1995). As established in earlier chapters, students of diverse backgrounds benefit from instruction that focuses on higher level thinking (Taylor, Pearson, Peterson, & Rodriguez, 2003) and develops their ownership of literacy (Au, 1997). Coburn's concept of depth includes changes in teachers' beliefs about students and their abilities, and their expectations for students. Lipman's (1998) study of reorganization in two middle schools serving African American students verified the importance of changing teachers' attitudes and expectations. Restructuring in these schools was conceptualized as an "at-risk" project. Unfortunately, using the "at risk" label permitted teachers to view their African American students as deficient in terms of mainstream norms, without considering their cultural and linguistic strengths. In Lipman's view, a change effort with depth helps teachers to see that it is educational institutions and their systems that need fixing, not students of diverse backgrounds.

The second dimension identified by Coburn (2003) is sustainability. Coburn found few studies of schools that had been involved in the same reform for 4 years or more. In my experience, it takes schools from 2 to 3 years to make significant changes, and the longer a school can move in a consistent direction, the better. For example, the principal of a successful school in a rural, low-income community in Hawaii reported that his school had worked for 8 years to raise their reading achievement scores. When I asked what his school had done that less successful schools had not, he replied that his school had not chosen a whole-school reform model or a package program. Instead, his school decided to stick to its own plan because students were beginning to make good progress. However, he and the teachers examined these models and programs for ideas and concluded that they needed to increase the amount of time students spent in small-group instruction. This consistency of direction and leadership over a long period of time is noted as well in other schools that beat the odds, those that have attained higher than expected reading achievement scores within their demographic category. For example, Mosenthal, Lipson, Sortino, Russ, and Mekkelsen (2002) described two successful rural schools that had begun the change process about 10 years earlier.

Because schools are embedded in districts, which in turn are embedded in states, schools have a better chance to sustain reform when their efforts are supported by these larger systems. A few coordinated state and district efforts seem to have led to substantive change at the classroom level (e.g., Connecticut, described in Darling-Hammond, 2003; Michigan, described in Dutro, Fisk, Koch, Roop, & Wixson, 2002; and Nebraska, described in

Gallagher, 2004). However, because these efforts are rare, strong leadership at the school level is likely to be a more reliable route to positive change in the classroom. Principals, curriculum coordinators, resource teachers, and other leaders who can maintain a consistent focus for a period of years are particularly important for the many schools located in large, highly politicized, urban districts.

The third dimension of change identified by Coburn (2003) is spread. Certainly, spread involves the idea that reforms should move out to a growing number of classrooms and schools. However, Coburn noted that it is also important to look at the spread of new norms and instructional principles within classrooms and schools. She argued that spread of this nature can be especially important with reforms that challenge conventional teaching approaches. If the goal is to close the literacy achievement gap, reforms that challenge conventional teaching approaches are the right choice. According to Coburn, reforms must show spread in the sense that new practices become embedded or institutionalized in the school's policies and routines. At the classroom level, spread can be indicated by the extent to which teachers apply the new instructional principles and norms of interaction to subjects and activities beyond those originally targeted.

The final dimension identified by Coburn (2003) concerns the shift in the ownership of reform. Many, but not all, reforms are initiated externally, rather than internally by the administrators and teachers at a school. However, if a reform is to be sustained for the length of time required to make significant improvements in student achievement, it must be valued and taken over by the school itself. Coburn pointed out that discussions of ownership typically focus on the early stages of reform, such as teachers' "buy-in," rather than on sustainability over the long term, such as how the school will maintain its direction in the face of new mandates. A key feature identified by Coburn was the capacity of the school and district to provide reform-related professional development and other mechanisms for promoting ongoing teacher and administrator learning. Too often, professional development related to the reform continues to be supplied by an external provider, a situation that prevents ownership from shifting to educators in the school and district.

In considering how to move their whole school forward, staff members at schools enrolling a high proportion of students of diverse backgrounds will want to remember Coburn's (2003) four dimensions. In schools with a history of poor performance on large-scale measures of literacy achievement, accountability pressures have made change a necessity, not an option. Because these accountability pressures are often associated with standards, that is the next topic I address.

Standards and the Staircase Curriculum

When the standards movement began in the 1980s, standards were proposed as a means of establishing a public conversation about the goals of education, and that intent found continued expression as the years went on (e.g., Pearson, 1993). Advocates of standards argued that goals for student learning were too often implicit in textbooks and the minds of educators and therefore inaccessible to parents and the general public, not to mention students. In my view, this original vision of standards and the public conversation about the goals of education remains a powerful and potentially beneficial concept, especially for students and families in marginalized communities.

Unfortunately, standards have come to be associated, not with a public conversation about the goals of education, but with accountability pressures and mandated testing. In many cases, these tendencies have had devastating effects on schools serving large numbers of students of diverse backgrounds. Darling-Hammond (2003) found that, in several states, standards and accountability were equated with high-stakes testing, and not with policies related to improving the quality of teaching or the allocation of resources. With high-stakes testing, crucial decisions about students are made on the basis of test results, often in the absence of other evidence about student performance. For example, students whose test scores fall below the bar may not be able to advance to the next grade or to earn a high school diploma. Darling-Hammond pointed out that, in states relying on high-stakes testing as the major policy reform, disproportionate numbers of students of diverse backgrounds experience failure in school. In these cases, expectations for the performance of students and teachers have been raised without provisions for the resources that would enable success, such as professional development for teachers or up-to-date textbooks for students.

Haney (2000), Gordon and Reese (1997), Paris, Lawton, Turner, and Roth (1991), and others have documented the negative effects of high-stakes testing, especially on students of diverse backgrounds. Because of pressures to raise test scores, schools can be tempted to resort to such measures as retaining students in their present grade or encouraging them to drop out of school. Some states, including Florida, Georgia, Massachusetts, New York, and Texas, have seen rising dropout rates as an apparent effect of such policies as holding students back in the same grade (Darling-Hammond, 2003).

Furthermore, high-stakes testing, when unaccompanied by adequate support for teachers and students to meet rising expectations, often results in the sanctioning of schools with low test scores. Often, the sanctioned schools are those serving large numbers of students of diverse backgrounds. Sanctioned schools, and those about to be sanctioned, have an even more difficult time recruiting the well-qualified teachers who could turn the situation around. In the words of a principal, "Is anybody going to want to dedicate their lives to a school that has already been labeled a failure?" (Darling-Hammond, 2003, p. 2). In this way, the vicious cycle created by high-stakes testing can inflict further damage on the students already least well served by schools.

Darling-Hammond (2003) emphasized the need for midcourse corrections if standards are to promote greater equality, rather than inequality, in educational outcome. According to Darling-Hammond, successful reforms do not emphasize high-stakes testing. Instead, these efforts focus on the use of standards to guide and upgrade teaching and learning. Standards, curriculum, and assessment are aligned and oriented toward higher level thinking. Multiple measures of student achievement are endorsed, including portfolios containing samples of completed classroom assignments. Teachers receive extensive professional development that gives them the knowledge to use standards to change their schools and improve their instruction (Dutro et al., 2002). These changes contribute to school-based systems that improve student achievement through standards.

Rationale for the Standards-Based Change Process

The SBCP is designed to help schools implement a system for improving student achievement through standards. The SBCP leads schools to develop their own staircase curriculum in reading and writing, as well as in other content areas. The logic of the SBCP is that every school, but especially one serving many students of diverse backgrounds, should take charge of its own future and create its own system for closing the literacy achievement gap. A school that successfully implements the SBCP arrives at an ongoing, schoolwide conversation about what everyone at the school is doing to improve student achievement. Over time, participation in this schoolwide conversation results in a closer coordination of teachers' efforts across grade levels and departments and leads to improved teaching and learning and steadily rising expectations for student performance.

The To-Do List

The SBCP centers on a nine-step To-Do List, shown in Fig. 10.2. Many teachers have knowledge of most, if not all, of the steps. However, in conducting SBCP workshops with leadership teams from over 100 public schools in Hawaii, I did not encounter any school that already had all the steps in place. The To-Do List is shown in a circular form, with arrows going back and forth between the steps, to show that the process of working through the To-Do List is recursive. That is, as they gain new insights, teachers often go back and forth between the steps. For example, after teachers have scored students' work with rubrics, they often see ways of strengthening their procedures for collecting evidence. The following description of the SBCP assumes that the school has decided to focus on reading, the subject area most often addressed first. The exact same steps are followed when the SBCP is applied to writing, mathematics, science, and other areas.

Philosophy.   The starting point in the To-Do List is the philosophy or underlying beliefs of the teachers at the school. In the SBCP, the focus is on beliefs about teaching, learning, and literacy. Teachers work in small

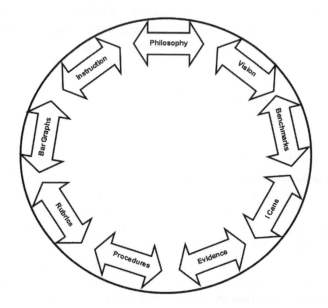

FIG. 10.2.   The To-Do List as a recursive process.

groups, usually by grade levels or departments, to arrive at two key beliefs about teaching, two about learning, and two about literacy. For example, a typical belief about teaching is that the teacher must be able to adjust instruction to reach all children, whereas a typical belief about learning is that all children can learn, although they may learn at different rates and through different means. Beliefs about literacy often center on the importance of reading and writing for different purposes, including school, work, and personal enjoyment, and on literacy as a process of lifelong learning. Each small group records its beliefs on chart paper and then shares its beliefs with the whole school. The leader or facilitator of the meeting highlights common beliefs that cut across the small groups and appear to be held by most of the faculty.

A discussion of philosophy is necessary to establish the foundation for the SBCP, or, for that matter, any other whole-school change effort. Although this step in the change process is often neglected, it is especially important at schools serving students of diverse backgrounds. Many of these schools experience high rates of teacher turnover. As a result, teachers usually know little about the educational philosophies of the other teachers in their own grade level or department, much less outside that immediate circle. Furthermore, rifts sometimes exist between grade levels or departments, due to earlier misunderstandings and differences in perspective. When a discussion of philosophy is conducted, beliefs about teaching, learning, and literacy can be made explicit. This process often allows teachers to see that they have much more in common with one another than they had assumed. The discussion of philosophy also serves as the occasion when the principal and other leaders can affirm the school's unwavering commitment to helping students of diverse backgrounds reach high levels of literacy.

Vision of the Excellent Reader.   The philosophical beliefs of the faculty serve as the springboard for creating a vision of the excellent reader who graduates from the school. The vision centers on the kind of reader teachers want their students to become by the time they exit at Grade 5, 8, 12, or other, depending on the highest grade level in the school. The purpose of the vision of the excellent reader is to provide a common overall goal to which all teachers will be directing their instructional efforts in reading. Most schools already have a general vision statement developed during strategic planning or for the purposes of accreditation. This statement often describes what the school—not students—will do or be (for example, provide a safe and nurturing environment) and so does not eliminate the need for a separate vision of the excellent reader.

Teachers work in the same small groups to draft their vision statements. At this point, all groups focus on the excellent reader who graduates from school, not on the outcomes for their particular grade or course. For example, if the school goes up to Grade 5, kindergarten teachers draft a vision of the excellent reader who graduates at Grade 5, not of the excellent reader at the end of the kindergarten year. As before, each group writes its vision statement of the excellent reader on chart paper, and the results are shared and discussed by the whole faculty. Because it is difficult to work out the precise details of wording in a large group, the appropriate committee in the school, usually a language arts or curriculum committee, takes responsibility for developing the wording of the final vision statement. The committee's proposed statement is brought back to the whole faculty for approval, and the vision statement of the excellent reader is posted in a prominent spot for continued reference.

Here is the vision statement created by teachers at a middle school in Hawaii:

> The successful reader who leaves Wheeler Middle School will be able to read with a clear purpose, engage in an ongoing process of questioning to understand big concepts and generalizations, and continue to apply and make connections.

The teachers at this school were familiar with the definition of reading and levels of reading performance used in the NAEP (NAEP, 2004), and their vision statement reflects this knowledge. Vision statements of the excellent reader frequently include such ideas as the following: students will read for different purposes, read with understanding and confidence, enjoy reading, make personal connections, and be lifelong literacy learners. In my experience, the vision statements of successful schools with many students of diverse backgrounds often include both cognitive and affective dimensions by incorporating the notions of higher level thinking with text and students' ownership of literacy.

Grade Level or Department Benchmarks. Once teachers have agreed on the vision of the excellent reader they will all work to achieve, they are ready to develop benchmarks. Benchmarks are defined as the expectations for the hypothetical average student at the end of the year in an elementary school, or at the end of a course in a secondary school. To decide on the benchmarks, teachers think about the kind of performance they would hope to see from the typical student who has been well taught throughout the year. Teachers create five to seven benchmarks in reading. Of course, the benchmarks do not reflect everything that is taught in reading, only the most important outcomes. I recommend that teachers develop reading benchmarks to address three areas: (a) attitudes, (b) comprehension, and (c) strategies and skills.

Here are typical reading benchmarks developed by teachers at schools in Hawaii. Examples of primary- and upper-elementary grade benchmarks are shown for each of the three areas:

- Attitudes.
  - ○ Children will enjoy reading everyday. (Kindergarten)
  - ○ Students will have favorite authors and topics for voluntary reading. (Grade 5)
- Comprehension.
  - ○ Children will identify the problem and solution in the story. (Grade 1)
  - ○ Students will construct the theme for the story and give reasons for their idea. (Grade 4)
- Strategies and skills.
  - ○ Children will read a grade-level text aloud with 90% accuracy. (Grade 2)
  - ○ Students will monitor their comprehension and seek clarification when necessary. (Grade 6)

Developing benchmarks is the most challenging item on the To-Do List, for good reason. Teachers have no difficulty when the task is to brainstorm a long list of benchmarks. However, they must think long and hard when forced to limit the list to a handful of the most important outcomes. Teachers should take their time when creating benchmarks, because sound benchmarks are crucial to the successful implementation of the SBCP.

Once they have a good draft, teachers check their benchmarks against state, district, or other standards to which their benchmarks should be aligned. This process of alignment is important for two reasons. First, teachers must make certain that they are teaching the appropriate content, with the appropriate degree of rigor, according to state, district, and other guidelines that their school should follow. Second, teachers need to build confidence in their own professional judgment. On checking these documents, they almost always receive validation that they are thinking along the right lines. Teachers revise their benchmarks for content and rigor, and in my experience, only minor revisions are usually required.

Then teachers share their benchmarks with the whole school. The purpose of sharing is to help everyone in the school become informed about the end-of-year targets being proposed by each grade or department. In this first round, no pressure is put on teachers to coordinate benchmarks across the whole school. However, teachers often notice inconsistencies and make the appropriate adjustments. For example, the first-grade teachers at one school learned that the second-grade teachers expected their students to read informational text to write a simple research report. As a result, the first-grade teachers decided that they would add a benchmark on the reading of informational text as well as fiction.

"I Can" Statements.   Grade-level benchmarks are written in the professional language of educators. However, particularly in the primary grades, children may have difficulty understanding this language. To foster greater student understanding, teachers translate the benchmarks into "I Can" statements for the students (cf. Cleland, 1999). Here are examples of "I Can" statements based on the primary-grade benchmarks presented earlier:

• I can tell about the problem in the story and how it was solved.
• I can read the words in a story written for second graders.

Teachers may work with their colleagues to reword the benchmarks as "I Can" statements, or they may hold class discussions to enlist students in developing wording for the "I Can" statements. "I Can" statements serve as an essential link between standards and students, because discussions of "I Can" statements help students become familiar with what they are expected to learn at each grade level.

Many teachers put the "I Can" statements on charts or posters where they can easily be seen in the classroom. When they teach a lesson, they refer to the "I Can" statement being addressed. Through the use of "I Can" statements, teachers can make the connection between instruction and standards explicit for students. In chapter 6, you read about a comprehension strategy lesson that began with the teacher identifying the "I Can" statement being addressed. Similarly, in chapter 9, you read about a skill lesson that opened with the teacher stating the two "I Can" statements being covered. As these examples illustrate, "I Can" statements play a central role in the SBCP, because they keep the attention of both the students and the teacher focused on important learning outcomes.

An added bonus of "I Can" statements is that they can serve as a useful communication tool with parents. During an open house or during parent–teacher conferences, teachers can refer to the "I Can" statements when explaining to parents what their children are being taught. In this way, standards for student learning become clear to parents as well, and parents are better able to assist their children in meeting the benchmarks.

Evidence. After teachers have decided on the benchmarks and "I Can" statements, they identify the kinds of evidence they will collect to monitor students' progress toward meeting the benchmarks. In general, classroom work is the type of evidence most likely to provide teachers with information useful for analyzing strengths and weaknesses in students' performance and improving instruction. Teachers can select assignments typical of the ones students are often asked to complete. For example, if the benchmark addresses summarization, the evidence might be the summaries students have written about a chapter of a novel.

Table 10.1 shows examples of benchmarks with the evidence that teachers might collect. Most teachers working with the SBCP do not rely on tests developed by outsiders, such as the end-of-unit or end-of-level tests often found in package reading programs. For example, if the benchmark addresses summarization, students' progress cannot be measured by a test that consists of multiple-choice and fill-in-the-blank items. Teachers come to prefer their own classroom-based measures because they can tailor these measures to assess the benchmarks directly.

Procedures for Collecting Evidence. Teachers must not only identify the kinds of evidence they will use to assess students' progress—they must also identify the procedures for collecting the evidence. The importance of this step on the To-Do List became clear to me one day when I was working with a group of third-grade teachers. The teachers had previously agreed that they would use story summaries as the evidence that their stu-

TABLE 10.1
Benchmarks and Evidence

Benchmark	Evidence
Students have the habit of daily reading.	Book logs for SSR and home reading.
Students comprehend informational text.	File cards with notes for research reports.
Students understand the characteristics of different genres.	Completed matrices for biography, historical fiction, fantasy.
Students monitor their own comprehension.	Double-entry journals showing questions and reflections on the novel.

dents could comprehend a text at the third-grade level. In one of the four classrooms, the teacher had obtained written summaries far superior to those of her colleagues. All of the teachers had given their students the same directions, and students in all classes had read the same text. However, in three classrooms, the students went straight from reading the text to writing their summaries. In the fourth classroom, the teacher had led the students in a discussion of the story before they wrote their summaries. Apparently, this scaffolding helped the students in this class to write stronger summaries.

In my opinion, either procedure for collecting evidence about students' comprehension—with or without the class discussion—might be appropriate at the third grade. The point is that all the teachers in a grade level or department must agree on the procedures to be followed, so that they will be able to aggregate their results. Groups of teachers working with the SBCP usually create a list of the exact procedures they will follow in collecting evidence for a particular benchmark. Teachers forge agreements about the wording of the directions students will be given about the task, the amount of time students will have to complete the task, and the degree of scaffolding or assistance students will receive. For example, students might or might not be allowed to consult a dictionary or other resources.

An important issue centers on how often evidence should be collected. In most schools in the SBCP, evidence is collected three times: at the beginning (pretest), in the middle (midyear check), and at the end (posttest) of the school year. Most schools establish a 2-week window for each of these evidence collection periods (for example, first 2 weeks in September, first 2 weeks in January, and last 2 weeks in May), when all the teachers gather evidence on their students' performance. Teachers at many schools are accustomed to collecting pretest and posttest results. The SBCP includes a midyear check to allow teachers time to make any necessary adjustments to instruction before the high-stakes, large-scale testing that occurs in the spring in most districts. Some schools in the SBCP collect evidence on a quarterly basis, but many schools do not, because the results for the first and second quarters tend to be quite similar.

Rubrics. Once teachers have collected their evidence, the question arises of what this evidence indicates about student progress. Thus, the next step on the To-Do List focuses on the development of rubrics or procedures for scoring the evidence. In some cases, I work with experienced teachers who already have in place suitable rubrics matching their benchmarks and evidence. In this situation, teachers show students the rubrics in advance, so that knowledgeable students can address the rubrics in their work.

In many other cases, I work with teachers who need to develop new rubrics. These teachers follow the procedure of first collecting student evidence. On the basis of their own professional judgment, they sort the evidence into stacks representing three levels of performance: working on (below grade level), meeting (at grade level), or exceeding the benchmark (above grade level). Focusing first on the student evidence that appears to be meeting the benchmark, teachers identify the characteristics of this work. After teachers have settled on the characteristics of work that meets the benchmark, they usually do not have a difficult time deciding on the characteristics of performance that indicate students are working on or exceeding the benchmark. In the SBCP, the category of exceeding the benchmark is reserved for work that indicates students are performing at a level typical of those in the grade level above. For example, to show work exceeding the benchmark, a third grader must demonstrate comprehension of a fourth-grade text by writing a summary comparable to one written by a typical fourth grader.

Rubrics play a critical role in the SBCP because they represent the clearest and most detailed statement of teachers' expectations for students' end-of-year performance, based on grade-level benchmarks. Teachers find rubric development challenging, because to develop a sound rubric, they must be extremely clear in their own minds about the kind of performance they want to see. In essence, a sound rubric should read like a list of minilessons. If the rubric is sufficiently detailed, teachers can easily identify students' strengths and weaknesses and the kind of instruction they need.

A group of third-grade teachers worked with the following benchmark: "Students will be able to summarize a story." The "I Can" statement for this benchmark was "I can summarize a story." The evidence was a written summary of a story at the third-grade level. The procedures for collecting evidence were that students would independently read the text and write their summaries. The teachers taught students story elements and familiarized them with the rubric. However, when collecting the evidence, they decided not to cue students about story elements required, because they believed that students should be able to include the required elements on their own. Here is the rubric these teachers developed:

- Above grade level.
  - ○ The response shows a clear understanding of the story and includes the elements of setting, character, problem, solution, and theme.

- ○ The response provides accurate and relevant information and shows sound reasoning about the story.
- • At grade level.
  - ○ The response shows an adequate understanding of the story and includes the story elements of setting, character, problem, and solution.
  - ○ The response provides accurate information, although not all of this information may be central to the story.
- • Below grade level.
  - ○ The response is incomplete and shows little understanding, or inaccurate understanding, of the story.
  - ○ The response may include random details and unimportant information.

Although these teachers were targeting the comprehension strategy of summarization, a kind of higher level thinking, they kept their rubric brief and to the point.

Bar Graphs.   In the next step in the SBCP, teachers prepare and present their scored student evidence in the form of bar graphs. In my experience, this is the step most unfamiliar to many teachers. The bar graphs serve several purposes. First, they provide teachers and administrators with a clear picture of students' progress on targeted benchmarks at the beginning, middle, and end of the year. Second, bar graphs give teachers and administrators an easy way of sharing the overall results of instruction with a variety of audiences, including fellow teachers, parents, community members, district administrators, and policymakers. Third, bar graphs send a clear message that accountability and improving student achievement are central concerns of the school.

In the bar graphs, teachers map out the number of students whose evidence has been rated as working on, meeting, or exceeding the benchmark at each of the three assessment points. Figure 10.3 presents a sample classroom bar graph. These results, for a second-grade class in reading comprehension, are typical of those seen at Title I schools during their second year in the SBCP. At the beginning of the school year, most of the students scored below the benchmark, an expected finding given that benchmarks are set for the end of the school year. At the midyear check, some students had progressed from the working on to the meeting category. At the end of the school year, the majority of students could produce work showing they met the benchmark, and the number of students working on the benchmark

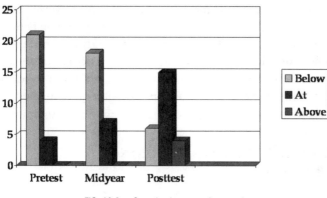

FIG. 10.3. Sample classroom bar graph.

had fallen. A small number of students had exceeded the benchmark. In my observations, teachers in Title I schools frequently focus on moving students from the working on to meeting categories. Teachers will also want to be aware of moving students from the meeting to the exceeding category.

Instructional Improvements. The final step in the SBCP involves instructional improvements. I am often asked why instruction appears at the end of the To-Do List, when instruction is obviously the way to improve student achievement. The reason that instruction comes last is because gains in achievement do not occur as a consequence of making changes to instruction willy-nilly. Instead, in efforts to close the literacy achievement gap, the starting point for instruction must be teachers' clear understanding of the kind of performance they want to see in their students by the end of the year—their grade-level or department benchmarks. Once the benchmarks have been identified, teachers need to know how well students are performing on these benchmarks, hence the need to identify evidence and procedures for collecting evidence before making changes to instruction.

To focus instruction to move students forward, teachers must carefully analyze student evidence according to their rubrics. This analysis reveals to teachers the content, strategies, and skills needed by the whole class or by small groups of students. Teachers can then design lessons to be given to the whole class or a flexible skill group. For example, a group of fourth-grade teachers learned from their pretest results that their students could not determine important information when they read nonfiction text written at the fourth-grade level. They decided that they should teach whole-class comprehension strategy lessons on determining importance when reading nonfiction. In terms of the comprehension of fiction, these teachers found that most of their students did quite well. However, a few of their students could not determine the important information in fiction because they did not know story elements well, particularly the concept of theme. The teachers decided to conduct small-group lessons for these few students. They knew that whole-class lessons would not be a good solution in this case, because most of their students did not require further instruction in story elements.

REGULAR REPORTING AND RISING EXPECTATIONS

SBCP schools establish a regular schedule in which teachers report on their bar graphs and plans for instructional improvements at three times during the school year, following the collecting, scoring, and analysis of student evidence for the pretest, midyear check, and posttest. Successful schools often use a day when teachers can meet together in the morning to revise their rubrics, score and analyze their evidence, and arrive at instructional improvements. Teachers in each grade level or department then prepare a presentation reflecting everything they have done on the To-Do List and including as well their reflections on the whole-school change process. After lunch, the whole school gathers to hear and discuss the department or grade-level presentations. Some teachers prefer to create their presentations on a computer, using a program such as Microsoft PowerPoint. Others prefer overhead transparencies or large charts. The exact form of the presentation matters less than the fact that these thrice-yearly reporting events foster an ongoing, schoolwide conversation about what all the teachers are doing to improve students' literacy achievement through standards.

How does the SBCP contribute to improvements in students' literacy learning? Teachers' clarity about exactly what they would like their students to learn—as indicated in grade-level or department benchmarks—is the key to rising achievement in literacy. Experienced teachers who are crystal clear about their goals for student learning are willing and able to acquire and apply the instructional strategies needed to move students in the right direction. As teachers teach to the benchmarks, they help more and more students to reach these goals. As an increasing number of students are able to meet the benchmarks, teachers see that they can aim for higher levels of learning. Teachers in SBCP schools benefit from the work of teachers at the lower grades in finding that their students arrive better prepared than ever before. Over time, teachers in these schools establish a cycle of rising expectations, allowing steady improvement in literacy achievement.

In my experience, schools that use the SBCP generally have strong, positive relationships with parents and the community. Parents indicate that they appreciate the "I Can" statements, which make expectations for their children's performance clear to them. Parents and community members attend gallery walks or curriculum fairs where they can view displays prepared by grade levels or departments, showing rubrics, anchor pieces, bar graphs, and other products stemming from work with the To-Do List. These events show parents and the community what the school is doing to address standards and how students are progressing. In the future, it will be important for schools in diverse communities to involve parents and community members not only as consumers of standards-based reform but as full participants. For example, parents and community members can contribute to the school's vision of the excellent reader and writer by informing educators about literacy practices valued in the community.

CONCLUDING COMMENTS

In concluding this chapter and the volume, I address the SBCP and the four dimensions of change identified by Coburn (2003) and connect these concepts to the goal of closing the literacy achievement gap. The SBCP enables schools to implement a system for improving students' literacy learning through standards. This approach to school change centers on the notion that each school should have its own literacy curriculum, developed by its own teachers for its own students. This approach represents the antithesis of the usual situation in schools serving students of diverse backgrounds, in which the norm is to adopt an externally developed program to solve the problem of low achievement.

In terms of Coburn's (2003) four dimensions, the SBCP has "depth" in leading to significant changes in classroom instruction, as teachers become clear about their end-of-year outcomes for students' literacy achievement and focus their instruction, especially on comprehension strategies and higher level thinking with text. The SBCP has "sustainability" in establishing a direction for change that teachers take responsibility for maintaining—because they see the difference in their students' learning. The SBCP has "spread" in helping schools to institutionalize a system for improving student achievement through standards. With the SBCP, schools keep to a schedule in which teachers collect, analyze, and report on evidence of student progress three times a year, year after year. This consistency of direction allows schools to stay the course for the period of time necessary to bring about improvement in students' literacy achievement. Finally, the

SBCP leads to a "shift in the ownership" of reform, as teachers develop their own curriculum, tailored to their students' needs as literacy learners. Teachers recognize that, although externally developed models and programs may provide useful materials and lessons, these models and programs must match their school's own literacy curriculum, not the other way around. In short, the best chance for closing the literacy achievement gap lies in strong schools staffed by expert teachers who set higher and higher expectations for students of diverse backgrounds and provide the powerful instruction that allows students to meet these expectations.

References

Achor, S., & Morales, A. (1990). Chicanas holding doctoral degrees: Social repro-
duction and cultural ecological approaches. *Anthropology and Education Quarterly, 21*(3), 269–287.

Allington, R. L. (1983). The reading instruction provided readers of differing abilities. *Elementary School Journal, 83*, 548–559.

Allington, R. L. (1991). Children who find learning to read difficult: School responses to diversity. In E. H. Hiebert (Ed.), *Literacy for a diverse society: Perspectives, practices, and policies* (pp. 237–252). New York: Teachers College Press.

Allington, R. L. (1997, August–September). Overselling phonics. *Reading Today*,
pp. 15–16.

Allington, R. L., & Walmsley, S. A. (1995). *No quick fix: Rethinking literacy programs in America's elementary schools*. New York: Teachers College Press.

Anderson, R. C., & Pearson, P. D. (1984). A schema-theoretic view of basic processes
in reading comprehension. In P. D. Pearson (Ed.), *Handbook of reading research* (pp. 255–291). New York: Longman.

Atwell, N. (1987). *In the middle: Writing, reading, and learning with adolescents*.
Portsmouth, NH: Boynton/Cook.

Au, K. H. (1992). Constructing the theme of a story. *Language Arts, 69*, 106–111.

Au, K. H. (1993). *Literacy instruction in multicultural settings*. Fort Worth, TX:
Harcourt Brace.

Au, K. H. (1994). Portfolio assessment: Experiences at the Kamehameha Elementary
Education Program. In S. W. Valencia, E. H. Hiebert, & P. P. Afflerbach (Eds.), *Au-
thentic reading assessment: Practices and possibilities* (pp. 103–126). Newark,
DE: International Reading Association.

Au, K. H. (1997). Ownership, literacy achievement, and students of diverse cultural
backgrounds. In J. T. Guthrie & A. Wigfield (Eds.), *Reading engagement: Moti-*

vating readers through integrated instruction (pp. 168–182). Newark, DE: International Reading Association.

Au, K. H. (1998). Social constructivism and the school literacy learning of students of diverse cultural backgrounds. *Journal of Literacy Research, 30,* 297–319.

Au, K. H. (2000). Literacy education in the process of community development. In T. Shanahan & F. Rodriquez-Brown (Eds.), *Forty-ninth yearbook of the National Reading Conference* (pp. 61–77). Chicago: National Reading Conference.

Au, K. H. (2001). Culturally responsive instruction as a dimension of new literacies. *Reading Online, 4*(8). Available: http://www.readingonline.org/newliteracies/ lit_index.asp?HREF=au/index.html

Au, K. H., & Carroll, J. H. (1997). Improving literacy achievement through a constructivist approach: The KEEP Demonstration Classroom Project. *Elementary School Journal, 97,* 203–221.

Au, K. H., Carroll, J. H., & Scheu, J. (2001). *Balanced literacy instruction: A teacher's resource book.* Norwood, MA: Christopher–Gordon.

Au, K. H., & Kawakami, A. J. (1994). Cultural congruence in instruction. In E. R. Hollins, J. E. King, & W. Hayman (Eds.), *Teaching diverse populations: Formulating a knowledge base* (pp. 5–23). Albany: State University of New York Press.

Au, K. H., & Mason, J. M. (1981). Social organizational factors in learning to read: The balance of rights hypothesis. *Reading Research Quarterly, 17,* 115–152.

Au, K. H., & Mason, J. M. (1983). Cultural congruence in classroom participation structures: Achieving a balance of rights. *Discourse Processes, 6,* 145–167.

Au, K. H., & Raphael, T. E. (1998). Curriculum and teaching in literature-based programs. In T. E. Raphael & K. H. Au (Eds.), *Literature-based instruction: Reshaping the curriculum* (pp. 123–148). Norwood, MA: Christopher–Gordon.

Au, K. H., & Raphael, T. E. (2000). Equity and literacy in the next millennium. *Reading Research Quarterly, 35,* 170–188.

Banks, J. A. (1995). Multicultural education: Its effects on students' racial and gender role attitudes. In J. A. Banks & C. A. M. Banks (Eds.), *Handbook of research on multicultural education* (pp. 617–627). New York: Macmillan.

Barrera, R. B., Thompson, V. D., & Dressman, M. (1997). *Kaleidoscope: A multicultural booklist for grades K–8.* Urbana, IL: National Council of Teachers of English.

Bartoli, J. S. (1995). *Unequal opportunity: Learning to read in the U.S.A.* New York: Teachers College Press.

Baugh, J. (1999). *Out of the mouths of slaves: African American language and educational malpractice.* Austin: University of Texas Press.

Baugh, J. (2002). *Beyond Ebonics: Linguistic pride and racial prejudice.* Oxford, England: Oxford University Press.

Bear, D. R., Invernizzi, M., Templeton, S., & Johnston, F. (2000). *Words their way: Word study for phonics, vocabulary, and spelling instruction.* Upper Saddle River, NJ: Merrill.

Bennett, K. P., & LeCompte, M. D. (1990). *The way schools work: A sociological analysis of education.* Hillsdale, NJ: Lawrence Erlbaum Associates.

Berliner, D. C., & Biddle, B. (1997). *The manufactured crisis: Myths, frauds, and the attack on America's public schools.* White Plains, NY: Longman.

Bishop, R. S. (1994). *Kaleidoscope: A multicultural booklist for grades K–8.* Urbana, IL: National Council of Teachers of English.

Boggs, S. T. (1972). The meaning of questions and narratives to Hawaiian children. In C. Cazden, V. John, & D. Hymes (Eds.), *Functions of language in the classroom* (pp. 299–327). New York: Teachers College Press.

Brock, C. H., Boyd, F. B., & Moore, J. C. (2003). Variation in language and the use of language across contexts: Implications for literacy learning. In J. Flood, D. Lapp, J. R. Squire, & J. M. Jensen (Eds.), *Handbook of research on teaching the English language arts* (pp. 446–458). Mahwah, NJ: Lawrence Erlbaum Associates.

Brown, J. S., Collins, A., & Duguid, P. (1989). Situated cognition and the culture of learning. *Educational Researcher, 18*(1), 32–42.

Bryk, A. S., Sebring, P. B., Kerbow, D., Rollow, S., & Easton, J. (1998). *Charting Chicago school reform.* Boulder, CO: Westview Press.

Burbules, N. C., & Torres, C. A. (2000). Globalization and education: An introduction. In N. C. Burbules & C. A. Torres (Eds.), *Globalization and education: Critical perspectives* (pp. 1–26). New York: Routledge.

Calkins, L. M. (1994). *The art of teaching writing.* Portsmouth, NH: Heinemann.

Campbell, J. R., & Ashworth, K. P. (Eds.). (1995). *A synthesis of data from NAEP's 1992 integrated reading performance record at grade 4.* Washington, DC: U.S. Department of Education, Office of Educational Research and Improvement.

Carnoy, M. (1974). *Education as cultural imperialism.* New York: McKay.

Carrasco, R. L., Vera, A., & Cazden, C. (1981). Aspects of bilingual students' communicative competence in the classroom: A case study. In R. P. Duran (Ed.), *Latino language and communicative behavior.* Norwood, NJ: Ablex.

Cary, S. (2000). *Working with second language learners.* Portsmouth, NH: Heinemann.

Cazden, C. B. (1988). *Classroom discourse: The language of teaching and learning.* Portsmouth, NH: Heinemann.

Clay, M. M. (1985). *The early detection of reading difficulties.* Portsmouth, NH: Heinemann.

Cleland, J. V. (1999). We Can charts: Building blocks for student-led conferences. *The Reading Teacher, 52*(6), 588–595.

Coburn, C. E. (2003). Rethinking scale: Moving beyond numbers to deep and lasting change. *Educational Researcher, 32*(6), 3–12.

Cohen, P. A., Kulik, J. A., & Kulik, C. C. (1982). Educational outcomes of tutoring: A meta-analysis of findings. *American Educational Research Journal, 19*(2), 237–248.

Cole, A. D. (2003). *Knee to knee, eye to eye: Circling in on comprehension.* Portsmouth, NH: Heinemann.

Compton-Lilly, C. (2003). *Reading families: The literate lives of urban children.* New York: Teachers College Press.

Crowell, D. C., Kawakami, A. J., & Wong, J. (1986). Emerging literacy: Reading–writing experiences in a kindergarten classroom. *The Reading Teacher, 40*, 144–149.

Cushman, E. (1998). *The struggle and the tools: Oral and literate strategies in an inner city community.* Albany: State University of New York Press.

D'Amato, J. (1986). *"We cool, tha's why"*: A study of personhood and place in a class of Hawaiian second graders. Honolulu: University of Hawaii, Department of Anthropology.

D'Amato, J. (1988). "Acting": Hawaiian children's resistance to teachers. *Elementary School Journal, 88,* 529–544.

Darling-Hammond, L. (1995). Inequality and access to knowledge. In J. A. Banks & C. A. M. Banks (Eds.), *Handbook of research on multicultural education* (pp. 465–483). New York: Macmillan.

Darling-Hammond, L. (2003). *Standards and assessments: Where we are and what we need.* Retrieved, from the World Wide Web: http://www.tcrecord.org

Delpit, L. (1988). The silenced dialogue: Power and pedagogy in educating other people's children. *Harvard Educational Review, 58,* 280–298.

Delpit, L. (1995). *Other people's children: Cultural conflict in the classroom.* New York: New Press.

Delpit, L. D. (1986). Skills and other dilemmas of a progressive Black educator. *Harvard Educational Review, 56,* 379–385.

Delpit, L. D. (1991). A conversation with Lisa Delpit. *Language Arts, 68,* 541–547.

Dewey, J. (1944). *Democracy and education: An introduction to the philosophy of education.* New York: The Free Press.

Diamond, B. J., & Moore, M. A. (1995). *Multicultural literacy: Mirroring the reality of the classroom.* White Plains, NY: Longman.

Dole, J. A., Duffy, G. G., Roehler, L. R., & Pearson, P. D. (1991). Moving from the old to the new: Research on reading comprehension instruction. *Review of Educational Research, 61*(2), 239–264.

Duke, N. K., & Pearson, P. D. (2002). Effective practices for developing reading comprehension. In A. E. Farstrup & S. J. Samuels (Eds.), *What research has to say about reading instruction* (pp. 204–242). Newark, DE: International Reading Association.

Dutro, E., Fisk, M. C., Koch, R., Roop, L. J., & Wixson, K. (2002). When state policies meet local district contexts: Standards-based professional development as a means to individual agency and collective ownership. *Teachers College Record, 104*(4), 787–811.

Ehri, L. C. (1987). Learning to read and spell words. *Journal of Reading Behavior, 19,* 5–31.

Ehri, L. C. (1994). Development of the ability to read words: Update. In R. Ruddell, M. Ruddell, & H. Singer (Eds.), *Theoretical models and processes of reading* (pp. 323–358). Newark, DE: International Reading Association.

Ehri, L. C., Nunes, S. R., Stahl, S. A., & Willows, D. M. (2001). Systematic phonics instruction helps students learn to read: Evidence from the National Reading Panel's meta-analysis. *Review of Educational Research, 71,* 393–447.

Erickson, F. (1993). Transformation and school success: The politics and culture of educational achievement. In E. Jacob & C. Jordan (Eds.), *Minority education: Anthropological perspectives* (pp. 27–51). Norwood, NJ: Ablex.

Erickson, F., & Mohatt, G. (1982). Cultural organization of participation structures in two classrooms of Indian students. In G. B. Spindler (Ed.), *Doing the ethnog-*

raphy of schooling: Educational anthropology in action (pp. 132–174). New York: Holt, Rinehart & Winston.

Ferreiro, E., & Teberosky, A. (1982). *Literacy before schooling.* Portsmouth, NH: Heinemann.

Fitzgerald, J. (1995). English-as-a-second-language reading instruction in the United States: A research review. *Journal of Reading Behavior, 27,* 115–152.

Florio-Ruane, S. (2001). *Teacher education and the cultural imagination: Autobiography, conversation, and narrative.* Mahwah, NJ: Lawrence Erlbaum Associates.

Fordham, S., & Ogbu, J. U. (1986). Black students' school success: Coping with the burden of 'acting white'. *Urban Review, 18,* 176–206.

Foster, M. (1997). *Black teachers on teaching.* New York: The New Press.

Fountas, I. C., & Pinnell, G. S. (1996). *Guided reading: Good first teaching for all children.* Portsmouth, NH: Heinemann.

Freeman, D. E., & Freeman, Y. S. (2000). *Teaching reading in multilingual classrooms.* Portsmouth, NH: Heinemann.

Freeman, D. E., & Freeman, Y. S. (2001). *Between worlds: Access to second language acquisition.* Portsmouth, NH: Heinemann.

Friedman, T. L. (2000). *The Lexus and the olive tree: Understanding globalization.* New York: Farrar, Straus & Giroux.

Galda, L. (1998). Mirrors and windows: Reading as transformation. In T. E. Raphael & K. H. Au (Eds.), *Literature-based instruction: Reshaping the curriculum* (pp. 1–11). Norwood, MA: Christopher–Gordon.

Gallagher, C. W. (2004). Turning the accountability tables: Ten progressive lessons from one 'backward' state. *Phi Delta Kappan, 85*(5), 352–360.

Gallimore, R., Boggs, J. W., & Jordan, C. (1974). *Culture, behavior and education: A study of Hawaiian-Americans.* Beverly Hills, CA: Sage.

Gaskins, I. W., Ehri, L. C., Cress, C., O'Hara, C., & Donnelly, K. (1996). Procedures for word learning: Making discoveries about words. *The Reading Teacher, 50,* 312–327.

Gaskins, I. W., Ehri, L. C., Cress, C., O'Hara, C., & Donnelly, K. (1997). Analyzing words and making discoveries about the alphabetic system: Activities for beginning readers. *Language Arts, 74,* 172–184.

Gaskins, R. W., Gaskins, J. C., & Gaskins, I. W. (1991). A decoding program for poor readers—and the rest of the class, too! *Language Arts, 68,* 213–225.

Gay, G. (2000). *Culturally responsive teaching: Theory, research, and practice.* New York: Teachers College Press.

Gee, J. P. (1989a). Literacy, discourse, and linguistics: An introduction. *Journal of Education, 171,* 5–17.

Gee, J. P. (1989b). What is literacy? *Journal of Education, 171,* 18–25.

Gee, J. P. (1990). *Social linguistics and literacies: Ideology in discourses.* London: Falmer Press.

Gee, J. P. (1994). First language acquisition as a guide for theories of learning and pedagogy. *Linguistics and Education, 6,* 331–354.

Goatley, V. J., Brock, C. H., & Raphael, T. E. (1995). Diverse learners participating in regular education "Book Clubs". *Reading Research Quarterly, 30,* 352–380.

Gollnick, D. M., & Chinn, P. C. (2002). *Multicultural education in a pluralistic society*. Upper Saddle River, NJ: Merrill.

Goodman, K. (1965). A linguistic study of cues and miscues in reading. *Elementary English, 42*, 639–643.

Goodman, Y., Watson, D., & Burke, C. (1987). *Reading miscue inventory: Alternative procedures*. New York: Richard C. Owen.

Goodwin, M. H. (1982). Processes of dispute management among urban black children. *American Ethnological Society, 9*, 76–96.

Gordon, S. P., & Reese, M. (1997). High stakes testing: Worth the price? *Journal of School Leadership, 7*, 345–368.

Graves, D. (1983). *Writing: Teachers and children at work*. Exeter, NH: Heinemann.

Graves, D. (1994). *A fresh look at writing*. Portsmouth, NH: Heinemann.

Graves, D., & Hansen, J. (1983). The author's chair. *Language Arts, 60*, 176–183.

Grigg, W. S., Daane, M. C., Jin, Y., & Campbell, J. R. (2003). *The nation's report card: Reading 2002* (NCES 2003-521). Washington, DC: U.S. Department of Education, Institute for Education Sciences.

Haney, W. (2000). The myth of the Texas miracle in education. *Education Policy Analysis Archives, 8*(41).

Hansen-Krening, N., Aoki, E. M., & Mizokawa, D. (2003). *Kaleidoscope: A multicultural booklist for grades K–8*. Urbana, IL: National Council of Teachers of English.

Heath, S. B. (1982). What no bedtime story means: Narrative skills at home and school. *Language in Society, 11*, 49–76.

Heath, S. B. (1983). *Ways with words: Language, life, and work in communities and classrooms*. Cambridge, England: Cambridge University Press.

Henderson, E., & Beers, J. (1980). *Developmental and cognitive aspects of learning to spell*. Newark, DE: International Reading Association.

Henry, J. (1972). *Jules Henry on education*. New York: Random House.

Hirsch, E. D., & Trefil, J. S. (1987). *Cultural literacy: What every American needs to know*. Boston: Houghton Mifflin.

Hoffman, J. V., Assaf, L. C., & Paris, S. G. (2001). High-stakes testing in reading: Today in Texas, tomorrow? *The Reading Teacher, 54*, 482–492.

Holdaway, D. (1979). *The foundations of literacy*. Sydney, Australia: Ashton Scholastic.

Hollins, E. R. (1982). The Marva Collins story revisited. *Journal of Teacher Education, 33*(1), 37–40.

Howard, A. (1974). *Ain't no big thing*. Honolulu: University of Hawaii Press.

Howard, E. R., & Christian, D. (2002). *Two-way immersion 101: Designing and implementing a two-way immersion education program at the elementary level*. Santa Cruz: University of California, Center for Research on Education, Diversity, and Excellence.

Hull, G., & Schultz, K. (2001). Literacy and learning out of school: A review of theory and research. *Review of Educational Research, 71*(4), 575–611.

International Reading Association. (1999). *Using multiple methods of beginning reading instruction: A position statement of the International Reading Association*. Newark, DE: International Reading Association.

Jacob, E., & Jordan, C. (1993). Understanding minority education: Framing the issues. In E. Jacob & C. Jordan (Eds.), *Minority education: Anthropological perspectives* (pp. 3–25). Norwood, NJ: Ablex.

Jimenez, R. T., Moll, L. C., Rodriguez-Brown, F. V., & Barrera, R. B. (1999). Latina and Latino researchers interact on issues related to literacy learning. *Reading Research Quarterly, 34*, 217–230.

Johns, J. L., & Lenski, S. D. (2001). *Improving reading: Strategies and resources.* Dubuque, IA: Kendall/Hunt.

Johnson, D. W., Johnson, R. T., & Holubec, E. J. (1994). *New circles of learning: Cooperation in the classroom and school.* Washington, DC: Association for Supervision and Curriculum Development.

Jordan, C. (1985). Translating culture: From ethnographic information to educational program. *Anthropology and Education Quarterly, 16*, 105–123.

Kamehameha Schools Office of Program Evaluation and Planning. (1993). *Native Hawaiian educational assessment 1993.* Honolulu, HI: Kamehameha Schools Bernice Pauahi Bishop Estate.

Kincheloe, J. L., & McLaren, P. (2000). Rethinking critical theory and qualitative research. In N. K. Denzin & Y. S. Lincoln (Eds.), *Handbook of qualitative research* (2nd ed., pp. 279–313). Thousand Oaks, CA: Sage.

Kindler, A. L. (2002). *Survey of the states, limited English proficient students and available educational programs and services: 1999–2000 summary report.* Washington, DC: The George Washington University and National Clearinghouse for the English Language Acquisition and Language Instruction Educational Programs.

King, S. H. (1993). The limited presence of African-American teachers. *Review of Educational Research, 63*, 115–149.

Knobel, M. (2001). "I'm not a pencil man": How one student challenges our notions of literacy "failure" in school. *Journal of Adolescent and Adult Literacy, 44*, 404–414.

Kong, A., & Fitch, E. (2003). Using Book Club to engage culturally and linguistically diverse learners in reading, writing, and talking about books. *The Reading Teacher, 56*, 352–362.

Koskinen, P. S., Blum, I. H., Bisson, S. A., Phillips, S. M., Creamer, T. S., & Baker, T. K. (1999). Shared reading, books, and audiotapes: Supporting diverse students in school and at home. *The Reading Teacher, 52*, 430–444.

Kozol, J. (1992). *Savage inequalities: Children in America's schools.* New York: HarperCollins.

Krashen, S. (1985). *Inquiries and insights.* Haywood, CA: Alemany Press.

Labov, W. (1969). The logic of nonstandard English. In J. Alatis (Ed.), *Georgetown Monograph Series on Languages and Linguistics* (Vol. 22, pp. 1–44). Washington, DC: Georgetown University Press.

Ladson-Billings, G. (1994). *The dreamkeepers: Successful teachers of African American children.* San Francisco: Jossey-Bass.

Ladson-Billings, G. (1995). Toward a theory of culturally relevant pedagogy. *American Educational Research Journal, 32*, 465–491.

Lambert, W. E. (1987). The effects of bilingual and bicultural experiences on children's attitudes and social perspectives. In P. Homel, M. Palij, & D. Aaronson (Eds.), *Childhood bilingualism: Aspects of linguistic, cognitive, and social development* (pp. 197–221). Hillsdale, NJ: Lawrence Erlbaum Associates.

Larson, J., & Irvine, P. D. (1999). "We call him Dr. King": Reciprocal distancing in urban classrooms. *Language Arts, 76*, 393–400.

Leslie, L., & Caldwell, J. (2001). *Qualitative Reading Inventory—3*. New York: Longman.

Lindholm-Leary, K. J. (2001). *Dual language education*. Clevedon, England: Multilingual Matters.

Lipka, J., Mohatt, G. V., & the Ciulistet Group. (1998). *Transforming the culture of schools: Yup'ik Eskimo examples*. Mahwah, NJ: Lawrence Erlbaum Associates.

Lipman, P. (1998). *Race, class, and power in school restructuring*. Albany, NY: State University of New York.

Lipman, P. (2002). Making the global city, making inequality: The political economy and cultural politics of Chicago school policy. *American Educational Research Journal, 39*, 379–419.

Loewen, J. W. (1995). *Lies my teacher told me: Everything your American history book got wrong*. New York: Touchstone.

Lomowaima, K. T. (1995). Educating Native Americans. In J. A. Banks & C. A. M. Banks (Eds.), *Handbook of research on multicultural education* (pp. 331–347). New York: Macmillan.

Lopez, M. E. (1999). *When discourses collide: An ethnography of migrant children at home and at school*. New York: Peter Lang.

Lowe, L. (1996). *Immigrant acts: On Asian American cultural politics*. Durham, NC: Duke University Press.

Lum, D. H. Y. (1990). *Pass on, no pass back!* Honolulu, HI: Bamboo Ridge Press.

Manyak, P. C. (2001). Participation, hybridity, and carnival: A situated analysis of a dynamic literacy practice in a primary-grade English immersion class. *Journal of Literacy Research, 33*, 423–465.

Mason, J. M., Stahl, S. A., Au, K. H., & Herman, P. (2003). Reading: Children's developing knowledge of words. In J. Flood, D. Lapp, J. R. Squire, & J. M. Jensen (Eds.), *Handbook of research on teaching the English language arts* (pp. 914–930). Mahwah, NJ: Lawrence Erlbaum Associates.

McDermott, R. (1993). The acquisition of a child by a learning disability. In S. Chaiklin & J. Lave (Eds.), *Understanding practice: Perspectives on activity and context* (pp. 269–305). New York: Cambridge University Press.

McMillon, G. T., & McMillon, V. D. (2004). The empowering literacy practices of an African American church. In F. B. Boyd, C. H. Brock, & M. S. Rozendal (Eds.), *Multicultural and multilingual literacy and language: Contexts and practices* (pp. 280–303). New York: Guilford.

Mehan, H. (1979). *Learning lessons: Social organization in the classroom*. Cambridge, MA: Harvard University Press.

Mehan, H., Hubbard, L., Lintz, A., & Villanueva, I. (1994). *Tracking untracking: The consequences of placing low track students in high track classes* (Research Report No. 10). Washington, DC, and Santa Cruz, CA: National Center for Research on Cultural Diversity and Second Language Learning.

Mehan, H., Hubbard, L., & Villanueva, I. (1994). Forming academic identities: Accommodation without assimilation among involuntary minorities. *Anthropology and Education Quarterly, 25*(2), 91–117.

Meyer, R. J. (2002). Captives of the script: Killing us softly with phonics. *Language Arts, 79,* 452–461.

Moll, L. C. (1992). Literacy research in community and classroom: A sociocultural approach. In R. Beach, J. L. Green, M. L. Kamil, & T. Shanahan (Eds.), *Multidisciplinary perspectives on literacy research* (pp. 211–244). Urbana, IL: National Conference on Research in English, National Council of Teachers of English.

Moll, L. C., & Diaz, S. (1987). Change as the goal of educational research. *Anthropology and Education Quarterly, 18*(4), 300–311.

Montes, T. H., & Au, K. H. (2003). Book Club in a fourth-grade classroom: Issues of ownership and response. In R. L. McCormack & J. R. Paratore (Eds.), *After early intervention, then what? Teaching struggling readers in grade 3 and beyond* (pp. 70–93). Newark, DE: International Reading Association.

Morrow, L. M. (1992). The impact of a literature-based program on literacy achievement, use of literature, and attitudes of children from minority backgrounds. *Reading Research Quarterly, 27,* 251–275.

Morrow, L. M., Pressley, M., Smith, J. K., & Smith, M. (1997). The effect of a literature-based program integrated into literacy and science instruction with children from diverse backgrounds. *Reading Research Quarterly, 32,* 54–76.

Mosenthal, J., Lipson, M., Sortino, S., Russ, B., & Mekkelsen, J. (2002). Literacy in rural Vermont: Lessons from schools where children succeed. In B. M. Taylor & P. D. Pearson (Eds.), *Teaching reading: Effective schools, accomplished teachers.* Mahwah, NJ: Lawrence Erlbaum Associates.

Nakanishi, P. (2002). *Interview with Pat Nakanishi* (videotape). Honolulu: University of Hawaii.

National Center for Educational Statistics. (2004). *The NAEP reading scale.* Retrieved, 2004, from the World Wide Web: http://nces.ed.gov/nationsreportcard/reading/scale.asp

Newmann, F. M., Smith, B., Allensworth, E., & Bryk, A. S. (2001). Instructional program coherence: What it is and why it should guide school improvement policy. *Educational Evaluation and Policy Analysis, 23*(4), 297–321.

Ngo, B. (2002). Contesting "culture": The perspectives of Hmong American female students on early marriage. *Anthropology and Education Quarterly, 33*(2), 163–188.

Nieto, S. (1999). *The light in their eyes: Creating multicultural learning communities.* New York: Teachers College Press.

No Child Left Behind. (2001). *Public Law No. 107-1110, 115 Stat. 1425, 2002.* One Hundred Seventh Congress of the United States of America. Retrieved, 2004, from the World Wide Web: http://www.ed.gov/policy/elsec/leg/esea02/beginning/html

Oakes, J., & Guiton, G. (1995). Matchmaking: The dynamics of high school tracking decisions. *American Educational Research Journal, 32*, 3–33.

Ogbu, J. U. (1981). School ethnography: A multilevel approach. *Anthropology and Education Quarterly, 12*(1), 3–29.

Ogbu, J. U. (1990). Cultural model, identity, and literacy. In J. W. Stigler, R. A. Shweder, & G. Herdt (Eds.), *Cultural psychology* (pp. 520–541). Cambridge, England: Cambridge University Press.

Ogbu, J. U. (1993). Frameworks—Variability in minority school performance: A problem in search of an explanation. In E. Jacob & C. Jordan (Eds.), *Minority education: Anthropological perspectives* (pp. 83–111). Norwood, NJ: Ablex.

Orellana, M. F., Reynolds, J., Dorner, L., & Meza, M. (2003). In other words: Translating or "para-phrasing" as a family literacy practice in immigrant households. *Reading Research Quarterly, 38*, 12–34.

Osborne, A. B. (1996). Practice into theory into practice: Culturally relevant pedagogy for students we have marginalized and normalized. *Anthropology and Education Quarterly, 27*(3), 285–314.

Padilla, A. C. (2003). *"Who's in charge here? Aren't I the teacher? Don't I make the rules?" Book clubs in a fifth grade classroom: Using a student-centered reading curriculum to increase student ownership of literacy.* Honolulu: University of Hawaii, College of Education.

Palincsar, A. S., & Brown, A. L. (1984). Reciprocal teaching of comprehension-fostering and comprehension-monitoring activities. *Cognition and Instruction, 2*, 117–175.

Paris, S. G., Lawton, T. A., Turner, J. C., & Roth, J. L. (1991). A developmental perspective on standardized achievement testing. *Educational Researcher, 20*(5), 12–20.

Pearson, P. D. (1993). Standards for the English language arts: A policy perspective. *Journal of Reading Behavior, 25*(4), 457–475.

Pearson, P. D., & Gallagher, M. C. (1983). The instruction of reading comprehension. *Contemporary Educational Psychology, 8*, 317–344.

Philips, S. U. (1983). *The invisible culture: Communication in classroom and community on the Warm Springs Indian Reservation.* New York: Longman.

Piestrup, A. M. (1973). *Black dialect interference and accommodation of reading instruction in first grade.* Berkeley: University of California Press.

Pittman, T. S. (1998). Motivation. In D. T. Gilbert, S. T. Fiske, & G. Lindsay (Eds.), *The handbook of social psychology* (4th ed., Vol. 1, pp. 549–590). New York: McGraw-Hill.

Raphael, T. E. (1982). Question-answering strategies for children. *The Reading Teacher, 36*, 186–190.

Raphael, T. E. (1986). Teaching question answer relationships, revisited. *The Reading Teacher, 39*, 333–340.

Raphael, T. E., Florio-Ruane, S., & George, M. (2001). Book Club Plus: A conceptual framework to organize literacy instruction. *Language Arts, 79*(2), 159–168.

Raphael, T. E., Florio-Ruane, S., Kehus, M. J., George, M., Hasty, N. L., & Highfield, K. (2001). Thinking for ourselves: Literacy learning in a diverse teacher inquiry network. *The Reading Teacher, 54*, 596–607.

Raphael, T. E., & Goatley, V. J. (1997). Classrooms as communities: Features of community share. In S. I. McMahon & T. E. Raphael (Eds.), *Book Club: Literacy learning and classroom talk* (pp. 26–46). New York: Teachers College Press.

Raphael, T. E., & McMahon, S. I. (1994). Book Club: An alternative framework for reading instruction. *The Reading Teacher, 48*, 102–116.

Rasinski, T. V., Padak, N. D., Linek, W. L., & Sturtevant, E. (1994). Effects of fluency development on urban second-grade readers. *Journal of Educational Research, 87*, 158–165.

Rayner, K., & Pollatsek, A. (1989). *The psychology of reading*. Englewood Cliffs, NJ: Prentice Hall.

Reyes, M. (1991, April). *The "one size fits all" approach to literacy*. Paper presented at the annual meeting of the American Educational Research Association, Chicago.

Reynolds, R., Taylor, M., Steffensen, M., Shirey, L., & Anderson, R. (1977). Cultural schemata and reading comprehension. *Reading Research Quarterly, 17*, 353–366.

Richardson, E. (2003). *African American literacies*. London: Routledge.

Rong, X. L., & Preissle, J. (1998). *Educating immigrant students: What we need to know to meet the challenges*. Thousand Oaks, CA: Corwin Press.

Routman, R. (2000). *Conversations*. Portsmouth, NH: Heinemann.

Rynkofs, J. T. (1993). *Culturally responsive talk between a second grade teacher and Hawaiian children during writing workshop*. Unpublished doctoral dissertation, University of New Hampshire, Durham.

Samuels, S. J. (1979). The method of repeated readings. *The Reading Teacher, 32*, 403–408.

Sato, C. J. (1985). Linguistic inequality in Hawaii: The post-creole dilemma. In N. Wolfson & J. Manes (Eds.), *Language of inequality* (pp. 255–272). Berlin: Mouton.

Scherer, P. (1997). Book Club through a fishbowl: Extensions to early elementary classrooms. In S. I. McMahon & T. E. Raphael (Eds.), *Book Club connection: Literacy learning and classroom talks* (pp. 250–263). New York: Teachers College Press.

Schmidt, P. R. (1999). Focus on research: Know thyself and understand others. *Language Arts, 76*(4), 332–340.

Schmitt, M. C. (1990). A questionnaire to measure children's awareness of strategic reading processes. *The Reading Teacher, 43*, 454–461.

Schunk, D. H., & Zimmerman, B. J. (1997). Developing self-efficacious readers and writers: The role of social and self-regulatory processes. In J. T. Guthrie & A. Wigfield (Eds.), *Reading engagement: Motivating reading through integrated instruction* (pp. 34–50). Newark, DE: International Reading Association.

Schwarzer, D., Haywood, A., & Lorenzen, C. (2003). Fostering multiliteracy in a linguistically diverse classroom. *Language Arts, 80*, 453–460.

Shannon, P. (1989). *Broken promises: Reading instruction in twentieth century America*. New York: Bergin & Garvey.

Shannon, P. (1990). *The struggle to continue: Progressive reading instruction in the United States*. Portsmouth, NH: Heinemann.

Shujaa, M. J., & Afrik, H. (1996). School desegregation, the politics of culture, and the Council of Independent Black Institutions. In M. J. Shujaa (Ed.), *Beyond desegregation: The politics of quality in African American schooling* (pp. 253–268). Thousand Oaks, CA: Corwin.

Slavin, R. E., & Madden, N. A. (1994). Whenever and wherever we choose: The replication of Success for All. *Phi Delta Kappan, 75*, 639–647.

Smith, M. C. (2000). What will be the demands of literacy in the workplace in the next millennium? *Reading Research Quarterly, 35*, 378–383.

Smitherman, G. (2000). African American student writers in the NAEP, 1969–88/89 and "The blacker the berry, the sweeter the juice." In G. Smitherman (Ed.), *Talkin that talk: Language, culture, and education in African America* (pp. 163–191). London: Routledge.

Snow, C. E. (1990). Rationales for native language instruction: Evidence from research. In A. M. Padilla, H. H. Fairchild, & C. M. Valadez (Eds.), *Bilingual education: Issues and strategies* (pp. 60–74). Newbury Park, CA: Sage.

Spindler, G., & Spindler, L. (1990). *The American cultural dialogue and its transmission*. London: Falmer.

Spivey, N. N. (1997). *The constructivist metaphor: Reading, writing, and the making of meaning*. San Diego, CA: Academic.

Spring, J. (2001). *Deculturalization and the struggle for equality: A brief history of the education of dominated cultures in the United States*. Boston: McGraw-Hill.

Stahl, S. A. (1997). Instructional models in reading: An introduction. In S. A. Stahl & D. A. Hayes (Eds.), *Instructional models in reading* (pp. 1–29). Mahwah, NJ: Lawrence Erlbaum Associates.

Staveteig, S., & Wigton, A. (2000). *Racial and ethnic disparities: Key findings from the National Survey of America's Families*. Washington, DC: The Urban Institute.

Stedman, L. C., & Kaestle, C. F. (1991). Literacy and reading performance in the United States from 1880 to the present. *Literacy in the United States: Readers and reading since 1880*. New Haven, CT: Yale University Press.

Street, B. (1995). *Social literacies: Critical approaches to literacy in development, ethnography, and education*. New York: Longman.

Strickland, D. S., & Ascher, C. (1992). Low-income African American children and public schooling. In P. W. Jackson (Ed.), *Handbook of research on curriculum* (pp. 609–625). New York: Macmillan.

Sulzby, E. (1985). Children's emerging reading of favorite storybooks: A developmental study. *Reading Research Quarterly, 20*, 458–481.

Taba, H. (1962). *Curriculum development: Theory and practice*. New York: Harcourt, Brace & World.

Tamura, E. H. (1994). *Americanization, acculturation, and ethnic identity: The nisei generation in Hawaii*. Urbana: University of Illinois Press.

Taylor, B. M. (1982). A summarizing strategy to improve middle grade students' reading and writing skills. *The Reading Teacher, 36*, 202–205.

Taylor, B. M. (2002). Highly accomplished primary grade teachers in effective schools. In B. M. Taylor & P. D. Pearson (Eds.), *Teaching reading: Effective schools, accomplished teachers* (pp. 279–288). Mahwah, NJ: Lawrence Erlbaum Associates.

Taylor, B. M., Pearson, P. D., Clark, K., & Walpole, S. (2000). Effective schools and accomplished teachers: Lessons about primary-grade reading instruction in low-income schools. *Elementary School Journal, 101*, 121–165.

Taylor, B. M., Pearson, P. D., Peterson, D. S., & Rodriguez, M. C. (2003). Reading growth in high-poverty classrooms: The influence of teacher practices that encourage cognitive engagement in literacy learning. *Elementary School Journal, 104*, 3–28.

Taylor, D. (1983). *Family literacy: Young children learning to read and write.* Portsmouth, NH: Heinemann.

Teale, W. H. (1987). Emergent literacy: Reading and writing development in early childhood. In J. E. Readence & R. S. Baldwin (Eds.), *Research in literacy: Merging perspectives (Thirty-sixth yearbook of the National Reading Conference)* (pp. 45–74). Rochester, NY: National Reading Conference.

Templeton, S., & Morris, D. (2000). Spelling. In M. L. Kamil, P. B. Mosenthal, P. D. Pearson, & R. Barr (Eds.), *Handbook of reading research* (pp. 525–543). Mahwah, NJ: Lawrence Erlbaum Associates.

The College Board. (1999). *Reaching the top: A report of the National Task Force on Minority High Achievement.* New York: The College Board.

Tse, L. (2001). *"Why don't they learn English?" Separating fact and fallacy in the U.S. language debate.* New York: Teachers College Press.

Turner, J. (1995). The influence of classroom contexts on young children's motivation for literacy. *Reading Research Quarterly, 30*, 410–441.

Turner, J., & Paris, S. G. (1995). How literacy tasks influence children's motivation for literacy. *The Reading Teacher, 48*, 662–673.

Ulichny, P. (1996). Cultural conflict. *Anthropology and Education Quarterly, 27*, 331–364.

U.S. Census Bureau. (2002). *Current Population Survey.* Washington, DC: Author.

U.S. Department of Education. (2002). *The condition of education 2002.* Washington, DC: U.S. Government Printing Office.

Venezky, R. L. (1991). The development of literacy in the industrialized nations of the west. In R. Barr, M. L. Kamil, P. B. Mosenthal, & P. D. Pearson (Eds.), *Handbook of reading research* (pp. 46–67). New York: Longman.

Viadero, D. (2000, March 15). Even in well-off suburbs, minority achievement lags. *Education Week*, pp. 1–7.

Vogt, L. A., Jordan, C., & Tharp, R. G. (1987). Explaining school failure, producing school success: Two cases. *Anthropology and Education Quarterly, 18*(4), 276–286.

Vygotsky, L. S. (1978). *Mind in society: The development of higher psychological processes.* Cambridge, MA: Harvard University Press.

Wagoner, S. A. (1983). Comprehension monitoring: What it is and what we know about it. *Reading Research Quarterly, 18*, 328–346.

Wagstaff, J. (1997). Building practical knowledge of letter–sound correspondences: A beginner's Word Wall and beyond. *The Reading Teacher, 51*, 298–304.

Watson, K. A. (1974). Transferable communicative routines: Strategies and group identity in two speech events. *Language in Society, 4*, 53–72.

Wenger, E. (1998). *Communities of practice: Learning, meaning, and identity.* Cambridge, England: Cambridge University Press.

Wilde, S. (2000). *Miscue analysis made easy: Building on student strengths.* Portsmouth, NH: Heinemann.

Wood, D. J., Bruner, J. S., & Ross, G. (1976). The role of tutoring in problem solving. *Journal of Child Psychology and Psychiatry, 17*, 89–100.

Yokota, J. (2001). *Kaleidoscope: A multicultural booklist for grades K–8.* Urbana, IL: National Council of Teachers of English.

CHILDREN'S BOOKS CITED

Cowley, J. (1990). *To town.* Bothell, WA: Wright Group.

Creech, S. (1996). *Walk two moons.* New York: HarperCollins.

L'Engle, M. (1962). *A wrinkle in time.* New York: Dell.

Lionni, L. (1991). *Swimmy.* New York: Knopf.

Lowry, L. (1990). *Number the stars.* New York: Bantam.

Martin, B. (1983). *Brown bear, brown bear, what do you see?* New York: Holt.

Martin, B., & Archambault, J. (1989). *Chicka chicka boom boom.* New York: Simon & Schuster.

Paterson, K. (1989). *Park's quest.* New York: Puffin.

Polacco, P. (1990). *Thundercake.* New York: Simon & Schuster.

Polacco, P. (1994a). *Babushka's doll.* New York: Simon & Schuster.

Polacco, P. (1994b). *The keeping quilt.* New York: Simon & Schuster.

Rattigan, J. K. (1998). *Dumpling soup.* New York: Little, Brown.

Shan, D. (2002). *A living nightmare* (Cirque du Freak series No. 1). New York: Little, Brown.

Simon, S. (1996). Wolves. In J. D. Cooper & J. J. Pikulski (Eds.), *Explore* (pp. 128–148). Boston: Houghton Mifflin.

Snicket, L. (1999). *The bad beginning: Book the first (a series of unfortunate events).* New York: HarperCollins.

Sperry, A. (1940). *Call it courage.* New York: Macmillan.

Young, E. (1990). *Lon Po Po: A red riding hood story from China.* New York: Philomel.

Author Index

Subject Index

A

Accuracy, 160–163
Acquisition, 55–56
Anthropological research, 77–87
Assimilationism, 2–4
Automaticity, 159, 163–164
Autonomous model of literacy, 38–39
Awareness, 158–160

B

Book Club Plus, xii, 34, 60–74, 96, 111,
  121, 123, 127, 147, 148
  dual obligations, 61–62
  literacy block, 68
Buddy sorting, 171

C

"Christmas tree" pattern, 176
Classroom literacy, 56–59, 87–93
Coaching, 109–110, 171
Codes of the culture of power, 38
Colonization, 20–21, 32
Community of practice, 76
Community share, 63–64, 67
Competition, 86–87
Comprehensible input, 149
Comprehension strategies, 96–99, 174
  determining importance, 100–101
  drawing inferences, 100
  generating questions, 102–103
  monitoring comprehension, 103–104
  predicting, 99–100
  summarizing information, 101–102
  teaching these strategies, 104–111,
    169–172
Core curriculum, 3
Cultural diversity, 5, 8–12
  and schools, 11–12, 22–23, 113–133
  sibling caretaking, 5, 11
Cultural imperialism, 21
Cultural inversion, 79
Culturally responsive instruction, 113–133
  curriculum content, 120–122
  social processes, 122–132

D

Deculturalization, 20, 32
Discourse, 45–48
  primary and secondary, 48–53, 56–59,
    71
Discrimination, 19–21

E

Embodied action, 71
English language learners (ELLs),
    133–134, 151–152
Essayist literacy, 38–41, 48
Explicit explanation, 104–106, 170

F, G

Fictive kinship, 23–25

213